# Separated, Acting Badly

# Separated, Acting Badly

## For the Love of Food, a Man, and Me

## BARBARA FLORES

A Russian Hill Press Book
United States • United Kingdom • Australia

Russian Hill Press

The publisher is not responsible for websites or their content that are not owned by the publisher.

The names and details concerning some people in *Separated, Acting Badly* have been changed. The author has on a few occasions changed the order of events, where those changes benefit narrative flow without altering a factual telling of the story. Otherwise all dialogue and events took place as the author remembers and recounts them in these pages.

ISBN: 9780999516256
LCCN: 2018961893

# DEDICATION

When I fell, you lifted me up.
Through grace
we don't all fall down on the same day.

# ACKNOWLEDGMENTS

When a book takes fifteen years to deliver, there are too many names to thank. But many talented and gracious midwives helped me birth this book, starting with Jim Kirkwood, my acting instructor, who taught me that the meaning of words comes from the heart, not from a script.

Huge applause for the wonderful women (and men) in Al-Anon. I've endeavored to respect anonymity by not identifying myself with specific Twelve Step Programs in the text. However, here I may shout the praises of this life-saving program for all the support, encouragement, and fellowship that it offers to friends and families of alcoholics. Also a shout out for Stand! For Families Free of Violence in Concord, California where I volunteered.

Thank you to my many editors: Marcia King-Gamble, Marilyn Willison, and the incomparable Dorothy Wall; and to my illustrious Bennington College instructors: Susan Cheever, Bernard Cooper, Wyatt Mason, and especially Phillip Lopate. When I enrolled in Bennington's Masters of Writing program at age 60 and left with a competed book draft, I was grateful no one even hinted that I might be too old to go back to college. Other remarkable teachers who deserve credit include Joyce Maynard, Jon Carroll, and my long-time teacher and one-time writing partner, Adair Lara.

I must also mention, author, Anne Lamott, who honored me by displaying my Pear Poster in her home and who never fails to inspire me with her brilliance, faith, and humor. *Muchas gracias* to all my writing students, writing group partners, and readers. You are too numerous to name, but when the rejection letters started piling up, you kept my head up and fingers on the keyboard. You proved that even an appreciative audience of one or two is more than enough.

Deep gratitude also goes to Paula Chinick of Russian Hill Press, and editor Jim Aikin; who both rescued my 300-page manuscript from being abandoned next to the six boxes of journals in my closet. Lastly I thank my husband George Canberg. Living with a writer-wife locked in her room isn't easy. He's fond of saying, "Barbara who?" And the kids—I tossed all of their dirty laundry on the front lawn, but not one of them (so far) has said, "God, Mom, you can't print *that!*" For their trust and faith, I'll be forever grateful. I hope someday they may read these pages and understand that this is not only a memoir, but a love letter.

# PART I

# CHAPTER ONE
## HOSPITAL

I wake up with a stiff sheet over my mouth smelling faintly of chlorine. I'm in a strange room, small and dark like an old motel. The window above my bed is covered with plywood. I sit up, woozy, still in a T-shirt and jeans. My feet hit the cold linoleum. Bent over, I notice the strange loopy-knit socks—beige with rubber skids on the bottom. Cheap, synthetic hospital socks. Where's my purse? My make-up? My shoes? Where's the blue-print hospital gown I had on last night? I remember Maya driving me to the Kaiser ER, but after that nothing.

I stand and steady myself with a hand on the chenille bedspread, then zigzag my way into the hall. My arm brushes the wall; I'm weaving like a drunk, though it's been fourteen years since my last drink. I'm drugged, Klonopin maybe. The door opens into a dim hall. But no hospital nurses in white uniforms bustle by. The nauseous air reeks of bacon grease, eggs, and burnt toast. No shiny metal breakfast carts in the hall either. Where the hell am I? Two open hall doors each reveal a bed occupied by a brown blanket mound. No elevators and no exit signs—must be a locked psych ward. I shudder.

This definitely isn't Kaiser, where I thought I would spend a night or two. Our Walnut Creek Kaiser was recently remodeled with an airy four-story lobby lit with skylights. Original oils, woven wall hangings, and impressionistic pastels of Mount Diablo adorn the hallways. I expected crisp white sheets, a TV remote with cable, meals served in bed, and good lighting—a modern window view room in white-on-white, chrome and glass against a cobalt sky. South Beach colors. A blurred memory of a black night in the back of an ambulance flashes through my brain. They outsourced me to a crappy hospital with windows boarded up with plywood?

A Band-Aid covers my right wrist. I peek under it carefully so as not to pull off the stuck part. The cutting wasn't deliberate or planned, just flicks really. The feathering of an X-Acto. A new number eleven blade. Graphic designers always have X-Actos, or we used to. Just a few scratches. I never intended to kill myself. But did my daughter, Maya, know that? It wasn't really an accident. It was a mistake, is what it was. I wasn't in my right mind yesterday. Love can do that to a woman. The words I overheard him say into the phone, "I love you. I'll call you tonight," loop over and over in my head, slicing deeper than any number eleven X-Acto blade ever could.

I follow the smell of bacon grease around a corner. A line of a dozen or so somber-looking patients advances toward a tiered cart with breakfast trays. They're so young; at fifty-six, I must be a freak in this place. But then I'm not staying one more night in this poor excuse for a loony bin hospital. I stand in line, not for the greasy food but for coffee. I have to shake this wooziness and convince whatever hack doctor is on duty to get me the hell out of here. A place like this could make you crazy.

A young couple stands side by side ahead of me in the breakfast line. "Where are we?" I ask. My tongue feels fat and my words roll out slow and lazy. There's a disconnect between my thoughts and my speech.

The boy pushes back a shock of oily black hair over a pierced eyebrow. "When did you get here?"

"Last night," I slur.

His green-haired girlfriend, who looks about fourteen, stares at the Band-Aid on my wrist. Just a small Band-Aid. I wish I'd worn long sleeves last night instead of a T-shirt. "This hospital, if you can call it that, is in Vallejo," she says.

I focus on enunciating. "How long have you two been here?"

"Been here ten days now." The boy moves forward in line, but allows the girl to go ahead of him. He doesn't look *that* crazy.

"Eight days." She looks up at him and smiles as if it was the best eight days of her life.

"You're kidding? You've really been here over a week?" I thought they just did seventy-two-hour holds.

The girl smirks. "Nobody gets outta this place before a week,"

I can't stay in this dump for a week. I have to speak at a twelve step meeting tomorrow, and Diego and I have a counseling session on Wednesday. "Who do you talk to to get released?"

"The doc don't show 'til afternoon," he says. I glance down at my watch, or where my watch used to be. "Must be after seven a.m., ma'am; we line up for breakfast at seven."

At the front of the line a stout woman in a neon pink T-shirt hands out small Dixie cups. Her nametag reads "Ruth Anne." I step to the side and ask her, "Ma'am, could you tell me what time the doctor comes in, please?"

She doesn't look up from her silver tray of paper cups. "Around one, hon. Stay in line."

*Damn, that's six hours.* She hands a Dixie cup to a tattooed girl with a nail in her nose in front of the line. No juice in the cup, only two red pills.

"Meds," the girl says as she downs them with water.

Damn. This is no breakfast line. It's a drug line.

"Take your meds, hon," Ruth Anne says to me like I'm a cocker spaniel. I raise my palm to refuse the Dixie cup and walk off. Her thick eyebrow shoots up in disapproval. Following the scent of coffee, I find a percolator bubbling and pour myself a cup.

"Hey, that's staff coffee." A dark-skinned man pushing a broom tries to stop me. The man shrugs and points to the blood spot on my Band-Aid. "Tch, tch, tch, shouldn't do that, lady." He shakes his head. The coffee tastes weak, tepid, and burnt. I want to tell the staff that percolating coffee boils the grounds and turns it bitter, but I don't want to be labeled as some troublemaker, a pill refuser, a coffee stealer. I remember when my son, Miguel was kicked out of his second rehab for stealing coffee. Will broom man report me?

I pick up a tray from the food cart, thinking the white bunny bread will soak up whatever drugs they gave me. *White bunny bread*, that's what Diego calls it. The young couple sits across the table from me, making moon-eyes over piles of yellow egg and limp under-cooked bacon. I've visited my kids in facilities like this. I know the rules: No contraband. No sex. No holding hands. This couple is holding eyes. Maybe it makes their days here in this sleazebag mental hospital bearable. Diego and I gazed at each other like that once. With adoring eyes. During our early Berkeley days in the seventies, when we couldn't keep our hands off each other.

I have an urge to cut the fat off the boy's bacon, but notice there are no knives. I used to do that for Diego until he told me that eating pork caused cancer. I wonder if this girl will someday cut the fat off this boy's bacon. I can tell these two want to touch each other, but can't. Will they call each other every day when they get out? If they get married, will they tell their kids that they met in a mental hospital? He's in his twenties, I guess, from the full dark stubble on his face. Stubble like Miguel has. When did my son get stubble on his soft cheeks? Sometime between algebra and his driver's license.

The girl could pass for thirteen, but I know she must be eighteen to be in with adults. Be careful, kid. Before you know it your children have left home, you've put on a few pounds, you've buried beloved pets, you're almost old, and you've given your whole life away to one person. You raise three kids, and they're all alive and haven't killed anyone (that you know of), you have a career, plant the impatiens, make supper every night, you even make your own salad dressings and grow your own arugula, and still he can crush you. Leave you for road kill. I want to warn her before it's too late. Before she falls in love. Just thinking the word *love* twists my gut. Their unspoken affection oozes out across the metal folding table, thick and sickly sweet, like pink cake frosting made with Crisco.

I can't eat this crap: dry rubbery eggs and foam-board bread. But I drink the slop coffee to clear my head. The shrink I'll see at one p.m. is my ticket out. The dining room has a sliding glass door, the only window I've seen. Outside is a gated cement courtyard flanked by two long one-story wings with boarded windows. I assume there was a pool and grass there once, but now it's flat gray concrete like a pitiful gorilla cage in an old zoo. I try to open the door for some air but it's locked. I shake the locked door and get a reprimand from Ruth Anne. "Don't touch that door, it's locked."

Shit. I don't belong here. These people don't know who I am. I design food art posters; I wrote two cookbooks—Alice Waters, the mother of California cuisine, signed her fruit book to me, "With admiration." I'm somebody, dammit.

I close my eyes wishing this were all a bad dream. I ache to be back home in my own bed with my sateen-finish turquoise sheets, hearing Tigger purring in my ear and Lola at my feet. Maya would be opening and closing the fridge a few times to satisfy her OCD before pulling out Eggos for breakfast, and Deanna would be singing outside my window on the swing set.

It's just a small cut, I'll tell the doc. A few scratches. No stitches needed. An accident. I'll take responsibility, they like that. I'll admit I did something stupid. Too much love for one man can do that.

· · ·

IT'S AFTER TWO WHEN I'm shown into a room with folding tables and told to wait for Dr. Cohen. Not the kind of psychiatrist's office I'm familiar with: no big mahogany desk, bookcases, or framed medical degrees on the walls. No windows either. Only bright fluorescent lights, the kind that turn skin tones green. I look like crap anyway. My bed-head blonde bob feels flat and separated in the back, exposing dark roots; my eyes are red and swollen, and any mascara and concealer I had on yesterday from brunch with Diego has been cried off. I'm grateful mental hospitals don't take mug shots. Normally I never leave the house without lipstick, blush, mascara, and shoes. I want to appear accomplished and professional to Dr. Cohen—but that's not easy in jeans, a T-shirt that doesn't cover the Band-Aid, and loopy-knit mental patient socks. All I have going for me is good posture and the pretense of a cooperative, congenial personality. Sit up straight, and whatever you do, don't cry.

Dr. Cohen is bald, my age—mid-fifties—with Chuck Berry glasses. I lean forward and offer a firm handshake and steady eye contact. He glances between me and the manila folder in front of him, giving me a quick half-smile. I smile back. He flips through papers in his folder.

"Why do you think you're here, Mrs. Flores?"

Isn't it obvious? I glance at my Band-Aid.

"Yes, you cut yourself."

"Uh, my daughter Maya, she's twenty-three, got upset last night and called 911. It wasn't an attempt to ..." I can't say the word "suicide." This is a mental hospital. In my recovery meeting for families someone could say, "I feel like killing myself because my husband doesn't love me anymore," but not here, not in front of a doctor, a mandatory reporter. There are legal consequences.

"So after an argument with your husband Dago, you cut yourself and—"

"He uses the Spanish pronunciation. 'Diego.' Like San Diego."

"Has anyone in your family been hospitalized for mental problems, Mrs. Flores?"

"My mother has." He doesn't need to know about Miguel. "She's bipolar, she calls it manic depression."

"Yes, Mrs. Flores, manic depression was the clinical term before 1986."

This Mrs. Flores thing is getting old. "Please, call me Barbara."

He pushes his large, dark-framed glasses up on a large perfectly symmetrical nose. "So, Barbara, how many times was she hospitalized?"

"A few." Mom had always described her sanitariums so serenely. Big windows with views of grassy hills, lakes, and cows. A piano in the game room. Breakfast in bed.

"How many times? Guess."

"Mom? Maybe eight, ten hospitalizations. I lost count. Most were before I was in kindergarten." I picture the sweet smile that spreads across my mother's pretty face when she talks about her sanitarium days. Like it was a six-week health spa vacation with meals served in bed, no kids to take care of, no diapers to change. She'd come back six weeks later overjoyed to see us, bringing gifts—the mukluk slippers she made during craft period. We never lacked for mukluks. But that was in the fifties. Cohen doesn't need to know about my childhood. I'm not going to sound accusatory or he'll think I haven't forgiven her.

"And I have three grown children in their twenties and a granddaughter. My husband recently retired but he still teaches part time at a junior college."

"So Mrs. Flores, let me get this straight. Yesterday afternoon you overheard your husband on the phone with another woman, you confronted him, and after an argument, he left." Cohen's thick hairy finger traces down the report as if reading Braille. "Then last night you cut yourself with an X-Acto knife and at the ER you asked to be admitted, right?"

I wish he'd stop saying, "you cut yourself," like I'm some deranged wacko teenaged cutter. That was Maya over Jesse in her teens, but it isn't me.

"Dr. Cohen, it was an accident, really. I never cut myself before." What is Cohen writing? I pull at the gauze part of the Band-Aid to show him the small crisscross marks. Tiny crosshatches barely an inch long. But it's stuck where blood has seeped through the bandage, painting a stain the size of a blueberry. The gauze gives way and bright red droplets appear from the cuts. Quickly I press the Band-Aid back on, and stash my wrist under the tabletop. Cohen looks across the table at me, half smiles back, and puts down his fat pen. I smile with good straight teeth (Dad was a dentist) and tell my shoulders to relax.

"Perhaps it's best that you remain here for a few days, Barbara. Have a rest."

God, no! "Really, I'm better today, I'm fine. Absolutely fine." A stream of blood trickles down my little finger leaving two red drops on the linoleum floor. I swipe my hand across my jeans and smile, trying to look normal.

Cohen closes the folder. No gold band on his left finger. Probably divorced, after ten to twenty. He removes his dark-framed glasses and his eyes soften. "Okay, Mrs. Flores—uh, Barbara, sorry—so tell me about your husband."

I should talk. Make friends with him. Prisoners should get personal with their captors.

"I met Diego in Berkeley in '74."

*It was at a campus bar, the Cheshire Cat, a half block off the Berkeley campus. I was married then to Bob. In retrospect, I think Diego had more respect for my first two-year marriage than Bob did. Bob believed that marriage was only a piece of paper created by the establishment to benefit the military-industrial complex. Vietnam was winding down and, according to Bob, the next important issue was overpopulation. To save our planet and its inhabitants from starvation, all couples had to limit progeny to 2.6 children. Once I asked Bob if I could borrow a .6 of a child from someone else, but he said no. And I wasn't much interested in sex then, maybe because Mom said it was something you had to put up with and it messes up your hair—she went to bed with toilet paper wrapped around her sprayed blonde helmet. So I drank first to get in the mood for wifely duty. I think my brief marriage to Bob proved to be a post-war casualty—when Nam was over we had nothing else to talk about.*

*Somehow it started up with Diego. Afternoon beers at the Cat, Top Dog for lunch, toking a joint in his white VW bug. Once I even skipped my evening astrology class to meet him. After Diego's classes, he taught history and econ at an East Bay junior college, we'd spend las tardes hiking in Tilden Park or discovering little Mexican restaurants. For four months, all we did was talk. Once on a drive in his white VW, his hand brushed my leg as he shifted into third, and a sensation fluttered up my bare thigh like a feather. Embarrassed, I closed my knees and swiveled away from the gearshift. Maybe it took us time because I wore a ring, or because he wasn't pushy, or because I didn't think he was James Garner handsome enough.*

*But one afternoon, parked in the bug up on Grizzly Peak overlooking the blue expanse of San Francisco Bay, we were singing "Brown Sugar" along with The Rolling Stones blasting from the radio. Diego put down the joint smoldering in its little metal ashtray, its pungent incense scent blended with my White Musk perfume. Then Diego's hand, his long fingers as graceful as a pianist, yet strong as a boxer's, inched up my long smooth leg, just under the fray of my cut-offs. This time I didn't pull away.*

*Maybe it was the weed.*

*Or maybe I wasn't as frigid as Bob told me I was. But that day in Diego's VW on Grizzly Peak, I only knew that I didn't want his hand to stop. And I wasn't going to give that up, not for vows, not for my future 2.6 children with Bob, not for James Garner, not for anyone.*

"Barbara, do you want a Kleenex?" Cohen pushes the box towards me.

"Sorry."

"No problem."

"Dr. Cohen, I really think I'm ready to go home this afternoon." I say it sincerely and clearly—the drug stupor has worn off. After an eye dab, I put the tissue in my bloodied hand. What the green-haired girl said plays over in my mind: "Nobody gets out of this place in under a week." I *have* to fix things with Diego. Sort things out. Besides, tomorrow is Sunday and I'm a speaker at a recovery meeting and I'm a lectern, a speaker, at Mass. I can't waste time in a mental hospital.

"Dr. Cohen, I just made a rash decision."

"But Mrs. Flores, you *did* deliberately cut yourself."

"I mean last night, when I told the ER doctor I didn't want to go home."

Cohen taps the folders papers on his thigh. "You were given a choice."

"I just expected to stay at Kaiser one night."

"But you do know that you acted irresponsibly?"

I nod. Yes, it was a rash, impulsive act, and truthfully, wanting to stay in the hospital was also manipulative. I wanted Diego to know how badly this hurt.

"Consider the advantages you'll have here. Daily therapy sessions where you can talk with professionals. Get support. No responsibilities. Your meals are prepared—"

"Doctor, Diego and I have been together over thirty years, we've been through rough times before, especially with the kids. We've lasted, we always pull through ..." Cohen gazes at me blank-faced. He doesn't get it. Our thirty-year bond was built out of mutual jealousy, possessiveness, and scar tissue. I likened to one of those amazing free-form junk art sculptures in the Berkeley Marina mud flats, built out of throwaway materials.

"... and we have an alcohol and drug free home now." I don't mention that Diego likes to drink beer and smoke weed in his van. "Dr. Cohen, we'll survive this too. Diego's a good man, Hispanic, old-school. He can be impulsive. He's entitled. I get that. But I accept who he is today."

"Then, he's entitled to leave, and to have other interests?"

My bloody fist jerks under the table. He calls another woman other *interests?* I tighten my arm to hold my hand still. A phone rings. I glance down at the linoleum for my purse, but realize I no longer have my purse. Or shoes.

"Yes, Ruth Anne, I'll make a note of that," Cohen says into his cell.

I'm outnumbered.

"Excuse me for a few minutes, Barbara." He walks out of the room.

I rub my bloodied hand on the tissue trying to get rid of the evidence. I'm aware that Cohen's job is to evaluate how suicidal I am. The standard eval question is, "Is the subject a danger to themselves or others?" Same question that police asked about Miguel when I had him arrested. But I am no danger, I'll tell him. I attend three different Twelve Step Programs, and I've been sober fourteen years. That should do it. Fourteen years of sobriety holds weight in the mental health community. My get-out-of-jail-free card. My ace in the hand, outweighing a bloodied Band-Aid, I hope.

Cohen returns and opens his folder. I point out the fact that I've been a model bipolar patient taking Lithium, a naturally occurring salt, for thirteen years.

"Lithium isn't mood altering," I tell him. "Over the last decade, I've had more career success designing posters, cookbook deals, and winning awards than I ever did without medication." Doctors like positive feedback about their meds. It validates them. "And I've been sober for fourteen years."

"So you work for a publisher, Barbara?"

"I'm a freelance graphic designer, but my food posters segued into some garden cookbook deals."

Cohen's eyes perk up.

"Have you seen the Chile Poster? It's been on TV—as a set piece behind a chef in a deodorant commercial."

"No, can't say that I have. Sounds like you're a very busy woman, Barbara. Perhaps you need a rest. A break from it all."

"No, I slept really well last night."

"Ruth Anne says you refused your meds." He closes the manila folder. Serious. Like a high school principal.

"No really, I don't need meds, not today. I'm fine." Now I'm pleading. My palms are sticky with sweat and dried blood.

"Barbara, the pain passes. We get over it. You're lucky. It's more complicated when children are involved." His eyes stare into mine. "That's a different ball game."

"Deanna, my granddaughter, is only eight. She's lived with us since she was a baby."

Cohen leans forward. He has hazel eyes, like me. "Barbara, understand whether he comes back or not, it won't negate all the good you've done for your family. You'll get through this, you're stronger than you think."

For a moment I almost believe him. He's good.

"Focus on your family, on your granddaughter. Not as a gift to her, but as a gift to yourself."

He's speaking to me like a professional, an almost equal, so I lob his tone right back at him.

"You should write a book, Dr. Cohen."

"I have," he says proud as a teenager after his first shave.

"Really. What's the title?"

*To Thine Own Self Be True.*"

"Catchy. Is it under Cohen?"

"Harold Cohen. But I go by Harry."

"Who's your publisher?"

"I'm working on that."

And *voila*. I'm back in the game. Cohen says that I've stabilized and can be released that afternoon as long as I agree to a four-week Kaiser outpatient day program. I hold out my left hand—the clean one. We shake on it. The relief is indescribable. *I'm getting out.* I fold my tissue-wiped hands on the table, Band-Aid side down.

Ruth Anne, at discharge, looks perplexed, but she gives me back my watch, purse, shoes, and wedding ring. "Sign here," she says, pointing below the line that says I'm prohibited from owning a firearm for five years.

While waiting for Maya to pick me up, I'm thinking about Cohen. He implied my marriage wouldn't survive, but he believed *for sure* that I would. He's a *mensch,* Julie, my art studio partner, would say. A good doctor.

That afternoon Maya drives me home in her gray Sebring. She came alone, leaving her daughter, Deanna, with a friend. Even in plaid pajama bottoms and a long-sleeved tee my daughter is remarkably gorgeous. She resembles Drew Barrymore, only prettier. But Maya, who greeted me with smiles and hugs at the facility, seems uncharacteristically quiet in the car. I expect an outpouring of sympathy, or at least a few derisive remarks about her father, "that dirt worm," but she's not talking. Not taking sides. Something's wrong, but I shrug it off. Likely another late night phone fight with Jesse. Just about everything that goes wrong in our house is Jesse's fault. It's very convenient. But this time my problem can't be blamed on a boyfriend twelve hours away in Washington.

Looking out the passenger window I take in the view, breathing deep. I can't wait for my front screen door to slam behind me, smell a cup of Peet's French roast, and tickle my granddaughter to hear her giggle. I love our house: a spacious ranch, warm Southwest colors, and dark wood beams on its high living room ceiling. A grassy front yard bordered by yellow daisies, tall pines, and wild roses. Terra cotta pots on the porch overflow with impatiens. The side yard is Diego's small orchard, where we pick apples, plums, and citrus. Almost like being in the country with winding two-lane suburban roads and a hillside field with cows and goats, and a bike path alongside a shallow, flowing creek. Not just any house, for the last fourteen years it's been our beloved, appreciated, and well cared-for home. Diego maintains the fences, the retaining walls, and in the aftermath of the Oakland fire he added a simulated-red-tile fireproof roof that came with a fifty-year guarantee.

We cross the Richmond Bridge to Contra Costa County, and the glittering San Francisco Bay reflects a vast dome of clear blue sky. The skyline of San Francisco never looked so bright and regal. I catch the first glimpse of Mt. Diablo, in its summer gold, rising theatrically out of lush green foothills and valleys dotted with homes. The green spreads out from the base of the mountain like the skirt of a Christmas tree.

One of those dots is mine.

I'm going home.

Obviously, I wasn't psychotic, nor did I believe that staying ten days in the Bates Motel of mental hospitals would have done me any good. Those dark rooms with grandma-style chenille bedspreads may have offered the younger patients a safe place to veg out and hibernate, but for me it was San Quentin.

I had a marriage to save, dammit.

Looking back at my early release—was I really a danger to myself or others?

Yes, definitely.

# CHAPTER TWO
## QUAKES
*June 2004 Lafayette, CA*

What happened to us? After leaving the hospital I had to think back. Retrace our steps. I knew Diego's leaving was not the only quake that had fractured our family. Our roots dug deep into the East Bay suburbs where we had lived for over three decades. Not only were there fissures from within, but we also felt attacked by outside forces. Like the event that woke us up at three a.m. two years earlier, before Jesse left. What plays in my memory most about that night wasn't Maya's broken nose; it was her new puffy ski jacket, a shimmery powder-blue, its front red-streaked with blood.

Maya, our twenty-one-year-old, tiptoes into our bedroom while Diego and I spoon in bed, my left arm draped over his defined bicep.

"Mom. Mom, wake up, I'm bleeding," she whispers.

The moonlight through the patio window traces the silhouette of our daughter standing beside our bed holding her nose. I sit up and switch on the reading lamp. Blood streaks down the front of her jacket, dripping steadily from her nose—a perfectly adorable nose—slightly short and turned up like mine. I clench a handful of Kleenex for her.

"My God! What happened?"

Diego pushes himself up on his forearms and squints at her. Maya is ranting about being at a San Francisco bar with her boyfriend, Jesse, punctuating her story with sniffs, tears, and "ow-ow-ows," adding, "Some random Mexican dude punched me."

"You called the police, right?"

"The club did. They couldn't find him." Her words come out nasal in sniffy blood bubbles, yet somehow coherent. Not drunk or drugged. Of course she wouldn't drink or use drugs. Not Maya.

"Mom, my nose isn't where it's supposed to be. Why did he hit the top part? That's the only part of my nose I like." Maya, sniffing, plops on the bed beside me.

Diego leans over my nightgown for a closer look. He boxes as a hobby. He knows about uppercuts, brass knuckles, and out-of-place noses. "Hon, take your hand off, so I can see it," he says.

Maya's bloodied left hand lifts and quivers in the air two inches from her nose as if it's scared to go too far. Fresh bullet drops land crimson on her half-zipped baby-blue jacket.

"It looks broken," he says matter-of-factly.

He knows these things. I know she needs to see a doctor. *Now.* And the jacket needs Shout before the stain sets. Two washes.

"It's my nose, Mom! On my face," she wails. "I need my face." Sniff. She catches a rivulet of blood running over her lip and tosses the red-soaked tissue in the wastebasket under my graphic design table.

I look at Diego. Even half asleep and without his glasses, he looks professorial with his trimmed beard and thick gray curls.

"Should I drive her to Kaiser or you?" I don't know why I ask. My watch says 3:07 and Diego needs his sleep before his eight a.m. econ class. It will be me who drives to Kaiser Hospital.

"Why didn't Jesse drive you to the hospital?" Diego accuses.

She grabs a handful of tissues and stands. "I have to go check on Deanna—"

"Maya, don't!" *Good Lord.* I can't have six-year-old Deanna seeing her mother looking like she's just been shot.

"We have to go to the hospital, Maya, now! I have to be back here to watch Deanna before your dad leaves." My bare feet hit the cold, wood floor, my head groggy.

"I'm not going to wake her, Mom. Jeez. I'll just peek in."

The pale blue iridescence of Maya's jacket shimmers out the bedroom door. I rub the goose bumps rising on my forearm. Two wet red splotches bloom beside me on my floral comforter. More stains. Diego falls back on the pillow, his dark mahogany eyes ablaze. They fixed on the ceiling. I'm waiting for him to say something reassuring before I throw on some sweats.

He says with certainty, "Jesse did it."


Maya's nose is adjusted back to its God-given position by a Kaiser physician that early morning. Maya takes a personal leave from work as a server at Postino, Chef Cat Cora's restaurant, because as Maya says, her face is "unpresentable" for fine dining. She spends her hours on the phone reveling in the attention and sympathy from friends and co-workers, denying them no medical details.

I want to believe she's telling me the truth about what happened. After all, Jesse, Maya's boyfriend of eight years and Deanna's father, wouldn't do something this horrendous—breaking bones horrendous. Diego says I'm being naïve. Miguel, Maya's older brother, who is temporarily living at home, sides with his dad. He warned his sister, "Look, Maya, I'm staying out of it this time, but you tell that piece-of-shit boyfriend of yours that he just better not get in my face." The last time Maya sported a bruise after an altercation with

Jesse—and it wasn't the first time—Miguel gave him a split lip.

I overhear Maya on the phone complaining to her younger sister Mimi. I'm compelled to listen in on my bedroom fax line. I need to know the truth.

"My face is all puffed out on one side. I got two black eyes and four stitches. I look like one of those hospital shots on Jerry Springer ... and the doctor had to give me four numb shots in the broken part before he cracked it. Nose cracking sounds really, *really* loud, like a bomb going off inside your head. It really hurts, Mimi."

"Did Jesse do it, Maya? Miguel thinks it was Jesse." Mimi cuts to the mustard.

"Mimi, don't tell Miguel that Jesse's living in Concord now, 'kay?

"So Jesse *did* do it. He hit you?"

There's no BS-ing Mimi. Mimi (short for Magdalena), the baby, is in her fourth year at a two-year college in San Diego. Admittedly, she's biased against Jesse big time. Mimi's been plotting to break them up since junior high. Mimi's our one kid who lasted four years in Lafayette's highly rated public high school. And she had sense enough to leave home a year after graduation, despite her father's protests. Still, I do miss her—the clomp-clomp-clomp of her platforms down the hall, her classical piano filling the house, those Seinfeld reruns, and her eye-rolling insinuations that she must have been adopted.

"He didn't hit me, Mimi."

"Did he shove you? Hit you with something? What, Maya?" Mimi sounds aggravated.

"Uh, it was his head."

"He head-butted you! Jesse hit you with his pointy cue ball head? Ewwww! That's so-oo fucked up, Maya. Really fucked."

There it was. The knotty, sickly, putrid truth, rotting over the Pac Bell phone line. Damn. My own daughter lied to me. She looked me in the eyes and lied to my face.

"I shouldn't have been standing in his way, Mimi. He was drunk and I didn't want him to drive. It's my fault. I tried to stop him ..."

Now I hate the creep, but I cover my mouth so I don't scream and out myself over the phone. I always tried to be nice and welcoming to Jesse and overlook his ADHD mental health issues, since he's Deanna's father. But I don't give a rat's ass if he is the donor of half my granddaughter's genes, every mama-bear cell in my menopausal body wants to hunt down this creep and smack him upside his pointy shaved head.

*But a head butt?* Seriously? I don't remember any head butting growing up in Wisconsin. Can a head butt really break a nose? I mean, if you're not a goat?

In the following days, Maya insists her nose is still tilted and has me drive her back to Kaiser for another adjustment. I tell Dr. Yang that Maya admitted that Jesse broke her nose but he says he's not making a report, despite my insistence. Local police tell me that they can't help either since no one except Maya knows where Jesse is staying—he's temporarily homeless and jobless— and Maya's mouth is zipped. I'm a nonviolent person but I'm aware that Diego's "Personal Violence Code" (the one he worked on in his men's anger group) calls for some retaliation in this situation. I know how painful it is for him to see his daughter with both her eyes puffed and purple as an eggplant. The brass knuckles Diego keeps in his glove compartment ache for some payback—some small adjustment to Jesse's rather prominent schnozz. A lesson. But Diego admits, "My hands are tied. I'm an educator. I can't have an assault record." We both agree that his job security at the college comes before Jesse's ass-whipping. There's nothing either of us can do. Miguel bows out of defending family honor too.

"Not my business," he says.

I can't get my head straight. Yes, at first I believed Maya's San Francisco bar story although we cringed when she said, "It was some random Mexican dude." A tacky insult to our family's Mexican heritage. Since learning that Jesse was responsible, I've had spontaneous bursts of rage all week with flames I can't put out. As I battle through Maya's nose crisis, I find myself cycling through a mucky cesspool of emotions—anger, fear, guilt, humiliation, nausea. Why didn't I do more to end this sick relationship when Maya was fifteen? Now I'm whop-whop-whopping myself with a wooden baseball bat of shame.

Exhausted after days of beating myself up, I admitted I was powerless over this crap—including Maya's lies and her spectacular choice in men and the malignant shame I was lugging around on my back like a dead monkey.

I reasoned there were two truths here:

#1. Maya's boyfriend broke her nose.

#2. I am not defective.

Jumping from number one to number two took a giant leap of faith that doesn't come naturally. I can do this, I thought. I can make boundaries. As long as Maya is living in my house, Diego and I get to make the rules.

Here was my newborn, freshly baby-powdered boundary: "Jesse, you fucking piece of shit, don't you ever set one of your twitching feet in my house again."

I knew this wasn't Mother Teresa perfect.

Maya takes my advice and stops taking Jesse's calls. Two days later on Friday Jesse calls me on my business line. He's lost it. He's screaming at me. "Barbara, if you don't let me talk to Maya now, I'm coming over with a gun and I'll kill you and your entire family!" I hang up the phone, shaking. Diego asks Maya if Jesse owns a gun.

"No," she says, looking terrified. "But his roommate does. I know where Jesse lives. He'll be here in fifteen minutes!"

There's only one thing left to do. Time to pull out big guns. Fight fire with fire. And crazy with crazy.

I knock on my son's door. "Miguel, are you awake?"

I consider calling the police, but what if Jesse is bluffing? Why have the police show up, one more time, for nada? In our three-car garage neighborhood, it's embarrassing. And they never come with just one car either. Yes, I joke at twelve step meetings that the police visit our address more than my mother, but it's the truth.

Fifteen minutes later our home swarms like a kicked hornet's nest. Maya puts Deanna to bed early, then paces down the hall doing her OCD one, two, three, four. One, two ... back and forth steps in every doorway. Diego scouts out traffic from the kitchen window. The warmth of day cools at dusk and the green grass out front darkens to a deep olive. Miguel has been in his front bedroom with the door shut ever since I told him Jesse's threat word for word. I can't seem to concentrate on loading the dinner dishes in the dishwasher; I'm putting glassware on the bottom. I know what's coming.

Maya checks the kitchen clock. Eight-twenty. "Any minute now, Mom."

"Maya, this is an order. You are not going outside to talk to Jesse under any circumstance."

After we agree, I check on Deanna, who is sound asleep in Maya's bedroom. Her six-year-old auburn curls halo around her head on the white pillow.

*Barbara, I'll kill you and your entire family.*

I steady myself against the doorframe and close the bedroom door quietly. My knees melt like Jell-O. Through the front door screen, I see Diego out front in the semi-dark peeking at Glenside Drive from behind the pine tree. From the door I can see into Miguel's bedroom window. That's strange. He knows Jesse will be here any minute yet he's lying on his bunk, barefoot in his underwear. The jeans and shirt he had on earlier are hung neatly on the desk chair. But he's taut. His fists clench and the arm muscles he built up in jail bulge from his shoulders. Even prone in bed he looks like an ignited bomb about to detonate. Odd that he's undressed but I don't let him know I see him. I'm still edgy around my son, wary of the meth-induced manic episodes of his teenage past and his Houdini proclivities for picking locks with credit cards and escaping from mental hospitals. He's resented me for the past ten years, ever since I kicked him out of the house as a teenager for smoking pot. I feel a pang of guilt for getting him involved in a revenge plot. I know Diego wants me to call the police to keep Miguel out of trouble; Miguel's only been out of jail for three months for some nonviolent charge and he's still on probation.

Diego calls from behind the rose bushes. "He's here! His white Mercury is parking at the end of the block. Direction two o'clock. He's getting out of the vehicle." His voice lowers. "He's got a stick ..., no, it's a tire iron. He's heading toward the house!"

Freaked out, I head to the front door. "C'mon inside, Diego."

Suddenly, Miguel whips past me on the lawn, disappearing into the night wearing only his boxers and wife beater, a lightning flash in his eyes. Oh God, help us. I did it. I unleashed it—the mania gene. Invincible. Grandiose. All-powerful. Knowing no fear. The gene I gave him. The gene, in times of war, that you hope is on your side. Jesse, being merely ADHD, is no match for bipolar.

Diego darts out into the street after Miguel. "Diego, no!"

But he doesn't stop. Maya's at the front door and I block her exit. Through the screen we see nothing but black. I hear muffled voices, grunts, then ... clang, clang clang ... thud. "Ooof."

"Mom, you have to call the police! NOW!"

I stretch my arms across the door. A loud moan pierces my ear.

Diego appears in the driveway, out of breath, his dark eyes popping. "He came at Miguel with a tire iron but Miguel made him drop it. Miguel's got him pinned." More groans come from the street. "But I got my licks in. I kicked him a few times." Diego heaves, catching his breath. Maya runs down the hall, I presume to check on Deanna.

"Barbara, you better call the police before Miguel gets hurt!"

Why am I always the enabler in this family? "Damn it, Diego, you call the police. I'm watching Maya."

"Me?" He looks surprised, as if I just told him to darn socks.

More grunts from outside.

"*Ayyyy chingada*, somebody could get maimed out there, Barbara."

I stand my ground at the door. We glare at each other in a contest to see who will give in and pick up the kitchen wall phone first.

"AHHHH!" An agonizing scream shakes my bones.

"Okay, okay, I'll call." As I head for the phone, Maya runs out the front door in her powder-blue shimmer jacket. The one I just spot-soaked in Shout and washed. I race after her to the door but the screen slams in my face. Outside I look for Maya in the dark. What the hell is she doing? But Maya has disappeared and the street is eerily quiet. Over the rose bush I see our neighbors Bunny and Steve standing in their driveway looking up and down Glenside Drive. I duck so they won't see me. You'd think they'd be bored with seeing police cars in front of our house by now. Tires screech around the corner. I presume it's Jesse's car. Miguel appears in the dark driveway hunched over and panting. I try to help him to the door but he shoves my arm away.

In the kitchen Diego is giving instructions on the wall-mounted rotary.

"Glenside Drive. No, Glenside is one word, not two. Yes, yes that's right. Yes, he had a weapon. Okay. We'll wait." He hangs up.

Miguel's bare legs are bleeding and his knees are pebbled as if he'd taken a holy pilgrimage on gravel.

"Where's the *pinché cavrón?*" [jerk] Diego asks, agitated.

"He took off in his piece of shit car." Huff, huff. "Maya's with him."

Oh no, not again.

"Police are coming but he attacked you, Miguel, it's self defense." Diego checks out the window. "Hey, did you see when I kicked him?" he brags.

Miguel straightens up, talking to his Dad, not to me. "I had him down on the street like this." Miguel is on his knees demonstrating. "I told him, 'I don't like having to do this, but you give me no choice.' But see, both my arms were pinning him down. I, I, I didn't know what else to do so I." He shakes his head.

"What did you do to him?" I hate the guy but I don't want him in the hospital. A little maimed maybe.

"I bit him in the forehead. Little bitch."

"You bit his forehead?" I can't picture it.

"The skin doesn't come off, Mom; it just sort of stretches—like in cartoons." Miguel, standing now, uses his thumb and forefinger to measure the diameter of a large orange.

"Ewww!" I make a face. Miguel and his dad are high-fiving and back-patting, and the gap-toothed grin on my son's face is a mile wide. I go for some bandages for the blood trickling down his legs, then I remember we only have Barbie Band-Aids. I hand him some paper napkins from the table. I suddenly realize how much taller Miguel is than his Dad.

While Miguel and Diego continue to re-enact the fight, Maya saunters in looking dejected. Her jacket is still clean. "Don't ask," she says.

The police will be here any minute so I tell Miguel to get dressed. I want my son to look presentable.

Miguel scowls. "Mom, I handled it; why did you call the police?"

"Your dad did."

"Dad did?" he asks, surprised.

In minutes two vehicles with red lights flashing pull up behind the rose bushes. Police arrive fast and in great numbers in the burbs, probably because there's not much to do.

"Police again," Maya rolls her eyes. "Why do these things always happen to MEEE? Everyone is crazy in this house!" She throws her hands up in the air theatrically and stomps down the hall to her bedroom.

Miguel, still undressed, explains to the two officers at the door, "I was taking a nap when Jesse approached our house, sir. I ran outside and he came at me with a tire iron."

"A lethal weapon," Diego adds.

"You were in bed?" The officer takes notes.

"Yes sir, I was resting at the time. Look at me, I'm in my underwear. I didn't even have time to put my shoes on."

I can't explain how I knew that Miguel wouldn't get the worst of it, from Jesse or from the police who took down his story and left. Sometimes I think it's some extrasensory intuition that my son and I share after experiencing manic episodes. Or maybe it's my son's reputation in street fights. Maya said the Walnut Creek homeless population (all ten of them) is scared to death of Miguel—they call him crazy. I had to be optimistic because I was the one who signed him up for the fight. A female Donald King with better hair. I knew what I was doing. I wanted Jesse to have a lesson. Some small scar reminder to teach him you don't mess with the Flores family. I knew my thinking wasn't living up to my highest spiritual potential. Seeking revenge is lower-plane, bestial thinking. Disgusting like dog fighting. But seeing a daughter's broken nose can tarnish even a professed Gandhian's ideals.

I admit I was complicit.

I pulled out the Big Guns, the Sampson gene. I took the musket down off the shelf, cleaned it, loaded it, and set it by the front door. It was a matter of time.

To Diego it was a matter of Latino family honor. He tells Miguel, "If they start it, you finish it."

And Miguel did. The day after the street tussle, Jesse drove his Mercury across two state lines to live with his parents in Washington.

. . .

ON THE TWENTY-NINTH of June 2004, at 2:30 p.m., the big one hit. With aftershocks that did more lasting damage than the following night I spend in a mental hospital. Every married person muses about divorce and separation at sometime or another but my thirty-one years with Diego did not prepare me for what happened.

Every Friday, Diego's free day, we go out for brunch in downtown Lafayette, then we head our separate ways for the afternoon and meet again with the girls for dinner. On Fridays, Diego brings home Chinese. After brunch, he often drives off to Berkeley to see his friend Keith and I head downhill to Trader Joe's to shop.

That's what I'm doing when I spot Diego's silver Dodge van parked a half mile from the house at the bottom of Snake Hill Road. Hard to miss—his is the only car parked in the trail staging area.

*Aha! I bet I'll catch him smoking weed.* Deviously, I pull in on the opposite side of the parking lot more in "gotcha" fun than to shame him. I respect Diego's different methods of entertainment as long as he keeps it out of the house. The gravel crunches under my Echo flats as I sneak behind his van. Ducking behind the rear fender I barely see him leaning out his driver-side window talking on his gold metro cell. I bought him the cell so we could communicate during his afternoon, after-school excursions. The cell phone was our marriage counselor's idea.

I tiptoe behind the van, trying not to crunch gravel, then crouch behind the rear wheel of the van. He's talking to someone about picking up our friend Keith at the airport last night.

And laughing. "We're driving round and round ..."

Funny, he told me he went alone to the airport. After a few more chuckles he says distinctly, "I love you. I'll call you tonight."

Huh? *I love you. I'll call you tonight.* I'm stunned. It takes a moment.

Then I'm hit with a two-by-four realizing what I just heard.

The next second I'm in the passenger seat of his van yelling and swinging at him with both hands. In two minutes when I'm breathless and thwarted by his expert forearm defense and depleted of names to call him, I'm sprinting back in my Ford Escort, gunning up the hill, seeing red, and screaming obscenities to the windshield. Diego is right behind me. I have to arrive home before he does so I'll be the one to kick him out.

I stampede, fuming, into our two-car garage that we recently remodeled into a room with a gym for Diego.

I suspect every article of his clothing, every hat, every sock, every pair of boxer shorts is contaminated with *her*. I'm totally disgusted. This is way worse than lice. It all has to be out of my house. Every goddamn shred. I tear clothes out of his gym closet, tossing them into a bonfire size heap next to his incline board. Diego enters through the kitchen door to the garage.

"Get out! Get out of my house, you liar," I scream at him, "and take your whore germs with you." I'm flinging fast and furious. Short sleeve shirts first: the Mexican *guayaberas*, the seersuckers, then long sleeves and the jackets. Diego keeps all his clothes in order with all the hangers facing the right way, which makes tossing more efficient. The metal hangers cling-clang on the cement floor in percussion to my rage. I'm calling him every name I know, wishing for a better repertory than "liar" and "asshole."

Diego stands back, grumbling. "I'm sorry, but now you know." He makes no attempt to try to stop my Olympic shirt hurling. "Jesus, Barbara." His eyes look alternately guilty and enraged, as if he can't decide what emotional mode best suits the situation.

"Listen, I—"

"Why should I? Everything you say is a lie." I'm heaving khakis now. I can't throw fast enough. "You lied to me, you lied to the counselor, you even lied to your dead father, you swore on your father's honor you weren't seeing anyone." I toss three Dockers on the pile that's waist high now.

He sighs, his eyes darting within his immobility as if he's searching for the right words.

Then: "I don't have to use Viagra with her."

"Fuck you."

I reach for the nearest weapon off a workbench—a Zen meditation book—

and fling it at his face, landing it square on the left side of his salt-and-pepper beard. He's rubbing his chin (it was a paperback) when Maya and Deanna walk in looking bewildered. Diego stares at his clothes in a heap, then picks up an armful and runs it past the two girls out the kitchen to his van.

"Mom, what happened?"

I can't be bothered. It's so damn obvious that her father is an asshole. As fast as I toss, Diego runs armfuls out to his van in efficient assembly-line fashion. Diego has a lot of clothes. Maya and Deanna watch through the garage window as Diego, on the front lawn, trips over several of his dropped Cuba T-shirts. Normally this Herculean clothes-heaving effort would exhaust me more than two hours of Jazzercize, but I'm enraged. I'm pumped. I mound a leather jacket on the pile like a shot put. I'm ready for the forty pairs of shoes he stores in the cedar closet. The heap soon reaches shoulder height. Now I want lighter fluid. And matches. And blood.

# CHAPTER THREE
## HOME

I *love you, I'll call you tonight.*

"Who is she?" I ask him over the phone.

"Barbara, it's not what you think."

Talking to him over the phone feels awkward and wrong. After a fight he should be here in our bedroom, or out on the patio, or at least sitting in his van. Calling me from a motel the day after my hospital release feels cold and not quite real.

"Where did you meet her?" My interrogator voice—the one he says he hates.

"I deserve to know who she is." The black hyphenated scabs on my wrist peek out from the long-sleeves of my cotton nightgown. They deserve answers.

"Look, I just need some time. Barbara, you're just making this hard on yourself—it isn't necessary."

"Yes, it *is* necessary!" His words to her over the phone, "I love you, I'll call you tonight," replay over and over in my head like a scratched record—a form of torture.

I hear him breathing. He sounds tired.

"Who is she?"

"A student, but—"

"How old?"

He sighs.

"HOW OLD IS SHE?" I demand.

"I dunno, thirty-seven, thirty-eight."

"Jesus. Diego, you're sixty-three, for Christ sakes."

"Look, I have to go to my eight-thirty class. I'll call you this afternoon, okay? After my office hour."

"Wait. We have counseling day after tomorrow."

"Of course. Don't worry about it."

I hear the click. I know Diego will call me when he says he will. He always does. But this is confusing. Like he's here but he isn't here. Still, I also know he won't stay at the Lafayette Hillside Economy Suites for more than a week, two at the most. He'll come home. He always comes home after a fight.

Abruptly, the small, sweet voice enters through the crack of the bedroom door.

"Gramma, can you please make me my Eggos?"

My voice turns melodious. "Course, sweetheart."


. . .


*I LOVE YOU. I'll call you tonight.*

*I love you. I'll call you tonight.*

The words he said replay again and again and again.

What if it's true?

I'm balled up in bed clutching my belly. The nausea comes in waves, as if I'm standing on the ledge of a skyscraper looking down. After days in bed my body becomes a sheet blown on a clothesline, ripped and twisted in an emotional storm until I'm more holes than cloth. I can barely hang on. I call this pain *The Unbearable Endless*, a phrase borrowed from a woman's story of losing her lover. My grief is too violent, too demanding, and too frequent a visitor not to have a name.

*What if he's never coming home?*

I peek out from under the sheet just enough to stare at a framed photo of my mother on the wall. It's a black-and-white photograph of Mom at thirteen, even then a beauty. This is the only picture I've found of her that reveals a cosmetic flaw—one crooked right eyetooth. The snaggle tooth must have been corrected early, before all her pretty pin-up-girl photos in the 1940s. Across the country in my parents' Florida condo, two crumbling black paper albums are filled with my mother's stunning homecoming-queen beauty. Arm in arm with Dad in his Navy officer's white uniform, they could be a movie star couple. Of course, I can't call them; it's too humiliating, and too soon.

My grief during those first weeks seemed to model my mother's own paralyzing depressions. However, my mother was the last person on earth I'd consciously choose as a role model. Ironically, it was that imperfect snaggle-toothed portrait of her that stayed with me at my bedside.

• • •

DR. PHIL SAYS that after an affair, it's important to have "complete disclosure." That week Diego and I attended our weekly Wednesday counseling appointment with Judy, but I got no answers. Some months after Diego's retirement two years ago I felt something in our marriage shift and I sought Judy's help. She informed us that Diego was having a midlife crisis. He just needed space, he'd said. He swore on his deceased father's honor that he wasn't having an affair.

That Wednesday I hoped Judy would negotiate the terms of a short separation (to punish Diego), then we'd talk reconciliation. But after she learned that Diego had been lying to her too, she said that she never wanted to see him again and she thought I should feel the same way. "He can't be trusted," she said.

"She's right." Diego nodded, contented to agree with her

A lot of help she was. The session was a complete bust.

•  •  •

WE MEET AGAIN ON Friday for our usual brunch. Across the café table Diego looks the consummate professor in rose-colored glasses, trim in his blue seersucker shirt and short-shaved beard. I'm wearing a short white jean skirt and more makeup and hair gel than usual. We smile and I admire the pink carnations on the table. We talk nicey-nicey and order coffee and croissants. *We can get over this once I have the truth.*

*Who is she?*

"So what's going on?" My loaded question really means, *what's happening with us?*

"Barbara, don't worry. She's just a friend." Diego shrugs.

I know Diego, like many Latin men, can too easily say, "I love you" in a casual way, but how much of a friend is she? Do you leave your wife of thirty years and move into a motel for *a friend?* He appears calm and casual like this is our every Friday-morning brunch date. He's not the wide-eyed, deer-stuck-in-the-headlights guy who ducked the shirts, hangers, and books flying at him a week ago. Nor is he the hunched, guilty dog with his mischievous tail between his legs who showed up at our Wednesday counseling session.

Over croissants oozing butter and raspberry jam, we schmooze about the kids, the bills he says he'll continue to pay, his garden timers, and everything but the she-elephant in the curtained café. After breakfast we linger in the parking lot. He glances at my mini jean skirt I dug out of the back of my closet. "Barbara, you look beautiful."

*Does he want me?* Leaning against my car, not anxious to leave, I finally ask the question burning holes in my brain all week long.

"When are you coming home?"

He swipes the graying whiskers at the sides of his mouth with a deft thumb and forefinger. "I'm dating," he says.

*Dating?* The word lands like a bomb. I'm not sure any man married to me has a right to date. "What did I do?"

"Barbara, it's not you, it's me, okay." He opens his arms for a parting hug. I need a hug. A real loving hug. Then he does something unforgivable—the guy hug that avoids chest action. The A-frame hug. Then the worst part—he pats my back—the guy-patting thing. Being hug-patted crushes me. I can forgive his calling me a *ventajosa* (controlling bitch) in anger, and I can wait out the ambivalence he professed towards me in counseling, his needing space, he said, but never, *never* could I accept the patting thing.

"I'll call you tomorrow," he says. I turn quickly, get in my car, and roll up the tinted window. I can't let him see tears. He steps toward his van, then calls back, "Barbara, I just need time." He pulls out of the gravel driveway and I'm blinded by a whirlwind of defeat, confusion, and white dust.

Home, under the covers, I decide that the man I just met at the café isn't my real husband—the real Diego pulls me into him when he kisses me goodbye, he holds me in bed when I'm scared, and he looks into my eyes and tells me I have beautiful lips. That man was an impostor. He's confused. He only needs time, like he said.

My bed is my only sanctuary, a mattress island that separates me from a hostile real world. I don't want to hear people saying that I will survive without him. I drown in ruffled eyelet pillows, under gold, 600-thread-count, satin-finish sheets, recently purchased as an expensive enticement for Diego. The window valences match a floral comforter blossomed with large roses and full-headed peonies. They mock my agony; still, I take pride in having a marital bed worthy of a Martha Stewart pom-pom Award. Only sleep, especially at night, with its tangible dreams consistently turns back time and brings my husband back home.

*Our limbs entwine in a loose lazy weave, my nose rests in the crook of his arm. We're still warm, damp, breathing heavily from exertion. His breath is slightly faster than mine, and I pause to catch up, so that our exhales greet the morning air in unison. My fingers comb his thick, dark, wavy hair, graze the bristles of a salt-and-pepper beard; then I trace down his arm, pausing at the mound of a firm biceps and a mole the size of a dime on his shoulder that I know so well. His hand reaches for me, and he pulls me into his chest. Such incredible hands, long, smooth but strong, protective, tender and polite—always waiting for an invitation. I bury my nose in his chest, inhaling him. Clean, like a fresh towel after a summer shower.*

*"At sixty-two you have a better body than most men do at forty-five," I tell him truthfully.*

*"It's all in the abs," he says, rolling his chestnut eyes into mine. Then he pulls the sheet down to expose a lean, tight midriff. He grins showing the same crooked bottom teeth that I've loved for thirty years. My head rests on his shoulder, his arm wrapped around me; I count the few hairs on his tan chest. Six, no, seven.*

*Something about our mornings together melts me, the soft rumpled sheets at our feet, the smell of jasmine through the open window, the sound of his sprinklers going off—he has them on timers. Even before the clock and the kids stir, when he has an eight-thirty econ class on a weekday, it feels like a long, silky vacation morning. Like we've got all day together, like we have a lifetime.*

Then with no warning, morning light pierces through the lace curtains like rude neighbors who barge in without permission. And the intimacy, which seconds ago was tactile and firm and soap-scented, evaporates in a cruel instant.

I'm alone in bed—feeling amputated.

Waking up is now a recurring nightmare, one that seems to never end.

After every fight, hundreds of fights, we always worked things out by talking, by apologies, by making love. But this is the first time he said, "I'm dating." What do I do now? Judy terminated our counseling sessions and I'm embarrassed to ask him out for brunch again. I call, Joanna, my recovery program sponsor.

"Focus on yourself," she says. "It's secondary narcissism."

"Secondary narcissism?" I'm already having trouble understanding primary.

"It means you're so centered on the life of another that you revolve your life around them," she explains. "Barb, Stop making Diego your higher power."

Easier said than done. Joanna suggests that I skin priorities down to bare bones, "to avoid overwhelm." So I make a list:

#1. Give Diego his space so he can come to his senses.

#2. Don't do anything to put me in jail or mental hospital.

#3. Don't become addicted to tranquilizers.

#4. Make a gratitude list.

#5. Don't ask Miguel to borrow a gun.

· · ·

OVER THE NEXT FEW WEEKS I still speak with Diego daily on the phone; nothing's changed there. Prayer, rosaries, and going to Sunday Mass don't help. Even my Thursday twelve step meeting, where we bitch about drinking family members, isn't a jump-start into living life forward again.

He needs his space, he said. I'm doing time waiting for "his space" to be over.

In bed I watch Dr. Phil and Oprah and the talk-show guests who reveal all the particulars of their miserable lives: obesity, spousal abuse, self-mutilation, drug addictions, and quirky sexual proclivities. It makes me feel better. My Kaiser outpatient aftercare, a four-week depression group, is like a live version of the Dr. Phil show—yet I feel I don't belong there. I'm not depressed, I'm broken-hearted. There's a difference. Still, listening to the other adults in this three-day-a-week Kaiser group offers some relief, and I'm growing to like the other patients: Janice with her head in the lap of her skirt, the muscle guy who burned his own arm, and Ken, who's despondent over getting a pink slip after twenty years of devoted service. Ironically, he worked as a tech for Kaiser.

On the advice of a twelve step friend, I decide to join a "divorced and separated" Catholic group. I'm surprised to hear other women in their forties and fifties share variations of my story: *It was someone he met at work ... The babysitter ... He met her at doggie day care.*

We gather in a church basement with something in common: we're unexpected new-age widows whose middle-aged husbands, enticed by Internet porn and Viagra, were herded off to greener breeding grounds. There too, I feel that I don't quite belong. Because I still haven't given up hope.

· · ·

THE BEST PART OF THE day is picking Deanna up after swim lessons. With Diego gone, she's claimed rights to his side of our queen-size bed. My feet are growing used to finding her socks, doll dresses, or hard puzzle pieces under the sheets. My bottom dresser drawer has turned into a toy box for both of us, where we keep our puzzles, books, clean underwear (Deanna's), puppets, and Nerf guns.

This July morning we sit side by side, propped up on pillows, playing cards with Leona, our mountain lion puppet. Deanna's long auburn curls are in their usual tangle, syrup spills streak her T-shirt, and her socks don't match. I'm a grandma—I don't have to care.

Deanna's mom barges into the bedroom, and as usual, does a pirouette scrutinizing her size five body in the closet door mirror. She squints at herself from her blonde streaks down her flowered scrubs to her pink painted toes.

"Mom, do I look fat?" This question is Maya's mantra—a Zen koan we can never figure out.

"No, you don't look fat." Deanna and I drone in practiced unison. Obviously this is not the right answer because Maya will repeat this question to us multiple times a day. Deanna rolls her eight-year-old eyes, glances at the playing cards fanned in her hand, and says to the puppet on my right hand, "Your turn, Leona."

We're used to it. One morning, Maya ran screaming into my bedroom insisting that her pores were growing. Her daily crises involve germs, fear of AIDS, brown recluse spiders, and moth eggs. I know now to give my daughter a mama bear hug and just let her vent. Let Maya be Maya. Tickling does not help.

Now she works as a medical assistant for a local oral surgeon. She's like my own private duty nurse in scrubs who does OCD rituals. She's the only one of our three kids at home. Mimi is still in San Diego and Miguel, the oldest, is living with his girlfriend, Erika, and her parents in Vallejo, a half hour away. I haven't seen them since Miguel's auto accident a month ago. I hear through Erika that he's recovering.

Without my asking, Maya took all the photos of her father off the walls and hid them on my top closet shelf. With her around, I don't have to feel so neurotic alone. Maya with all her phobias, by the grace of God, is here for me.

She's my trusted post-mental-hospital caretaker—the person assigned to hide all the knives.

Both Maya and Deanna are at the top of my gratitude list. I still have two people to cook for. Pulling out my recipes for orange roasted chicken with sourdough stuffing or enchiladas *suizas*, Diego's favorites, is still painful but I keep cooking the same large portions for four anyway. I don't know how not to. So the freezer fills with leftovers.

I'm saving them. Lorraine, my new Kaiser therapist, diagnosed me with a "situational depression," which means when the situation (Diego's midlife crisis) is over, my regular put-together, married self will be back to normal.

The house is still full of land mines. Diego's handwriting turns up everywhere: on old notes to me, labels on boxes, even his Sharpie-drawn initials "DJF" on the bottoms of his socks. Coming across his compulsively neat, legible hand lettering, as articulate and well formed as his speech, feels gut wrenching. Though I emptied the closet in his garage/gym, I neglected his drawers. It's his antique mahogany dresser that tempts me most. He didn't empty his drawers. Does he think he's coming back? The tall dresser had belonged to his father, José Maria Flores, son of the mayor of Juarez, grandson of the governor of the state of Chihuahua. Each time I slide a drawer open, I breath in this indescribable macho scent of imported Spanish soap, old polished wood, and the stories of bygone wealth lingering in his neatly folded T-shirts, knee wraps, hotel matchbooks, and sock balls.

I already checked all the matchbooks for phone numbers.

. . .

SOFT KNOCKS ON MY bedroom door at mid-morning. I'm up designing a shoe ad in my robe.

"C'mon in, Deanna." I know it's Deanna. Maya doesn't bother to knock.

"Deanna! Don't you dare go into Gramma's room," Maya yells from the kitchen. I place my Ecco shoe illustration in the scanner, close it, exhale, and try to figure out what's the problem between Maya and Deanna. With my ear against the bedroom door I hear muffled voices, shushes. Was Deanna crying? Code orange alert. Deanna shouldn't be crying. I've told Maya in this house Deanna has consequences, not punishments. Timeouts, not spankings. I want Deanna's upbringing to be different.

I look for Deanna in the kitchen.

"Butt out, you're always interfering," she snaps. Maya opens and closes the freezer door multiple times.

"Was Deanna crying?" I catch Deanna's face in the hall peeking out her bedroom door.

"Okay, if you're not telling me what happened, I'll ask Deanna."

"Mom, stop!" She plants her bare feet in the kitchen doorway, blocking my passage to Deanna's room. "She's on timeout. Every time I try to discipline her, you always have to stick your big head in." Deanna's bare foot edges out into the hallway, then her head appears.

"I can spank my own kid if I want. Deanna, get back in your room and close the door." Deanna pulls back her foot and head but her shadow falls across the oak hallway floor.

"I should move to Seattle and live with Jesse."

"Real smart, Maya. Move back in with a guy who broke your nose."

"I wanna go live with Daddy," Deanna calls out.

"Dammit, Deanna, I said to close the door!" Maya scolds. The door slams. Deanna uses a tad more force than necessary.

"Okay, now I'm adding five minutes more to the timer, Deanna," she calls down the hall. But she doesn't move from her blockade to adjust the stove timer, which I see has five minutes left. Five minutes is okay, but sometimes Maya gives twenty and twenty is too long for an eight-year-old. It's a minute for each year of age, I tell Maya. She pulls the Eggo box from the freezer, shakes it. Only crumbs. "You need to buy more Eggos, Mom." She tosses the package in the stuffed trash compactor.

"Maya, we don't hit in this house."

"I didn't do anything," Deanna calls from behind her door.

"First she kicked me. Then she bit me," Maya says loud enough for Deanna to hear. "So I whapped her on the butt. She deserved it."

"I told you about that study, Maya. You can't hit a child. It's not effective. It causes trust issues and violent behavior later in life."

"Dad said the Child Protection Services worker told him spanking is not considered abusive. End of story. Go back to bed, Mom." That's Diego's pet phrase—"end of story."

"*Don't you dare* bring your father into this."

I remembered Diego's defense. "Barbara, spanking isn't violence," he preached. "And even violence is acceptable in certain situations. Everyone knows that." Damn, I hate when my head is still fighting with Diego, even when he's not here.

"Mom, I'm her mother, not you. I can spank Deanna if I want."

"Not in my house, you can't."

"Fine! We're moving to Washington!"

Ding! The kitchen timer announces a truce.

Deanna bounces out of her room looking like an innocent angel in her white nightgown. Lola, our Westie, follows with her happy windshield-wiper tail. Then Tigger, our cat, darts out like a low-flying bullet wearing a lacy pink doll dress.

· · ·

I PICK UP DEANNA FROM swim school and the thought of driving us back home suddenly feels unbearable. At home I'm forever hearing Diego coming in the front door or out in the yard watering his citrus trees. Sometimes I imagine he's tapping on my bedroom window with his trowel. Deanna, big enough to ride shotgun now, buckles herself in.

"Hey Deanna, how 'bout we go to the reservoir?"

"Yeah!" Her brown eyes, which somehow always look a bit sad to me, open wide as headlights.

"We have to get the bread first, Gramma." So we make a quick kitchen pit stop. Our freezer holds multiple, near-empty bags of stale sourdough and multigrain in various stages of freezer burn—saved for just such an impromptu occasion.

Deanna wants to bring Leona, but I get out of it by reminding her that Leona, a glove-size puppet, is too small for a life jacket. We consolidate the bread bags, and with wind in our sails and Dolly Parton in the tape deck, we're heading west to the Lafayette Reservoir, or "the res" as locals call it. A two-and-a-half mile scenic path circles the pristine blue water, home to fish, waterfowl, paddleboats, and a few stray party balloons. Stay-at-home Lafayette moms escape to the res when they're going bonkers trapped in their overpriced a million plus, four-bedroom, three-car-garage homes that are never shined enough, uncluttered enough, or remodeled enough.

Deanna runs ahead to the paddleboat dock and in minutes we're aboard our very own sun-bleached, fiberglass two-man craft. I steer and together we pump against the choppy current into the quiet center of the lake, as far away as possible from any human life: joggers, dog walkers, women (and men) pushing über-engineered strollers.

A mile in, we metaphorically drop anchor. Deanna, clad in an orange life jacket and flower print shorts, clamors onto the back deck, making our boat rock furiously. When I'm in pre-panic attack mode, like today, I find the sensation of being tossed around, like on a carnival tilt-o-wheel ride, to be incredibly soothing. I spread out in the plastic seat, close my eyes, and relax like Gramma's ball of warm dough being pleasantly punched and deflated on a floured board. Here, surrounded by indigo waters reflecting a cloudless sky,

I can breathe. I do absolutely nothing. For an hour of rented time my mind is set on drift.

I look overboard and notice a large white fish floating belly-up on my side of the boat.

"Gramma, Don't you dare touch it." She's already parroting her mother's phobias. Of course, I have to pretend to touch the fish and wag my finger at her, teasing Deanna with tainted, dead-fish finger. That's when we hear loud honking behind us.

"Here they come, Gramma!" Deanna, guardian of the bread bag, readies herself on the back deck. Across the dark blue lake an army of ducks advances at torpedo speed in V formation like the fleet of a thousand ships, half swimming, half flying.

"Oh my gawd, look at 'em all!" She sits up wide-eyed. Reaching into her arsenal, she picks off bread pieces and shoots tiny white cannonballs toward the advancing fleet. Some front-runners take to the air.

"Duck attack!" Deanna calls out gleefully. In seconds a mass of quacking ducks engulfs the waters off our back deck. She madly tosses out pieces that land like bombs, creating a frenzy of honking snapping yellow beaks and diving green feathers.

She aims behind the flock at the juveniles, but the big ducks in the front perform handstands on their wings to catch the pieces.

"Don't be so greedy," she reprimands. I notice she talks to birds the identical way her mother did at eight-years-old. Her every attempt, against the wind, to reach the younger birds in the back fails.

"Throw it out further, Deanna."

"This bread won't throw."

She pulls her arm back in a pitcher's windup over the side, but a large green mallard rushes in and snaps his flat gold beak inches beneath her fingertips. She screams, drops the crust, and backs away horrified. "Gramma, he tried to bite me."

"Honey, they don't have teeth." I laugh—the first good belly laugh I've had in weeks. And I can't stop chuckling. In the quiet center of the lake, amidst these noisy begging ducks, I notice how much my own "heh, heh, heh" laughter resembles quacking.

"Watch this, Deanna." I'm going to teach my granddaughter how to hand-feed a duck. I hold a baguette crust high over the side. A splashing flurry of ducks charges my side of the boat. A large brown female cranes her neck stretched like a pole, higher than I expect a duck neck to crane. I pull the bread piece higher.

"Gramma, what if it flies in the boat?"

"Watch. She'll eat it out of my hand."

But a huge snapping orange beak is inches from my arm. Slowly, I lower the baguette piece. The duck lunges, snaps and clamps onto my fingers like two wood paddles. Harder than I expect. "Ow!"

"He bit you, Gramma."

"He's a she." I show her my fingers, not red, but a bit wet. "Didn't hurt." I add cockily. Actually it was like a firm handshake—well, from a clothespin. I wag my wet duck-germ finger at Deanna again playfully.

The ducks switch to Deanna's side of the paddleboat. She lobs another piece into the air. But this time her crouton sails with the wind, flying farther than either of us can believe.

"Whoa, did you see that, Gramma?" It lands well behind the flock and a juvenile in the rear scoops it up. Deanna beams, looking amazed at her newfound throwing skills.

"Watch this one, Gramma!" Another home run.

"Good arm, Deanna."

Leaning back in the sun, hands behind my head, I'm thinking at least I'm a good grandmother. Deanna is tossing out the last crumbs and her final reprimands to our soon-to-be fair-weather feathered friends. Then I remember my camera in my bag under the seat. I'm snapping Deanna feverishly from every angle—her every move—wanting to capture her little girl-ness, her wind-snarled hair, her sweet beaver teeth, and most of all her bottomless reservoir of joy.

. . .

WHEN MAYA BECAME PREGNANT at age sixteen, she had a troubled teen history with OCD, eating disorders, and cutting, so a pregnancy seemed ill advised. But Maya thought differently. And the Kaiser nurse, who verified her pregnancy test, informed her that any girl over twelve has the right to choose.

"But she can't even remember to feed the hamster," I protested. Diego, chanting his mantra, "No more diapers!", agreed with me. He says diapers give him asthma. He even offered Maya two thousand dollars to terminate the pregnancy, but Maya declined her father's offer out of allegiance to her sister. "It wouldn't be fair to Mimi to take two thousand dollars, because she only gets a five-dollar allowance," she said.

I consulted with Gangaji, a Marin County lady guru, whose lectures I attended. She told me that my daughter was carrying the Christ child. Although I considered her word choice to be metaphorical, still, what theological interpretation gave me the right to tamper with the Second Coming? Jesse's parents complicated the matter even further by pushing to have the child adopted. Maya reasoned, "If I have to go through all that pain and fatness, I should at least get to keep it." And I thought in secret, what if the Virgin Mary's mother-in-law had butted in and told fourteen-year-old Mary that she had to put her baby up for adoption? What if Jesus had been raised by a nice Muslim family instead of a Jewish one? What then? Okay, I googled it. You're right. Christianity is 600 years older than the Qu'ran. But you get my point.

At first I had been campaigning for early termination (I couldn't say the

"A" word), but my mother objected. "This child is part of our family," she said, "and it deserves to suffer just like the rest of us." Direct quote.

Eventually, by Christmas, after Maya's first trimester, I was already buying booties and onesies. I'd joined sides with Maya, my mother, the Kaiser nurse, and Gangaji. Diego still insisted he wasn't changing any diapers.

. . .

THOSE FIRST FEW WEEKS after Diego left I'm camped out in bed. One afternoon Maya comes home early from her work at the dental office. She sits at the table in her purple flowered scrubs, eating a tortilla chip, biting off one corner at a time. I greet her still in my bathrobe. I've got a moment to chat with her because it's ten minutes before Oprah. I'm finding it strange that Diego being gone seems to have no effect on Maya, or on Deanna for that matter. And why isn't she justifiably angry with him for breaking up our family? Just the opposite, she seems to be growing impatient with me living in my robe and crying every day. It's been two weeks now since Diego left, and my nightstand is still so full of wadded-up tissues it looks like a Memorial Day float. Maya stares at me funny across the table, a look I can't quite place. Then I recognize it; it's the same expression on the faces of my program friends—it's pity.

"Mom ... I think there's something you should know."

"What's wrong?" I'm ready to listen to Maya's problems. After all, I'm still her mother. Today doesn't have to be all about me. I go to the cupboard for a cup and a tea bag.

"Um," she mumbles head down. "It's uh, that I think I overheard Dad on the phone talking to his girlfriend in the side yard."

"What?" The cupboard door closes harder than I intend.

"Mom, don't get mad at me, it was a long time ago, and I wasn't sure who he was talking to at first—"

"How do you know who it was?"

"I, I, I didn't at first. I thought it was Rena." Rena is Diego's daughter by his first marriage. "But he wouldn't be talking *like that* to Rena."

"When?" She examines the bitten sides of her tortilla chip, counting. "Maya, *when?*"

"I'm so sorry, Mom." I walk over and look directly into her mascaraed brown eyes. These eyes can't lie to her mother.

"Maya?"

"I dunno, two years ago, maybe."

"*Two years?*" I'm dumbstruck. "And you didn't tell me? I'm your mother, and you didn't tell me!"

Maya can't look at me. Her hung head wobbles back and forth. "I'm so-so-so sorry, Mom. I thought it would blow over and I didn't want Dad to be mad at me ... I didn't expect it would last and ..."

"You knew about her for *two years?*" My lips can't say the word "girlfriend." I stand abruptly, turn off the screaming teakettle, walk past the laundry hall into my bedroom and close the door. I'm feeling stabbed in the back, betrayed not only by Diego but also by my own daughter. Puzzle pieces swarm frantically in my head like Hitchcock birds. It's too strange to even think of him loving someone else. Foreign. Unreal. Obviously I still love Diego, but what if I'm not the only one? He said he was dating. What if it's serious? From the edge of my bed I stare at the palm tree on the patio.

*Two years? How could that be?*

I'm angry at Maya. I can't talk to her. The betrayal feels too thick. But at the same time I know she thought her silence was protecting me. I pick up the TV remote and notice that it's shaking on the end of my hand. I'm panting uncontrollably, like Lola, our Westie, after a long run. I need more than Oprah to calm down. I want a drink, or some legal form of annihilation, but I don't keep alcohol in the house. Besides, one brandy would only lead to a bottle. The framed photograph of my mother, the one with the snaggletooth, stares at me sympathetically. "You know you're sick, Barbara, like me. Take your pills."

I don't want to. I don't want to be like her. My mother's bottles of Seconal and Thorazine sat on her kitchen windowsill in our Wisconsin home. I loathed them.

"Take your pills, Barbara."

*No. I don't need them.*

An orange plastic vial lies unopened in the back of my nightstand drawer. I find this recent prescription and read the label. "Xanax. Take one to two pills as needed." I take out one white pill, and look at it in my palm; it's tiny, smaller than a currant. Taking it as needed isn't every day. I'm not like Mom. She ordered her pills herself from my dentist Dad's drug catalog. This is prescription. So I swallow it. So tiny it doesn't need water.

I lie down. Take deep breaths. Within minutes the screaming, heart-racing, hyperventilating edge tapers off, cooled with a refreshing mental paralysis. That tiny pill, my internal straitjacket, swaddles and calms my terrors with pinpoint accuracy.

It's hard to explain but at that time, the healthy, contented old-timer friends I knew from my regular twelve step meetings didn't work for me. I turned to grittier, druggier meetings in downtown Concord. Until Diego left, I had never identified with hard-core alkies and addicts. Originally I had quit drinking in 1990 because Miguel's adolescent treatment counselor had said I should. It was important for our son's recovery, she said. In Diego's view, one member of the family getting sober and attending meetings was enough.

But that summer in 2004, in Concord's smoke-filled rooms, I connected emotionally to those down-and-outers: bone-thin addicts who wore long sleeves to cover more than their tattoos, young women who had their toddlers taken away, and that pretty girl whose boyfriend hit her on the head with a television set. Although I no longer craved an after-five goblet of Chardonnay or a Courvoisier nightcap, I felt that the six criss-crossing scars below my watchband earned me the right to that Concord chair. I kept attending. Even fantasizing that some handsome graying Richard Gere with a home in the Bahamas would show up at a meeting and whisk me away. But the new male friends I met in my new Concord meeting all had missing teeth or prescriptions for methadone.

# CHAPTER FOUR
## THE PHILANDERER

"That's not love, that's attachment," Joanna tells me at our weekly program meeting. I can't argue with Joanna because you don't argue with your sponsor. Going to meetings is now a fourteen-year habit. Sometimes I'm asked why I still go to meetings since my kids (and I) no longer have alcohol issues (that I know of). I tell them because meetings are where my friends are. Being unskilled in the care and feeding of friendships, I find institutionalized friendships are convenient and timesaving. The twelve step credo states: "Any time, anywhere someone reaches out for help, I want the hand of (*name of program here*) always to be there." So day or night, in nearly every major city on the planet, I can locate a twelve step meeting where I'll find a room full of honest, compassionate, good listeners who have to be my friends whether they like me or not. And there's coffee. An acceptable drug of choice.

Joanna is a large, imposing woman who has the annoying habit of always being right. I chose her as my program sponsor partly because she's an accredited MD. That carries a lot of weight, and so does Joanna—she weighs in at over three hundred sixty pounds. And I admire her for being comfortable in her own ample freckled skin. My arms can barely stretch all the way around her middle, and when I hug her I feel six years old again, like I'm in the arms of my late, large, Swedish grandmother. I love every pound of Joanna and, selfishly, I hope she'll never get skinny.

Also, her physician status makes her a mandatory reporter. I tell her all the off-the-wall behavior of my family, including me, and I don't have to be the judge if someone steps over a boundary line that looks iffy and blurry to me. With regular weekly meetings with Joanna and my full disclosure of events, I can count on her professional judgment to define the parameters of addiction, abuse, and insanity. She's required by law to make a report if someone crosses a line. But in all the years she's sponsored me, about four, Joanna never reported any of my family crises—which, she says, were not really crises but incidents. To me she is Dr. Joyce Brothers and the plump Disney fairy godmother Merryweather all wrapped up in one perfect sponsor.

After this morning's Thursday meeting, we're meeting in Cherubini's, a cozy café. Joanna starts with the usual barrage of physician questions:

Barb, did you attend OPT for four weeks? *What's OPT?*

Your outpatient treatment. *Yes.*

Are you taking your meds? *Yes.*

How are you sleeping? *Okay, I guess.*

Did you call a lawyer yet? *Uh, no.*

Why not? *It's too soon.*

She pauses and gives me one of her soul-searching looks that make my insides squirm. "Barb, why even talk to Diego on the phone if you know he's having an affair?"

I never use the word *affair*. It sounds too much like a party.

"You know he's a philanderer."

Our waiter sets our sandwich platters on the table, giving me a moment to respond. She doesn't know Diego. She's jumping to conclusions. "Actually, in our last counseling session he said he'd been faithful to me over our middle twenty years." Twenty years of faithfulness over three decades must count for something.

"Did he ever wear a wedding ring?"

"What does that have to do with it? Diego wore his father's ring on his left hand."

"*Philanderers* don't wear wedding rings."

"But he says he's not *in love* with her. He sounded sincere."

"Barb, every time you say or think 'Diego,' I want you to say *philanderer.* Say, *the philanderer* sounded sincere," she directs.

"*The philanderer* sounded sincere," I parrot back to her. It sounds stupid.

Joanna bites into her thick dripping sandwich, sending a tsunami of mayo and bacon oozing out the sides.

"And he did tell me that his life would be easier if we reconciled."

"Say philanderer."

"Well, I think *the philanderer* wants to reconcile."

"Barbara, this isn't about what he wants, it's about what you want."

"Philanderer doesn't sound right." I can easily call my husband an asshole but philanderer isn't in my vocabulary. Philanderer sounds like a high-class cheater. Joanna's blank stare tells me I'm not trying hard enough. Her straight, waist-length brown hair is pulled back into a tight bun, no wisps, and her blue dot eyes are centered in her wide, full moon face. I'm not sure if she looks like a cartoon Betty Boop or Buddha.

"But that's what he is, isn't he, a philanderer?" she asks setting her sandwich down. She wipes her mayo-glossed fingers with a napkin, then trims off a tongue of bacon hanging out of her chicken, bacon, and Swiss. "Just call him the cheater then, that works. Just keep calling him that until it sinks in." She taps the side of her skull with her forefinger.

Perhaps I need practice. Cheater, cheater, cheater, cheater, cheater, I think. He's a cheater, you know he's a cheater. "Diego is a cheater." I say it out loud to try it on for size.

"That's better. Remember once a cheater, always a cheater."

"That dirty no-good shit-faced lying cheater. F- him," I say a bit too loudly.

"Bravo!" Joanna cheers. Two women in pink jogging outfits at the next table turn around and stare. I don't care. I'm beginning to feel a little lighter already.


That summer of 2004 was not the only time I had to deal with Diego's philandering. Our early years, from 1972 to May 1979, were peppered with battles, flings, leavings, broken stained-glass cabinets, doors, and windshields. I was not responsible for the doors. The seventies were the decade of pot smoking, women's lib, and free love. But love had a cost for us. After infant Maya was diagnosed with spinal meningitis at eight days old, Diego admitted to multiple flings and brief affairs. He believed that God was punishing him with tiny Maya at the brink of death.

Our daughter recovered and so did the marriage. Diego swears on his father's honor that he remained faithful for the next twenty years and he gave me no reason to doubt him until this year. Contrary to prevailing public opinion and my program girlfriends, who want to slap me silly, I still believe he was faithful for those two decades.

My weekly meetings with Joanna were a godsend. At first it seemed unfair, having fourteen years of program under my codependent belt, that I had to start step one over again. But I had to admit the truth. Step one: I really was powerless. I've had plenty of practice with powerlessness already: with a mentally ill mother, Miguel's beer bottles under the bunk bed, and a sixteen-year-old's positive pregnancy test. Now I was powerless over Diego's—I mean cheater's—philandering penis and where ever he chose to put it.

Calling Diego a cheater, a full-time cheater, not a past cheater or a summer-blip cheater but a full-fledged, bona fide, thoroughbred cheater, offered relief and a measure of sanity. However, I also felt guilty—as if I was rewriting in indelible ink smudgy slurs over all the wonderful times we had together.

"Cheater, cheater, cheater, that asshole cheater." Eventually the words fell trippingly off my tongue and I began to feel the bravado of a bullied child who stands up for herself on the playground. Joanna's magic mantra worked. My shoulders rose from their slump and strength returned. There were even some fleeting, exhilarating moments of freedom. Maybe even hope.

· · ·

IT'S A WARM JULY MORNING, trash pickup Friday, and I decide it's going to be a new day. Today I'm not going to cry over Diego's stupid two-year fling. After all, it's been a month since he moved into the motel, and with no new information about *her* from him, I've survived so far.

I pull the over-stuffed trashcan up our inclined driveway as if I'm lugging a dead horse. Putting out the trash is his job. I stuff the mushrooming bag down into the full, ripe-smelling bin and try to close the lid. My body has no muscle memory for trash bags, or bringing in the mail, or handling garden hoses and door locks—all Diego's jobs. Carrying out the trash feels like an unnatural act.

Our mailbox is as stuffed as the garbage cans, as if we haven't been home for a month. I intercept Maya's Victoria Secret catalog before the wind sends it flying across Glenside Drive into Bunny and Steve's front yard. These July weekends, I often see Steve out mowing his lawn or washing his red convertible Corvette. And I smell his barbecue grill on Sundays. Steve is safe, because he won't ask me anything about Diego's missing van.

But Bunny, with her sparkling, no-crumbs-on-the-counter, no-dishes-in the-dish-drainer kitchen, is another matter. Bunny has a kitchen full of ducks: duck plates, duck potholders, duck pottery, duck magnets, and Delft blue ducks marching across her wallpaper. I'm not about to trust a woman with a theme kitchen—a woman with all her ducks in a row. I have to be on the lookout for Bunny. If I see her picking up newspapers on the drive, I duck behind the hedge. Her sad, blue-eyed, compassionate "where did it all go wrong?" expression is too much to bear.

So far she hasn't asked me about Diego's missing van. Or why on Saturdays my Ford Escort is gone when he shows up to water his citrus trees or clean the pool filter. Does she wonder why my car stays in the drive on Sunday mornings instead of heading to St. Perpetua's? She'd notice, even though they're Lutherans.

But this Friday is a new day. Like Joanna says, take the magnifying glass off Diego and put it on Barbara. On my needs. No more sobbing. No more living in bed. I don't want much. Just a bathrobe without stains, hair without gray roots, a body without cottage cheese thighs, and a non-philandering husband with his car in the driveway. Today I'll wash this bathrobe.

I put all of Diego's mail into a fresh brown paper Trader Joe's bag, then place it on our greenhouse kitchen window between the bromeliads and the three-foot marble statue of Mary. The first mailbag I made disappeared last Saturday morning when I went to Jazzercise. I labeled it "asshole" in black marker, but today being a new day, a civil day, I simply and courteously write "Diego" on the paper bag, and turn it to face out the window, toward the empty spot in the drive.

This trash pickup Friday I contemplate doing laundry, and wearing a fresh white robe without coffee stains, and having clean pillowcases that don't smell like him. Then I think I'll Windex my kitchen appliances and mop the sticky spots off on the floor, so I'll have a kitchen that shines like Bunny's.

I'll start after *The Tyra Show.*

. . .

WEDNESDAY AFTERNOON I walk into the kitchen carrying groceries. Maya's sitting at the kitchen table, dabbing at a strawberry jam stain on her pajama bottoms. She looks up excited.

"Mom, there was a sighting."

"What sighting?" I wipe my feet and set my Trader Joe's bags on the counter.

"Annalisa said she saw them in Dad's van in Berkeley."

"When? You talked to Annalisa?" Annalisa is Sara and Bill's daughter, we've been friends forever.

"Annalisa told me last night on the phone."

"When did she see them?" My heart is pounding. My face hot.

"I dunno. A few days ago."

Oh, no. We've known Sara and Bill since our kids were in grade school together in Berkeley. Now they know. I sit at the table across from Maya. Groceries can wait. "So what did she look like?"

"She said she was a pretty black woman. Short and old, over thirty." Maya reports enthusiastically. I'm taken aback, stuck on one unexpected word. *Pretty.* Diego always told me I was the prettiest woman he'd ever dated. *She was pretty.* It stings. Her race doesn't surprise me. When I confessed to Diego that I had a crush on Antonio Banderas, not too long ago, he admitted to having a thing for Halle Berry. Remembering how we would joke about such things, make love and talk and talk in bed after, I begin to feel dizzy, disoriented.

I turn away from Maya so she won't see tears welling up.

*I'm not crying. No. Not today.*

Facing the grocery bags on the counter, head back; eyelids open wide to drink back the growing puddles.

"Mom, you're crying again."

"Oh no, I'm not crying. I'm fine. I have to put away the ice cream." Maya gets up and hugs me from behind as I hide behind the freezer door.

*No, no. Don't hug me.*

"Sweetheart, please." I peel off Maya's painted nails from my T-shirt. Hugging makes me feel cared for, and then I'll really start bawling.

She backs off.

*Pretty.* The word twists like a knife in my back.

The next day I'm running to find the ringing cordless. Finally under the sofa afghan I feel the curvature of the plastic handset along with a Barbie doll and Lola's missing leash. Out of breath, I press the button.

"Barbara, you okay?" *It's him.* Hearing his voice shoots an adrenaline rush through my veins. I try to sound normal. I'm not going to scream at him for being outed by Sara's daughter.

"Maya didn't put my phone back. She was fighting with Jesse again last night."

"That *pendejo*." He sounds so close. Like he's sitting next to me in the La-Z-Boy I bought for him.

"She says they're broken up, again. But he's still calling her."

"What a cockroach."

I laugh. Hearing Diego call Jesse a cockroach feels safe and comfortable. He's still calling me every day. His sister Tita told me his girlfriend is probably in it for the money, and once she finds out that he doesn't have any, she'll leave.

Today I'm not going to grill him for information about her. Be nice. I walk to the bedroom and relax lying down on the unmade bed.

"Did you hear Arnold Schwarzenegger wants Davis impeached so he can run for governor?" I ask. "Can you imagine the Terminator as governor of California?" Politics are his favorite subject.

"That's never going to happen." He's serious. "Oh, uh, I have some news."

"Good news or bad news?" I tease.

"Uh, I got an apartment."

*An apartment?*

"Why?" Why does he call me every day if he wants to move out?

"Barbara, it's only a month-to-month. In Walnut Creek," he says. "No long-term lease. Just five minutes away."

I feel sick. Does that mean our marriage is month-to-month?

"I'll still come by twice a week to do the watering and clean the pool filter. And you can still go to Hawaii with the girls like we planned, I'll pay for the tickets and hotel." He says he'll pay the mortgage and utilities and I can have checkbook access to his retirement account.

We fought for months over my access to his retirement account. Now suddenly he's willing to share it with me? I don't get it. Tickets to Hawaii, or pool cleaning, or even his retirement checkbook isn't going to make up for an apartment and a two-year girlfriend.

I have the urge to run. To leave for Florida by myself and visit my parents, give myself a screen refresh. My going to Florida always piqued Diego's jealousy in the past.

"You mean you still need more time to decide?"

"Decide what?"

"If you're coming home. How much time?"

He pauses while the rest of my life holds its breath. "Uh, five months, I guess."

"Okay," I say as if I have a choice. I count the months. "That's Christmas. You're not coming home 'til Christmas?" My voice is barely audible.

"Barbara, you okay?"

In a flash I'm angry. "Maya told me she heard you talking to *her* in the yard—two years ago. And Annalisa saw you with some young black woman," I snap. "How long, Diego?"

"Barbara, if it wasn't her, it would be someone else."

Now I'm mad *and* crying. My fist rubs my eyes and I hear the squish of tears into the folds of my eyelids. They're overflowing like our gutters in a bad rain.

Maya rudely knocks at the door. "Mom, is that Dad? I need to talk to him about our lunch date." She bursts in, the queen of Sheba in a towel turban and a wrap-around sheath that barely covers her breasts. She takes one look at me. "Jesus, Mom."

"Give me a minute, honey."

Maya rolls her eyes and closes my door, but I don't hear her walk away— she's eavesdropping, which is normal in our family.

"Diego, is she the same one as last summer?"

"Barbara, it's not just one."

"What? How many are there?"

"Uh ... six." He doesn't even sound embarrassed about it.

"Jesus, six?" The swollen banks of my eyelids burst into a flood. I can't help it. "I told you Diego ... there cannot be ... any reconciliation ... until ... you ... stop ... seeing ..." The words squeak like a staccato violin.

"I know that." His voice is sincere, understanding, and soft. He's struggling with this too. In the vacuous silence, he sighs deeply. I recall an evening a few months back when he came home late and found me crying over not knowing his whereabouts. He sat beside me in bed and wrapped his arm around me. When I looked at him, his dark eyes were filled with tears.

*He's not coming home. Ever.*

Heaving sobs rise up out of my chest with a will of their own like labor pains, and I reach for a Kleenex from a pedestal nightstand that now resembles a miniature pharmacy: Lithium, Welbutrin, and Zyprexa (the zombie med *du jour*), various vitamins, and anti-wrinkle creams. Used tissues spill off the nightstand. They land on the wood floor like crushed white rosebuds. I can't stop bawling, nor can I hang up the phone.

"I have to go," he says finally. "I'll call you tonight before my tai chi class."

The handset is dripping wet.

"Barbara?"

Diego waits for me to compose myself before he can say goodbye.

But I can't say the word, goodbye.

The dresser mirror reflects a pathetic stranger looking back at me. A haunted, vacant face with dark bags under bloodshot eyes, hair hanging in wet strings, a red nose. The face of the bag lady I fear I'll become someday.

"I'll get Maya," I say.

I dry my face on the bed sheet, walk to the kitchen and place the handset down on the Mexican floral tablecloth for Maya. I try to look cheery.

Maya takes one look at me. "Jesus Mom, get a life."

.   .   .

AT LEAST WHEN A HUSBAND dies you get a funeral. You get red roses in the shape of some dumb horseshoe, and the cousins fly in from Wisconsin, and you wear a black sheath with no cleavage, and a veil to cover swollen eyes, and you have to suck it up and act like Jackie Kennedy. After the service they bring over lasagna and that awful fake Mexican salad with a layer of sour cream, and pink boxes of store-bought sugar cookies, and you collect the cards painted with tacky blue flowers that say too many times, "I'm sorry for your loss." But at least you get *something*. Some acknowledgment of the hurt. The outside world, with everyone in black milling around talking and weeping softly, matches your aching insides, and they hug you over and over in the air that smells like chilled, tight rosebuds.

"We all loved him," they say. "He was such a gentleman, so admired, so funny. I'll never forget him." Sara and Rosa, my friends from Mexico City would weep. *"Tiene corazón, mi amigo,"* and they'd pat their heart three times, cross themselves, and look up to heaven as if they could see Diego flying overhead. "You did everything you could, Barbara," Sara would tell me. "You were a good wife. You stood by your husband until the end."

But that's not what I get from my Anglo program friends. "Forget the asshole. Why would you stay with a cheater? It's for the best, Barb."

The best for whom? His new girlfriend?

I expected more sympathy. But they gave me slogans like, *One day at a time. Progress not perfection. Keep coming back. God has a better life in store for you,* yadda yadda yadda. In the nineties, those sayings and the Serenity Prayer had helped me quit drinking, cope with my son's addiction, and admit my own control issues. But after Diego left, those slogans felt empty, canned, cold. *One day at a time* and *let go, let God* didn't work anymore. My grief didn't need slogans. I felt as if my friends were talking to someone I used to be.

Actually, I identified more with widows than with divorcees. I didn't want to end up like the many divorced women I knew who found quick replacements and proceeded to repeat their marital mistakes. But grief knew a loved one could never be replaced. There was no easy fix. No substitute. Whether grief heals in quiet dignity, or in loud wailing and pillow-pounding— as in my case—grief irrevocably changes you.

So now, if I'm not who I was, then who am I?

# CHAPTER FIVE
## FAMILY

Mimi, Deanna, and I flew to Hawaii in July while Maya insisted she needed to stay home so as not to miss any insulting, name-calling phone calls from Jesse. Waikiki Beach was Mimi's vacation idea, but it was overcrowded and offered no seaside solitude, not even a free patch of sand to spread a beach towel. And floating in the surf proved dangerous, with too many amateur surfers taking lessons on puny two-foot waves—a head injury waiting to happen. Waikiki Beach with its crowds and skyscraper beach hotels felt alien, a far cry from the calm Palm Beach retirement community where my parents lived.

After Hawaii, I spent a month in the Bay Area before flying solo to Florida in mid-August. Entering my parents' condo with Dad, I'm greeted with the same pleasant smells of my childhood home: Folger's coffee, menthol cigarettes, Arpege perfume, and Ajax. Mom, now in her eighties, still looks lovely seated in her orange chair. Every curl is sprayed in place on her bubble of thinning white hair, and her powder-blue pantsuit matches her eyes. Everything is comfortably the same: same worn pink and tan sofa bed, same

Dad disappearing out the door with golf clubs or fishing gear, same dinner plates on the table at six. Mom's open living/dining room is clean, polished, uncluttered. Her thing is vacuuming. Every morning after makeup and sink scrubbing, Mom pushes a vacuum while singing, "What a friend we have in Jesus." Nothing different in Florida except Mom's metal cane leaning by the front door.

It's a ninety-degree morning, and after Dad leaves for an 8:30 tee time, Mom and I chat over coffee. I can't tell her Diego moved out. It's too soon. And I didn't come home to Mom for sympathy. That's like going to the hardware store for bread.

"I fell down on the way to the mailbox. Did your father tell you that?" Mom blows smoke out the side of her mouth.

"No, he didn't say much on the ride here."

"That's your father for you. I had to crawl the whole distance from the mailbox on my knees carrying his junk mail." Sometimes Mom exaggerates. "The problem is my back," she goes on, "but the doctor won't give me anything for it; he wants me to do *exercises*. Can you believe it? I'm not doing any damn *exercises*." Mom has the same negative view about the group therapy prescribed for her. Exercise, to Mom, is a weird, foreign word like *yoga* or *hot tub*. Glamorous ladies of the fifties didn't lift weights or whine in therapy circles. They crossed their pencil-skirted legs, played bridge, smoked, and solved their *downers* with after-five martinis. Today Mom wears pastel pantsuits and drinks brandy old-fashions timed not to mix with her tranquilizers.

"Your father won't drive me to get a handicapped sticker. He made me drive by myself all afternoon looking for that damn DMV until the car finally ran out of gas. The police had to come. I bet he didn't tell you that!" Mom shakes another cigarette from her pack of menthols. "Sometimes that son of a bitch makes me so mad I could just spit."

My mother's face can contort from compassion to disgust in a blink of her robin's-egg blue eyes.

This is our routine. Mom complains. I listen. Our favorite topics are husband-griping and being mentally ill. We share the original, true bipolar diagnosis, not the current namby-pamby ones given to four-year-olds. My sweetest childhood memories of Mom are of her at my bedside during my stays in the hospital for childhood surgeries.

We seem to be getting along well although this morning she did ask me to move into Aunt Alvina's empty condo so she can sit on the hide-a-bed-couch when she can't sleep.

"Barbara, I really need help with that handicapped sticker."

"Yep." I nod, avoiding the issue. I don't ask her about the cane. I noticed in church yesterday that she used it more for whacking people out of her way than for balance. I think she likes the look of it. She lights up another menthol using the worn silver cigarette lighter engraved with her initials in a flourish script.

"So, Barbara, how are Diego and the kids?"

"Fine."

I can't talk about Diego's affair, not to my mother. She'll blame me for not letting Diego keep beer in the kitchen refrigerator, or for working too much. She thinks jobs are for poor single women—women like Aunt Ginny, whose rat husband ran out on her in Texas, leaving her with two kids, so she had to work at a Bowl-A-Rama. "Horrible. Just horrible," Mom commiserates whenever Aunt Ginny is mentioned. She's always been very transparent with me, even as a little kid. I learned all the family dirt: the rat husbands, suicide attempts, extramarital affairs, and teen pregnancies. During kissing, she said, a boy's sperm can climb up your thigh.

But Mom is partial to Diego. It didn't take her long to get over the fact that he was half Mexican. In waspy, corn-fed Wisconsin, the word "Mexican" was always preceded by the qualifier "greasy." But cultured, well-bred Diego is the polar opposite of the greasy wipe-the-beans-off-your-shirt stereotype.

And whenever Diego and Mom get together the jokes flow as copiously as the brandy. I'm the outsider.

"I really like your mom," Diego told me once with a devilish crooked-tooth grin, "We both have a mean streak." I'm surprised that he admitted it.

"So why didn't Diego come with you?" Mom asks.

"Uh, he starts work this month." A lie by omission. I'm feeling a tad guilty not telling her that he moved out, but then she'll want to talk about it, and I'll start crying. Worse, she'll tell my dad. Then I'll really feel like a failure.

"Barbara, we could go together for the handicapped sticker to the place out on Military Trail." She smiles sweetly.

"I'll look into it, Mom." I know my father won't be the least bit happy about a disabled placard displayed on the windshield of his Ford station wagon.

"We can go tomorrow." Her blue eyes look so imploring, so innocent and needy. Makes me feel protective. Like today I'm her best friend.

I call Diego from Dad's bedroom on his old princess phone. It's August 14th, our twenty-ninth wedding anniversary. I always count the two years we lived together to edge our relationship over the thirty-year mark. It's clear from Diego's cheery voice, with no hint of regret, that he forgot what day it is. He says he's going to a jazz concert today; he bought tickets, he says. *Tickets. Plural.* I choke back my anger. Since when does he like jazz? Salsa is our thing. I hang up and grief overcomes me. I stifle my sobs in Dad's pillow.

I can't cry in front of them—they're Wisconsinites.

I leave the condo ASAP and cross the road, A1A, to the beach. Palm Beach is a long narrow barrier island known for its wealthy socialite elites, like that reality show millionaire, Donald Trump, whose Mar-a-Lago residence is five miles north of us. South Palm Beach, where my parents live, is a narrow one-road strip that had once been a foul sulfur-smelling swamp until low-rise condos appeared in the fifties. My grandmother, Mom's mother, was an original owner of a three-story unit on the Intracoastal Waterway side.

The walk is familiar. I've done it since I was thirteen. A narrow pathway, lined with a wall of sea grapes with fan-shaped leaves as large as dinner plates, leads to the beach. I climb the half flight of stairs at the Imperial, the condo where my aunt Alvina used to live. The metal gate floods with a brilliant Disney-esque gold light that spills onto the faded green AstroTurf. This is the back door to heaven. The fresh salt sea air greets my lungs. A few steps more to the Imperial's back deck, where an endless aqua sea spreads before me. Waves billow toward shore like a bed-making mother tossing a white comforter.

Even as a child back in cow-patty Wisconsin, I dreamt of a far-away ocean. I planned to build a raft and paddle across the state and down the Mississippi River to find it. I loved to swim and fantasized that I was really a mermaid who was born in land-locked farm country by mistake.

I spread my towel on the vacant beach and close my eyes to listen. The waves, one after another, sound like a succession of distant airplanes taking off. I lie back letting the warm, briny air embrace me.

· · ·

NO ONE WILL SAY IT out loud in front of Mom, but Dad looks much younger than she does. He's tall, with straight Bob Barker posture and a tan, smile-lined face. Dad's not much of a talker unless you want to talk about the weather, the Packers, or golf. He's in his eighties, but shoots in the seventies, which I'm told is pretty damn good. Cousin Bob Miller golfs with Dad and says he still can't beat him. In Wisconsin we had a sunroom full of dad's golf trophies until Mom threw them out. Dad didn't object.

Note: *The American Basketball Association (ABA) Handbook* says Ken Buehler, my dad, was rookie of the year in 1943. He's listed on quite a few pages of basketball history, including the page listing the most important games ever played. Top of the list is the first game where blacks and whites played together. Dad played in that game. But we never knew Dad had a famous history when we were kids. Mom kept his scrapbooks high up on their bedroom closet shelf. We only knew about our parents' lives from Mom's photo albums. We saw pictures of Mom and Dad as UWM's homecoming king and queen and snapshots of Mom's boyfriends before Dad—the one I remember was Grover who wore a white V-neck letter sweater. We didn't know that Dad had played pro ball for the Pistons, or that his Sheboygan team, the Redskins, had won the national championship. Dad was high scorer. We didn't learn these things until my brother Bob sent Dad an *ABA Handbook* not too many years ago.

When my parents moved from Wisconsin to Florida they only took only what Dad could fit in the station wagon. Patsy and I rescued Dad's basketball and WWII scrapbooks before they hit the dumpster. Dad always looks slightly embarrassed talking about his sports-hero past, and there's something about his chagrin that reminds me of Johnny Carson. Everyone likes my dad. Even today, as I write this, when you ask him, "How ya doin', Ken?" he says, "Never better." He turned ninety-nine last November.

I'm blessed to have had a father like that in my life for seventy years. Sitting next to him with some game on TV is just about the most comfortable spot on God's green earth. This is home base. Dad's couch is where he'll examine my molar for a cavity, discuss the stock market, or pick up his harmonica and play me a near-perfect "Yankee Doodle Dandy."

There, beside Dad, nothing has changed.

When I enter my parents' condo, refreshed after the beach, I plop next to Dad on the couch watching golf on TV. Mom is already down for her afternoon nap. I'm nervous about asking him about Mom's handicapped sticker. He believes in toughing it out, in illnesses as well as marriages. Although he's a retired dentist, he seldom sees a doctor. When we were kids he didn't like us walking around in pajamas past noon, even if we were sick. Actually I don't recall ever seeing my Dad in pajamas, a robe, or lounge wear. Only collared shirts, pants, shorts, or swim trunks. His younger self was a tall, dark, and handsome Ken doll Dad with the pants molded on.

I do have to give him credit for sticking it out through Mom's depressions and hospitalizations. They've been married sixty years, "in sickness and in health." Dad does the health part and Mom has the sickness part covered. He never complains. He told me he once played an entire basketball game with a broken ankle. He's a boot-strap, buck-up, raised-in-the-Depression era Navy man. No nuance there. Not where you'd expect sympathy, but he's always been proud of me. I can't afford to lose that.

On the couch I plan in my head how to word it. The handicapped placard doesn't have to hang on your windshield, I'll say. We'll store it in the glove compartment. I'll drive her to the DMV tomorrow and afterwards I'll take her to the Dune Deck for lunch. A real mother/daughter day. How can he say no?

I'm about to explain tomorrow's plan when Dad turns to me. His blue-gray eyes look uncharacteristically serious behind his thick-framed glasses.

"Barb," he says, "Don't let him destroy you."

*Damn.* He must have heard me crying on the phone with Diego.

"Uh, okay," I say, feeling guilty as a four-year-old. The charade is over. My own damn grief outed me to Dad. For a second Dad wears this doctor, you'll-survive-this expression, not unlike confident Dr. Cohen. Then he turns back to the sports channel. And I'm just sitting here on the couch, a big lump blinking. Not knowing what to say. Feeling exposed. And horribly, childishly ashamed. He's thinking, Barbara can't hold a marriage together. Now she has two filed marriages. Christ I can't even hold myself together.

Christ, I can't even hold myself together.

*Don't let him destroy you.* I can't stop thinking about what Dad said yesterday. Meaningful words. Tear-worthy, hug-worthy words. But just as he said them and the door to intimacy opened, it slammed shut again. He was there for a moment, then poof, like a UFO, Dad was gone. Back to the TV set.

. . .

THE NEXT DAY I DRIVE Mom and her physician-signed form to the DMV. Driving on the Military Trail, Mom is as giddy as a kid going out for a malted milkshake. We used to go out for malteds when I'd accompany her to her psychiatrist appointments in downtown Milwaukee. I still remember feeling bad that day in Macy's basement restaurant when I finally admitted to her I didn't like malted milk.

In the torrid August heat we keep the AC on, the windows up, and she does me a huge favor by not smoking. Military's street numbers are impossible to read as we zip past multiple strip malls full of Dunkin Donuts, chiropractors, and gas stations that advertise beer, smokes, and ammo. I make several U-turns, doubling back searching for the address.

*Don't let him destroy you.*

I bet Dad told Mom already, which means all my aunts and cousins will know by tomorrow. But she doesn't mention it in the car. She's yapping about her bridge club. Mom has always been a whiz at cards, I'll grant her that. Bridge, knitting, telling jokes, and reading Danielle Steele and Andrew Greeley novels are her thing.

"Ever since Shirley moved into the fancy-pantsy Carlisle, she thinks she plays so much better than us. Who does she think she is ..."

*Don't let him destroy you.*

"... and I'm not the only one. Dinah feels the same way about Shirley. One rotten egg spoils the whole barrel."

"*Apple*, Mom. One rotten *apple*."

After a wasted half hour of driving in circles, we finally spot the nearly invisible "Tax Collector" sign where the DMV distributes license plates and placards. We pull into the strip mall. She's pulling a cigarette pack out of her white clutch purse and shakes out a smoke.

"Well, Barbara, we made it."

"You betcha." I hand her her shiny new cane. Together we'll conquer Florida strip malls, New York drivers, DMV lines, and my father's fear of handicap placards in his Ford.

Today Mom and I are a team.

. . .

WHEN DAD DRIVES ME to the airport, he has other concerns than the new blue handicap placard in his glove compartment.

"Did you know your mother's bridge club friends don't want her to play with them anymore?"

What? Mom always had bridge club on Wednesdays as long as I could remember.

"Shirley told me she can't remember the cards," he says with his steely, straight-ahead look he uses to hide embarrassment. "Did she tell you?"

"No, she didn't mention it."

I was so focused on my own life upheaval that I didn't notice my parent's lives were changing as well. But after that trip to Florida, for whatever reason, neither of my parents ever mentioned Diego to me again.

I was grateful for that.

# CHAPTER SIX
## PARTY TIME

After returning home to California in early September, I dial the 707 area code for the North Bay, wondering how long my son is going to ignore my calls.

He picks up. "Hello."

"Miguel?"

"Hi, Mom," he says with little affect. I cut to the chase. "Since next weekend is your birthday, I thought maybe you'd like to come over and we'll barbecue." Miguel is an expert barbecue-er and horticulturist, two hobbies I hope might turn into job opportunities.

"Uh, no thanks, Mom. I'm cooking tri-tip here for Erika's family. Thanks anyway." He sounds normal. Calm. Not talky-crazy manic, nor mad at me.

"Honey, you know your father left." What I really mean is, what do you know about your father's affair?

"I don't wanna talk about it, Mom."

"Your dad told me that you knew." I deserve some sympathy at least.

"I'm really tired Mom. I should try to get some sleep." It's almost noon.

"Are you taking your Depakote?" A synthetic lithium substitute.

"Yeah. Bye, Mom."

"Say hi to Erika and—" Click.

I'm thinking, well, that's positive. At least he talked to me. Since Miguel was fourteen, I've been running after my soon-to-be twenty-nine-year-old son, trying to set him on the straight, drug-free and narrow. Six drug programs so far. They don't stick. It seems like I can never quite catch him; he always slips right through my hands. The police have better luck than I have. I've lost count of his arrests. Minor charges. I don't remember most of them. Theft, drugs, possession of a semiautomatic AK-47, something like that. I think he does this to torture us. Still Erika, his girlfriend, is an improvement over the last one. And it's been months since he's been tasered.

. . .

IT'S BEEN ONLY THREE months since Miguel's accident. On my fifty-sixth birthday, three weeks before Diego left, Maya rushed into our bedroom trembling.

"Miguel's car crashed on Highway 4 between Martinez and Vallejo."

Diego was not home from work yet so I immediately called him on his new cell phone. In minutes the five of us headed in shocked silence to John Muir Hospital during Friday afternoon rush hour traffic. I screamed in my head at every green light, TURN GREEN NOW!

Diego, Maya, Deanna, and I were ushered into a waiting room on the fourth floor. "Wait for the doctor," we were told. Erika, Miguel's girlfriend of four years, was already seated, still in her Safeway uniform. She looked up. "He's alive." she said softly. Her teary blue eyes were innocent. Naïve. Her long blonde hair cascaded over her slumped shoulders like a protective cape. Sometimes I wondered with all the trouble Miguel had been in, how could this sweet girl love him so much. Maya hugged her and sat beside her with Deanna on her lap. Diego and I took two seats further down to give Erika some space. We were all in a line facing the double doors. The room was small, windowless, and cold as a meat locker. I was still in shorts and the burgundy plastic chairs felt like ice blocks on the backs of my thighs. No one spoke except for Deanna, who was reading aloud from a picture book. "Hop, hop, hop goes the rabbit. Jump, jump, jump goes the frog."

Was he conscious? Did he break bones? Was he drunk? Could my tough, hardware-store-working, pot-smoking, best barbecue-er in-the-world son be seriously injured? I prayed that Miguel was okay. He had to be okay. He had always come through scrapes, I thought. Jump-ins, overdoses, mental hospital escapes, holdups, scraps with the police, being tasered, hit in the head with a brick, shot at. My son has nine lives. I prayed this was one of them.

Diego wasn't watching Wolf Blitzer on the overhead TV. Hunched over, eyes cast down behind his rose-colored glasses, he looked distraught. His hands were lost and helpless in his lap. I wanted to comfort him but couldn't find the words. Diego had planned to celebrate my birthday that night by taking me to my favorite Indian restaurant. He didn't deserve this.

"He's tough. He'll come through," I told him.

I caught him wiping an eye. "Allergies," he said. When his hand fell to his lap, I reached over to squeeze it and hold on.

After the longest forty-five minutes of my life, a, young, thin-haired doc in a white coat pushed through the double doors.

"Mr. and Mrs. Flores?" The beanpole of a doctor held a clipboard. He looked too young to be saving my son's life. We were instantly on our feet crowding around him. Deanna pushed to the front.

"Will he be okay?" Diego asked. The three girls behind us were mute and wide-eyed like fawns frozen in headlights.

"According to the paramedic's witness reports, his vehicle rolled over six times. The sun roof was destroyed, leaving no skin on the top of his head," the doc said flatly. He pulled out an 8-by-10 photo of a bloody scalped head. We gasped in unison. He lowered a grisly photo right under Deanna's little nose. I wanted to cover her eyes like it was a TV sex scene but it was too late. She saw it. We all did.

The doctor continued, "... ten stitches, no internal bleeding, no obvious brain damage but we don't know yet ... we have to wait and see. It's a miracle he's alive. They had to use the Jaws of Life to get him out of the car," he said. "He was helicoptered here. If he hadn't been driving a Lexus he'd be dead."

How I had criticized Miguel for buying a Lexus, a used "luxury" car. I thought it was pretentious, extravagant and macho. Not now.

"Can we see him?" Diego asked. The doctor talked directly to us, his parents, the official family members. His back was to Erika, the woman Miguel lived with. She looked desperate, lost. Uncounted.

He motioned for us to follow and Diego and the girls paraded behind him mute as a funeral procession. I was last in line. I couldn't get the picture of that gory photograph pushed in little Deanna's face out of my mind.

The girls entered the hospital room first. My son was halfway sitting up in the hospital bed, his face cut and bruised; his head bandaged. Erika rushed to his bedside and held his hand. The others circled around. He seemed calm, sedated, awake and quite alive, thank God.

Then he spotted me.

"Get her out," he shouted. His swollen eyes burnt holes through my heart.

"Get Mom out of here!" Diego shot me a sympathetic glance that meant we had better placate him. I backed out into the hall and stood silent behind the open door, feeling again too tall. Like I was consuming too much air.

"GET HER OUT!" he screamed as if he knew I was standing outside his door.

"But Miguel, she's your mother ...." Diego was doing his best to convince him.

"AND KEEP HER OUT!"

I dragged myself head down back to the waiting room. An outcast demon. He's never forgiven me for kicking him out of the house when he was sixteen. Over ten years ago. The truth was proclaimed with deafening trumpets down the fourth floor hallway of John Muir Hospital.

My son hates me.

. . .

THURSDAY IS MY HOME meeting day. The Thursday Morning Danville Group, where we don't hide the ugly truth of our disastrous lives. After Florida it feels great to be back among friends in cool, dry California weather. Ahhh, so refreshing. After the meeting we gather for lunch at Pasqual's, a French café in downtown Danville, with print curtains, tabletop sunflowers, and the erotic aroma of fresh baked pastry. Joanna and I are the first to arrive. She's wearing an elegant, flowy copper tent dress that could fit three of me inside. I'm in shorts and "A Bug's Life" T-shirt.

Out the wide glass windows, I spot Doris striding down the Danville shopping district sidewalk toward the café. She's a retired psychologist with admirable style, always impeccably dressed in calf-length Chico skirts and matching chunky jewelry. She takes a seat next to me.

"You know, Barbara, our meeting uses only conference-approved literature."

Jesus, give me a break.

Doris is annoyed because I quoted from the AA Big Book. *"... we pause, when agitated or doubtful, and ask for the right thought or action. We constantly remind ourselves we are no longer running the show."* A huge no-no. I hate all these new rules. You can't share this, you can't share that, you can't say the Lord's Prayer, you can't go over three minutes, and I hate, hate, hate that stupid timer Doris brought in. Ding! The ding means shut up, Barbara.

Your share is over. You hogged too much meeting time. I could point to the handbook page that says small quotes from outside sources are acceptable at meetings, but why start a controversy? No way am I arguing with a Ala-Nazi like Doris. Too dangerous. I'd rather keep Doris and her little entourage of sponsees as my friends. She calls them her FROGs. Another acronym: *Fully Reliant On God.* I'm not big on program acronyms either, or sponsors who label their sponsees by some animal name like Ducks or Bunnies. But Doris and many of her Frogs are my lunch friends. And Frogs have parties. Upscale Danville catered lawn parties with crepes and wheels of baked brie. Defending two lines in the Big Book isn't worth giving up garden parties with baked brie and virgin grape juice sangria. I just wish she wouldn't have called me out at the meeting in front of the newcomer, Carrie.

Joanna, seated beside me, waves through the wide café-curtained window at a cute thirtyish blonde in a baseball cap as she climbs down from her SUV. It's Carrie wearing a plastered-on grin. I've heard program members call that smile an Al-lobotomy. We all come into program with the same plastered-on expression. No one gets to program on a good day.

Gail, an old-timer like me, walks beside Carrie, pointing to the café. Gail's red hair is short-cropped and she wears sneakers. She dresses like a teeny-bopper but she was a manager at a big Silicone Valley 500 company before she retired. Now she drives around in a red convertible with the top down even in the winter. In spite of differences, we're a family. We all came in wounded and we recognize other wounded as one of our own. Carrie doesn't have to spell it out at her first meeting for us to know she's desperate and fed up with the alcoholic husband who's ruining her life. We know she's miserable and has no where else to go or she wouldn't be here. Gail, bless her, always says to newbies, "Come to at least six meetings, and if you don't want to stay, we'll gratefully refund your misery."

"Hi, everybody!" Carrie bounces in ahead of Gail as bubbly as a cheerleader. It's a front. She puts her oversize purse on the table. The outside has plastic photo sleeves with pictures of Carrie's family. Doris's eyebrow shoots up at Joanna in an expression of disguised horror. We're all thinking the same thing. Carrie obviously doesn't realize that "anon" in any program name refers to "anonymous." That includes family members.

"Nice purse," Gail says, probably to annoy Doris.

"Oh these are my kids: Caylee, five, and Tyler, he's three."

"Adorable," Gail says. Gail's not a Ala-Nazi or a frog. She has her own sponsees.

"And that's Jay at the gym."

Oops. Carrie just outed her hubbie.

Carrie turns to me. "Barb, I like what you shared at the meeting."

Touché, Doris.

"You're just so together. I mean your son was an addict, your teenager got pregnant, and your husband cheats on you. Wow!"

I feel a wee bit proud of myself.

Just then a tall expressionless waiter appears with his pen poised like a ballerina.

I tell him, "My usual. The roasted eggplant on sourdough. Half sandwich/half salad."

Joanna follows with the chicken and avocado on homemade country loaf. "And," she adds, "Bread pudding with whipped cream."

After ordering, Carrie excuses herself to make a phone call outside.

"Barb, have you talked to Carrie yet?" Joanna whispers. "She really needs a sponsor." Joanna fixes her dot eyes right at me. *Oh no, Not me. Not now.* Jesus, I can't even hold my own marriage together, and Oakland School for the Arts just offered me a new high school teaching job.

"I'm kind of busy." I know that's no excuse. "I don't know about sponsoring now, I'm still in grief mode," I say discreetly to Joanna.

"Barbara, that's not grief—that's self-pity," she whispers back. "The longer you sit on the pity pot, the stronger the suction. You need to stop thinking about yourself and think about others."

I hate it when Joanna's always right.

My heart goes out to Carrie. I wonder how long she's been living with addiction. Do they fight? Does it get physical? Do Caylee and Tyler hear? Or does she withdraw from conflict, make excuses for his behavior, and sit in it? Like the frog in a pot that's turned up degree by degree until it boils to death. Something must have happened recently. Something frightening enough to cause her to jump out of the denial pot and brave coming to a twelve step meeting. Is he a mean drunk behind closed doors so the neighbors won't hear? Does he throw plates or chairs? Did she ever have a broken bedroom door left hanging on a hinge like a dislocated arm? Maybe he's having an affair. Did he stop making love to her because he's too drunk and can't get it up any more? I've heard all the stories, the funny drunks, the crying sorry drunks, the angry drunks, and the ones who quietly pass out and disappear into the La-Z-Boy at nine o'clock. After fifteen years, I know all the right answers. You don't interfere with the alcoholic's drinking or try to change the situation. You allow them to hit their own bottom. Remember, I say to my sponsees, your qualifier has his or her own higher power, and it isn't you. Acceptance is key.

When I was a newcomer fourteen years ago, I blabbed all the gory details about Miguel's using, Maya's cutting hospitalizations, and fights with Diego. Joanna and the others listened. They didn't interrupt, criticize, or give me advice. They nodded, gave knowing smiles, and passed the Kleenex box. Even when I told them the most horrible, absolute worst things about myself, like how I once lost it and slapped Maya when she was little for talking back, they didn't judge me. These meeting women knew what I did, and they still liked me. I thought about my sponsors, Wendy (for alcohol) and Joanna. These women spent hours and hours and hours with me one on one, mostly just listening.

As the sun passed high noon in Danville that afternoon, a few good things in life reached critical mass. I was surrounded by good friends, served by a

French waiter, and Gail shared her turkey, avocado, and smoked bacon with me, and I shared bites of my crusty sourdough with roasted eggplant with melted provolone. We chose exquisite desserts from a gleaming silver and glass case: an opulent array of French pastries skirted with frilly paper doilies. Golden croissants as fat as my arm, custard-filled napoleons, tall seven-layer cakes, strawberry tarts and chocolate decadence cookies the diameter of a lunch plate. And before we left, Carrie asked for my phone number.

. . .

MAYA BLOWS INTO THE kitchen after work with a flushed face and a screen door slam.

"My car stalled and I tried to call Dad but did he answer? Nooooo! Where the hell is he, Mom? He doesn't work on Fridays." She wipes her sweaty brow with a handful of napkins. "I had to walk all the way home on the bike path. The sun's damn hot out there. Where *is* he?"

"What's his number, Maya?" I refuse to memorize *the cheater's* phone number. Lorraine, my therapist, says I should try not talking to him. Talk to him only when it concerns the kids, she says. But this is about car trouble and it concerns the kids. Maya recites his number and I get his recording. "I'll get back to you. Have a nice day." I hate that nauseating message that tells me "to have a nice day." After hearing his voice, how can I have an effing nice day?

"He has the message on."

Maya drinks water from the kitchen faucet, careful not to let her lips touch the metal. "I could have fainted out there in this heat."

I put the phone down calmly, ignoring a sudden dizziness. What if he saw "Barbara" on his caller ID and decided that after four months, it's time to stop talking to me? What if he's tired of me asking him if it's over with her? My breaths idle faster. Little gasps that can't find enough air. The telltale sign of a panic attack onset. Maya doesn't notice.

"Mom, he's fucking the crap out of that black bitch. That's where he is. Shit!"

I'm shocked Maya said it. "Maya, shhh, watch your language. Deanna's in the living room."

"We'll follow Dad from his work and find out where she lives. Then we go there, and when she comes to the door, we jump her. Beat the goddamn fuck outta that skanky-ass ho." Maya's cherub face turns demonic.

"Maya, that's crazy." I slide the kitchen door shut. Deanna is on the couch watching *The Little Mermaid* for the nineteenth time.

"Who does that fucking black bitch think she is? FUCK HER FAT ASS!" Maya slams her fist into her palm, fingers uncurled so as not to damage her acrylics.

"Nobody is going to hurt anyone. And don't say 'black bitch.'" I only allow myself to think it. I don't want Maya to pick up on the racism that had recently invaded my thoughts.

"Take that, beee-atch!" A left, then a jab, then a roundhouse to an ear and an undercut hook to the jaw. Maya's left foot kicks low in the air near the trash compactor, as if she's finishing off a victim already downed. Her street-fighting skills look impressive. I sip my chamomile tea solemn-faced, pretending not to enjoy my daughter's pummeling pantomime of the thirty-something adversary that I've never met. Suddenly I'm aware that my breath has slowed to normal.

"Seriously, Mom, we rent a car, tinted windows, twenty-five bucks, max. And we follow Dad from the college, like on Friday, to see if he goes to the skank's house. Hey, my friend Trey, the one with the pitbull, he's got a taser."

I'm a pacifist. I took Miguel to see *Gandhi.* I read Buddhist books. I don't believe in spankings, and I never eat lamb or veal. Still, I'm thinking, what Maya chooses to do on her own time is not my business—but if she got a couple of old friends from the dog-pound gang together and—

"Sweetheart, you know I'm not a violent person."

"Does she know he has a family? That dirt-bag douche deserves it." *Sweetness to my ears.* "Dad is such a perv." *Even better.*

My shoulders drift down like in a soothing hot shower.

"He's like way more twisted than I thought." *Finally. Maya sees the light.*

But no sooner do I realize that we are on the same team for once, and her head is back inside the refrigerator lickety-split. "So what's for dinner, Mom?"

On that warm October afternoon, the one and only time Maya suggested a joint mother/daughter smack-down, something in me shifted. Although an ambush was obviously impractical (and, I admit, morally questionable), Maya's impressive girl-on-girl mugging pantomime felt not only calming but healing. The pain inside me was so cellular and unreachable and buried so deep, it just couldn't scream its way out by itself. But Maya's "fuck that beeatch" slap-slam-kick-ass rap song seared through the kitchen no less than the beaming operatic chords of *Tristan und Isolde.* "Let's jump that skanky-ass ho" assuaged a place deep in my bowels, a rage that no Scripture, twelve step platitudes, or even Kaiser's psychotropic drugs could touch. More importantly, Maya blamed *her,* the other woman, the interloper, the home-wrecker, over her dad. Her allegiance with my blind-sided thinking was a welcome remission. For five precious minutes in the kitchen with my furious daughter, I finally felt I wasn't alone.

Maya didn't know it then but I had another secret reason for not renting a car and confronting Diego's friend. I didn't dare tell Maya, or the women at my Serenity Book club, or even my sponsor Joanna. That warm afternoon in the kitchen with Maya, I presented myself as good mom. The kind of mom who takes a protective arms-outstretched crossing guard stance against the evils of spying, stalking, and vengeance. The one who tells her kids don't be confrontational, don't get involved, let it go. The same principles taught to fifth graders to prevent bullying.

But the month before, before I went to Florida, I lost my senses. My obsession to find the home wrecker, or was it many home wreckers, overtook good mom, the mom who teaches by example. I searched the house for a college student disguise. In Miguel's old bedroom closet I found an oversize pair of orange basketball shorts that hit just above my knees and topped it off with a Raider's T-shirt, an oversize fleece, a baseball cap, and a long blonde wig that retired in the nineties along with my acting career. I drove to Diego's college campus in a black Enterprise rent-a-car and dark glasses. My plan was to arrive at the social science building parking lot before one p.m., when Diego's Thursday classes ended. I'd wait for him to get into his Nissan van and follow him. That way I'd stay unseen in the rental car and I wouldn't have to set one of my high-top sneakers on campus grass.

I'd follow him to her place. I'd shove the church portrait of our family in her thirty-something face. "Did he tell you we have an eight-year-old granddaughter at home, did he tell you that, did he?" Bitch.

I drove around the large parking lot, but I couldn't locate his van in the usual parking place. So reluctantly I left the safety of tinted windows, pulled the cap bill down over the long blonde wig, hiked up the oversize shorts, and bee-lined to the social science office building to find out if he had left. Please don't let me be spotted by Shirley, the school secretary, or one of Diego's colleagues.

I checked the gold doorknob on my husband's office door. Locked. A student with a sparse goatee passed me in the hall.

"Uh, Mr. Flores left over an hour ago," he said.

"Yo," I said and headed to the rental car. On the way out the side door I passed Charles Chin, a professor we knew. Head down I felt him staring at me. *Why did I leave the car?* On campus spiky-haired students with backpacks were scattered in clumps on the sunlit lawn. I realized my long blonde Barbarella wig and big purse were out of campus style. I was clearly no junior-college student but a wacko, old lady in a P-Daddy rapper outfit. And Charles

Chin saw me spying on Diego. I dashed to the rent-a-car, rolled up the windows, and clutched the wheel to hang on to my sanity. My hands shook uncontrollably, and my gold wedding band clinked rhythmically against the steering wheel.

*Never again.* I don't have the guts for espionage.

I pulled off the sweaty, damp wig and threw it on the front seat.


A few weeks before I left for Florida I met Hector Martinez in a restaurant ten miles away from our Lafayette suburb. No one knew me in Oakland. Mr. Martinez, a stocky ex-cop in a blue suit, smiled confidently. His detective service ad won me over with his friendly-sounding Hispanic name and his bright Yellow Pages smile. He slipped the signed contract and two photographs of Diego into his briefcase.

"You'll only have to follow him from the college once or twice because he knows I'm vacationing in Florida." This job was a slam-dunk. I felt relieved. Martinez also relieved me of five hundred dollars.

"More if we have to put a GPS tracking device on his vehicle," he said.

"Isn't that illegal?"

"No, you're married. It's your car too."

But I wasn't ready to bug Diego's Nissan Quest. Tracking devices fell over my rapidly eroding moral line. From my parents' Palm Beach condo I called Mr. Martinez every day for a report. I hoped my unreturned calls meant no action. Maybe they broke up; now that I was away, Diego missed me.

A week later Martinez called. "We have a problem. Your husband spotted me tailing him in the parking lot. I tried to follow him but his vehicle raced out of the lot too fast. I lost him in the chase." He explained this over the phone logically and patiently, like this scenario is typical. "He knows my car now. We'll have to put more men on the job. That'll be another five hundred."

I was speechless.

"Or we could go with a tracking device."

I panicked. Now Diego knows I'm having him followed. I told Martinez I had to think about it. I spoke with Diego at least every other day, but he never mentioned being followed or a car chase in his college parking lot. Now I wonder if it ever happened.

. . .

TODAY'S DISCUSSION AT OUR Serenity Book Club isn't about our self-help book *du jour, The Verbally Abusive Relationship,* but about spying on husbands. Yvonne admits to once putting on a costume to spy on Harold, and Leslie says when she was married and living in Texas, she hired a private investigator. What a relief it is to know other nice, church-going, suburban women check pockets, wear wigs in rented cars, and hire detectives. I'm rapt with attention as Leslie gives me the details of her PI story.

"My detective told me that Stewart spotted him in the parking lot," Leslie says. "Then he said Stew sped off, there was a car chase, and he lost him. After that," she says, "he asked for more money."

I tell her my story, that is line by line identical to hers. *What are the odds?*

"You guys were both scammed!" Gail says.

*I'm feeling violated all over again.*

"Did either of you get a referral or check to see if the guy was licensed?" Gail asks. Gail's a lawyer. "Most detectives are ex-cops," she explains. "It's easy for an ex-cop with four years to get a detective license. By the way, tracking devices are against the Privacy Act."

Jeez. How could I be so dumb? Why did I pick a Hispanic name and straight teeth out of the Yellow Pages? Why didn't I shop for a detective the same way I shop for a tile man?

"So Barb, did you report it to the California Office of Consumer Affairs?"

Doris asks. "You're the consumer."

"No." But I did prefer being called the consumer rather than the psycho, jealous, spying wife.

"Wait a minute, Doris. What woman is going to report some PI she hired to spy on her husband?" interrupts Gail. "Then she'd have to ask her cheating husband to sign some document declaring that he was never chased by a detective in a parking lot. She'd be outing herself. That's absurd."

I can't ask Diego to sign some government form that says he's suspected of cheating. And he'd be pissed if he knew I hired a detective. Now I don't feel like the consumer anymore. More like the dumb fourteen-year-old caught stealing gin out of the liquor cabinet.

"Funny. Stewart never said anything about a car chase either." Leslie looks astonished as if the PI scam is finally dawning on her.

I suspect that most detective business comes from desperate, scared, cheated-on women who feel shamed into secrecy. Dumb women (like me) who call detectives out of the phone book are sitting ducks. Makes me wonder how many of us have been scammed by disreputable PIs? Nevertheless my foray into espionage wasn't totally useless. I had to consider how I would have felt if I had succeeded and Mr. Martinez had brought back explicit photos or videos. Or what if, while in my rent-a-car, I came across the two subjects together, arm in arm, or worse. Real visuals would have slayed me. I was tortured enough already by my imagination.

Still, I couldn't close the case. I had to know.

Who was she?

HE SAID AT FIRST HER name was Sochi, a Latina, then Kay Kay, later it was Kathy Davis. Maya says it's one girlfriend, Diego says it's six. Six? Trying to make sense of Diego's dating life feels like looking through a kaleidoscope of constantly changing abstractions.

Diego gives me his new Sprint cell phone number. Armed with a marriage license and his social security number I call Sprint, and with the help of a kind, but not so bright, Sprint employee I learn his new cell number is linked to a LaShondra Jackson. I'm no whiz on the internet but an easy $4.99 computer search with Intellius.com reveals a LaShondra Jackson, age thirty-eight, with an address in Castro Valley near the college where he works. Now we're getting cookin'.

Diego calls the next day. I know it's him because the phone says "Restricted." All his calls read "Restricted," as if his phone access comes with yellow-taped parameters." I ask point blank, "So who's LaShondra Jackson?"

He laughs. "Oh her, she's just a friend. She's not even one-eighth of a girlfriend."

"Oh." *One-eighth of a girlfriend?* Does that mean he's screwing her one out of eight times and he has seven others, not six? Actually six or seven feels safer to me than one. And I want to believe him when he laughs her off as insignificant; but what if he's lying again? What if Maya's right and there is only one? So I store the Intellius search with the address for one LaShondra Jackson in an innocuous manila folder labeled *Dog Medical* where I keep copies of all Diego's bank and investment statements behind Lola's vaccination records.

I envision her as thin with flawless young skin and Angelina Jolie lips—a gorgeous Halle Berry that I could never compete with. Does she want to live with him? Marry him? Does she want his children? Suddenly a shock awakens me; self pity is replaced by indignation. Why should I divorce my husband for some LaShondra Jackson? Some low-morals student living in Castro Valley. Over my dead body. That's probably just what she wants—me dead, buried, and conveniently pushed out of her way. Well F you, LaShondra Jackson, or whatever your name is. Who the hell do you think you are bulldozing my life and the lives of my children?

Suddenly all those suicidal urges that never conclusively left my emotional bargaining table with God—pills, cement boots in the pool, asking Miguel for a gun—they all sound absurd. Why let her win?

## CHAPTER SEVEN
## GUESS WHO'S COMING TO DINNER?

Maya walks into the kitchen with a ski jacket over her scrubs. Deanna flies in from the living room and wraps her arms around her mother's waist. "Mama, guess what, Papa's coming for dinner."

"You have to be kidding." Maya spins around and stares at me standing over the stove. "Mom, why are you doing this?"

Humming the Rod Stewart song, "Tonight's the Night," I slide a pan of golden cornbread batter onto the oven's top shelf. "Well, we all have to eat."

"You know what I mean, having Dad for dinner." She dumps her stuffed Coach purse and two Macy's bags on the table.

"Don't put that there, honey. Deanna has to set the table."

"Mom, he has a girlfriend. He's lying about six women. Where's an old dude in his sixties with garlic breath going to find that many women? C'mon, Mom. He's not rich. He's no catch. He's trying to throw you off track. Like when he said six women."

"We had a talk this afternoon. It's not as though I don't have conditions." Diego knows my terms. With cornbread in the oven and a *posolé* stew on the stove, he had better be telling me the truth this time. Still, for a change, optimism feels delicious.

"You called him, didn't you, Mom? You said you weren't going to call him for a month. I knew it. I *knew* you'd call him."

"Honey, his garage refrigerator is leaking, there's water all over the floor, so I had to call." Our old, rusted refrigerator in the garage has no inside door to its freezer box, and when the power was on, the freezer gradually turned into one solid block of ice—like the kind I remember being sold to goat herders on desolate beaches in Greece. I can't have a leaking goat herder icebox in my garage, so I threw down the towel (literally on the wet cement floor) and called Diego.

Maya looks over the kitchen counter. "You made a pie? Sheeze."

I taste the pork *posolé* to make sure the Anaheim chiles don't make it too *picante.* Diego started complaining that too much chile gave him indigestion. And it's not as if I'm doing all this just for him. I started the stew before I called him about his leaky refrigerator. You can come for dinner but only on one condition, I said. I was clear about that. It has to be over between you and *her.* He chuckled at first, then paused realizing I was dead serious.

I never expected to invite him to dinner this afternoon, nor did I expect to deliver an ultimatum. But I'm tired of this pussyfooting around. Tired of his secrets. Tired of waiting for his five months of indecision time to pass. And tired of his T-shirts and sock balls taking up space in my garage and in my head. And I'm tired of being a doormat—Jesus, I'm wall-to-wall carpeting. Even if it is just one woman, like Maya says, it's time for Diego to choose. Either *her* or my *posolé.* He can't have both. No more wishy-washy Barbara. No free lunch.

When Diego lived at home, I figured out that he spent Sunday afternoons with his girlfriend. Yet he always, *always* arrived home by seven for dinner. That's the sickening part. The thought of him being with *her* and then eating *my food* made me physically ill. He defiled my food, my Greek salads, my *carnitas,* my enchilada casseroles, my ginger teriyaki chicken by bringing whore-germs into the house. Coming home to my table disgusts me far worse than coming home to my bed. An unforgivable betrayal. But not this time.

"So you'll call her and tell her you're ending it?" I told him over the phone.

"Okay," he agreed.

"I'm serious, Diego."

"All right."

"Okay then, you can come to dinner." After our agreement I could relax. I won, didn't I?

That afternoon for three glorious hours I cooked. I added finely chopped onions, cilantro, and tomatoes to my guacamole, along with a splash of pickled jalapeño juice (my secret ingredient). Then I threw in the pits the way Diego had taught me to keep the avocados from turning brown. While I mashed the avocados, Deanna sat at the table and decorated a ledger paper centerpiece with scented colored markers. The kids raised in my house may have lacked for consistency and discipline, but they never lacked for art supplies.

I foresaw the day when all three kids and their father would finally be home. The family would be sharing summer meals again from the upper patio that overlooked a turquoise pool. Our weekend pool parties would return with beach balls, salsa music, Diego's barbecued chicken, and my salads. Sara would bring her Mexican rice. Parties were what the Flores family did best.

I picture him home, happily watering his lemons and holding court at the dining room table for our upcoming Thanksgiving dinner when Mimi and Miguel would be home. And, of course, for Christmas. But I won't let him move back in that quick. We'll date first, returning to our regular Saturday date-night dinners out for Indian, Thai, or hot wings at the Pyramid. Then soon we'll be laughing again across the table, telling stories. Like our camping trip to Yosemite when Diego claims he fought off a ten-foot grizzly. We did hear a bear attack the cooler but really Diego never left the tent. We have so many stories to laugh about, but not now. One dinner is too soon for "remember when" stories. I'll save them like the top tier of a wedding cake that remains in the freezer frozen until the anniversary day arrives.

My kitchen is filled again with the aroma of refried beans and pan-roasted jalapeños. The Mexican rice is browning in butter, topped with a string-tied bouquet of leaf coriander; and the blender, with charred tomatoes and lime juice for the salsa, awaits the blackened jalapeños. Fresh garlic, clove, and anchovies infuse their flavors into a jar of virgin olive oil for a salad dressing, and a bouquet of parsley, grateful for a drink, soaks in a glass on the windowsill.

My joy in the kitchen, my exultation in front of a stove, doesn't come from just one perfect marinade, or mousse, or moussaka; it's in the orchestration. I like having all four burners synchronized going at once while I chop, blend, sauté, blacken, purée, bake, braise, and broil so that each dish is finished at exactly the same time. All in perfect balance. I conduct a meal in front of the stove and my apron is my tuxedo.

While the stew simmers, I shower, wash my hair, and exfoliate my face (it's supposed to make you look younger), then I spray Joy perfume, the big bottle Diego bought me in Juarez—but only a whiff so Maya won't rag on me. I pull out my new skinny jeans, with the size ten tags still on. They're two pants sizes smaller than the fourteens I wore last year and I shimmy them up my freshly shaved legs. For seven long years those extra twenty post-menopausal pounds wouldn't budge for love or money or hormones, yet when Diego marched out the door, my extra pounds just marched off with him. Now I weigh the same as in high school—the same weight as George Harrison. My Jazzercise friend Joyce calls it the "divorced and separated diet." I remind her not to use the "D" word—not yet. I twist my torso in front of the mirror to admire my butt, which retains its apple-round shape, then I slip an apron over my peach T-shirt and tie its strings around my new thin waist. Before he arrives, I'll sneak back to the bathroom vanity for a patch job: run a brush through my hair, dab on light lipstick, and pat powder to remove the oily sheen from standing over the stove.

Back in the kitchen I mix the guacamole, wipe the avocado off my fingers onto my apron, and peer over Deanna's shoulder. She drew a large rainbow springing out of a puffy cloud, and the top reads "Britney Rocks."

"That's beautiful, Dee."

She places her drawing in the center of the table and flashes her adorable beaver-tooth grin. Deanna sets the table with plates, bowls and silverware; I don't even have to ask her the usual three times. Our everyday mismatched ones will do. The gold-rimmed china or eating in the dining room would be too obvious. Deanna folds paper towels into square napkins. She surprises me with a bouquet of daisies that she picked from the yard. She puts them in a canning jar and sets them on her drawing as a centerpiece.

We don't have long to wait. Diego's always on time. I watch his Nissan van pull into the drive, and my knees dissolve into jelly. He's walking towards the front door and I notice how much thinner he looks. He's not eating properly. Careful, now the jelly is spreading to my brain. Don't make a big deal of this, Barbara. The metal screen door closes with a warm familiar clang and he's here in the flesh. Diego's home. He wipes his loafers excessively on the entrance mat, then says, "Hi, how are my girls?" He hangs his leather jacket in the hall closet. The jacket that my arm fits around so naturally, expensive black leather, soft and supple. He's wearing a wide grin and my favorite blue seersucker shirt—I love to trace my fingers down the back and touch the puckers. But I stay glued to my chopping station. Deanna has her little arms wrapped around him and Lola jumps up and down at his khaki pant leg like a furry white pogo stick. Eyes down, I chop the tomatoes, jalapeños, red onions, and epazote leaves for the *pico de gallo*. Now he's standing right next to me. I ache to throw my arms around him and bury my face into his grey beard and clean soap scent. *Don't leave. I'll be better, I promise.*

"How was your day?" I want to say like I've said for thirty-one years, but that feels too intimate, too wishful, too normal.

So I chop pretending that I'm okay—tat-a-tat-tat-tat-tat—with Diego's Tic-Tac breath only inches away. For a second, I look in his brown eyes and I lose it. "Kiss," I say. Ack! That word betrays me; it leaked out. He leans in and my right cheek turns to receive the soft, familiar touch of his lips. My knife stops, and my hand twitches on the firm crimson half of a tomato, sending a rivulet of red juice into the moat of my cutting board. He steps behind me and I remember how his trained boxer's arms would circle me from behind in the kitchen, and he'd whisper, "Let's have a date night."

He sniffs the covered pot on the stove. "Smells good, Barbara."

"*Posolé.*" A pork, corn, and charred green chile stew. Nearby is a pie, baked with cinnamon-dusted apples, cooling on the counter. These siren aromas swirl around my kitchen, alluring him, I hope, to his seat at the table.

"Papa, I set the table." Deanna drags him over to see it.

"Good job, Deanna!" he says. She pushes her Papa's chair from the corner over the dog dishes, back to its former position at the head of the table. *He actually kissed me.*

"Better check my refrigerator, Barbara. I thought I'd turned it off." Diego heads to the garage door with Deanna and Lola trailing behind.

Diego peeks through the garage door holding up a half-empty twelve-pack of Tecaté. "Look what I found in the fridge."

"Maya's friends must have left it there. Have one," I say, breaking my no alcohol in the house rule.

"Well, it *is* my refrigerator."

And legally he *is* still my husband. Joanna just doesn't get it. I have an obligation to try and bring him back, I think. Not just for me, but for Deanna, the kids, and all those generations of Mexican wives who stuck by their men for the sake of their families. I have to give Diego a chance.

At the table Diego sits at his place. The white marble Madonna, in the greenhouse window behind him, looks over his shoulder. Maya, still in her work scrubs, reminds Deanna to wash her hands. When she's seated we all hold hands for the blessing, "Bless us, our Lord, for these thy gifts ... " and for the first time no one picks up their fork until after we say the amen.

"Mmmm. *Muy sabroso.*" Delicious, he says and wipes red drips from his graying mustache. The cornbread is extra moist because I haven't scrimped on the butter, sour cream, or cheddar cheese, and the dark, rich *posolé* has simmered for hours. We talk about Diego's bumper crop of lemons, apples and plums, and how I'm saving energy by not running the heater at night. The conversation flows effortlessly and the normality of it all leaves me feeling mildly, pleasantly, apprehensively euphoric. As if these last four months were a bad dream. Everyone is on good behavior. Even Deanna, who separates her food lest a grain of rice touch her meat, is careful to place her milk away from the edge of the table. And tonight Papa isn't reprimanding her to "lean over your plate, use your knife instead of your fingers, and don't feed Lola at the table." Maya, as usual, pours on too much salt, and discreetly spits her chewed meat into pieces of napkin. But she neatly tucks the marble-sized, napkin-clothed spitballs under the rim of her plate away from her father's eye. We've already told her over and over that the fat comes out in the juice, but she evidently doesn't believe us. This evening, however, Diego doesn't mention his daughter's anorexic eating habits.

We commiserate lightheartedly over Bush's surprising second-term win in this month's presidential election. "How did that ever happen?" And we're laughing about having the Terminator as governor. I let him take the lead in political discussions, just like he does as a tour guide on his frequent college trips to Cuba. Diego is still the most interesting, brilliant, witty man I've ever met. We may have had angry raised-voice dinners, but never any boring ones. Wendy, my first sponsor, calls Diego a knee-jerk liberal, but I can overlook that. My husband can turn any topic into a fascinating history lesson: the Middle East, religion, boxing. Even our food is a reflection of Diego's politics. For fifteen years while the farm worker's grape boycott was on, I didn't buy grapes, and I never made a lettuce salad without paying homage to César Chávez.

I'm nodding and smiling through the dinner, but I catch myself holding back. Don't grin too wide, I tell myself, or laugh too loud at his Bush jokes.

He finishes his bowl of stew before I serve myself salad.

"Want more, Diego?"

"Well, maybe just half."

I fill his bowl nearly full. I know what half means. Then pass him the *pico de gallo* and the towel-wrapped hot tortillas. Ladling his soup bowl and hearing his voice back at the table where it belongs makes me feel hopeful, almost even relaxed. He always did come to dinner never complaining, always jovial, his manners meticulous. His napkin dabs drops of *posolé* juice off his goatee.

In the back of my mind I know that I still have to ask, did you call her? Did you do it this afternoon? But I can't say anything in front of the girls and not now when we're having such a good time. Maybe he'll stay after dinner and we can watch the MacNeil-Lehrer Report. When we're alone, I'll ask.

"Dad, you're coming over for Thanksgiving, right?" Maya asks.

Diego looks at me. I don't know what to say. Thanksgiving is a month away. "We'll see, Maya," he replies.

"Sara invited the family to go to the blessing of the special needs kids," I say. "It's after Thanksgiving. Bishop Cummings is presiding. It's for David." David is Bill and Sara's youngest. Diego isn't much of a church goer, but Sara and Bill are like family. Sara calls Diego her *compadre*, her Mexican buddy.

"Well, hmmm. I'm not sure Barbara." He places his bowl and silverware on his plate and stands.

"There's pie," I add. Maya rolls her eyes.

"I'm full. Barbara, dinner was great, as always." He grins at me, and pats his stomach, then pushes his chair in under the table. *Don't go. Please stay.*

"I turned off the garage refrigerator, and put a bucket under the freezer. I'll be back tomorrow to empty it."

"Diego, I can empty it. You don't have to drive all the way over." *He wants to come back.* Of course. His sock balls are still in his dresser, his jackets are still hung in the cedar closet, and his suede boxing bag still hangs next to his slant board near his six tool boxes.

"I should go. Dinner was great. You've always been a great cook, Barbara."

I fill a Tupperware container with *posolé*, then stretch out two pieces of sky-blue Saran Wrap to cover a wedge of cornbread and a slice of apple pie.

"I used your apples," I say, handing him his leftovers. I'm too scared to say we have to talk. He leans over and kisses me on the lips. A peck.

"What was that for?" One quick glance. Prolonged eye contact feels too risky.

"Well you wanted a kiss when I came in," he grins sheepishly. We say our goodbyes at the door as if everything is hunky-dory. It might have been hunky, but not quite dory. Not yet. I stand at the open door confused. Should I follow him out to the car? Pride won't let me. You kissed me? Twice. So what does that mean, Diego? Did you call her or not? I close the front door. I can't bear to watch him drive away again.

"I handled dinner very well, don't you think, Maya? And after he left, I didn't cry once."

"Yet," she says.

After cleaning up I'm still energized. Singing to myself, I load bed linens and my robe with its four months' worth of stains, still unwashed, into the washtub. I overhear Deanna telling her mom, "Gramma's happy again, because Papa *is* coming home." She doesn't say he *could* come home or he *might* come home. Deanna says Papa *is* coming home. I hold on tight to that slender grammatical straw.

And Maya saw him kiss me. Maybe now she'll get it that a man doesn't throw away a thirty-one year marriage with kids and grandkids for any pretty young chick enrolled in his Econ class. "They stray and come back," my friend Joyce says "After thirty years, they come back," she says. They come back for the money, or the memories, or the dog, or the lemon trees, or in this case, the stew.

. . .

DIEGO AND I ARRANGED A dinner date for Thursday at the Pyramid Brewery in Berkeley. I admit I suggested it, but he did offer to pick me up at the house. As I'm picking out clothes for date night—my push-up water bra, skinny jeans, a long sleeve cleavage-covering top—I'm excited about spending time with Diego. We need face time, our short dinner together wasn't nearly long enough. We've chatted briefly on the phone over the Schwarzenegger surprise win, and of course I've heard plenty of his rants on Bush, who Diego says resembles a stunned bird hit with a BB gun. But I miss his expressions, the way his teeth show when he gets worked up, the knowing looks, the thigh pats, the laughter that makes me bend over, clutch my stomach, and tear up.

I will admit that he's all political talk with no action, but no one can deny that Diego is entertaining. His full classes attest to that. He's always seeking a better textbook, the one that actually tells the truth about the Mexican American war, and he's forever typing new study guides and handouts and finding films for his class like *El Norté* and *The Hunt for Pancho Villa*. He's a gifted, charismatic speaker as well, with a passionate voice that captures an audience with no mike or a script, making his points with ardor, eloquence, and humor. Yet when it comes to attending a rally, a march, or an after-school Cesar Chavez meeting he can't be bothered to get his professor-ass out of bed if meetings interfere with nap time. I've learned over three decades that Diego will always choose free time over socialism.

Last Cinco de Mayo when he was invited to speak on campus in front of TV cameras, I encouraged him. "You should do it, Diego. The kids would like to see their dad on TV. Don't you want to be up there on stage with Edward James Olmos?"

Diego shook his head. "Barbara, it's on a Saturday."

I couldn't stop loving the easy-going, magnanimous, generous *carpe diem*, "my day is my plum," no ambition Diego.

As always he is prompt in picking me up. I don't mention *her* on the half-hour ride to Berkeley's Pyramid Bar; we keep conversation light. Why ruin an evening right off the bat? At the brewery, Diego suggests we sit at the bar. I enjoy seeing Jake the bartender again, several acquaintances from nearby Ten Speed Press, and Frank, who has a bar seat with his name on it. Frank and Diego were hired at the college together in the late sixties. Frank taught Black American Studies before he retired; he's also the godfather of our kids. Truthfully, my appearance at this brewery, Diego's turf, is less about *seeing* old friends and more about *being seen* together with Diego. My appearance stakes a claim, like a cat who marks her territory. Sitting next to him at the bar is broadcasting to the crowd, "Listen up, bitches, this is my man! Be warned." But no one except our old friends appears to take any notice of us.

We split a huge plate of chicken wings. What do I care if there's red hot sauce on my cheek—I'm not uptight. I'm totally relaxed talking with my husband about our kids.

"So is Maya staying home or going to see that 'shit for brains' boyfriend?" Diego waves a wand of celery. Such imaginative colorful language Diego comes up with for Jesse. Like the Eskimos with a hundred names for snow.

I swallow before speaking. "She's staying home, thank God. Nothing good ever comes of her going to Seattle. I'm surprised Jesse's parents put up with it."

"When is she going to learn?" He shakes his head. We've had this conversation a thousand times. This time it feels wonderful, feels like home.

"So the girls will be home for Thanksgiving, then."

"Yep." He wants an invite for Thanksgiving, but he's too embarrassed to ask. I lift my non-alcoholic beer up for a small victory toast. We clink glasses; he gives me a small smile and brief eye contact. But I need more than that before he gets turkey.

The clock is ticking. December, the month that marks his five-month deadline, is around the corner. Is he coming home or not? Did he tell her it's over? Tick tock. Tick tock.

The rest of the evening we're in a three-way with Frank; he's telling us about his last trip to Paris. I mention the Mass for Sara's son David—my Mexican girlfriend Sara would for sure approve of my wooing Diego back—but neither Diego nor Frank is willing to commit to the event. Still, this is going rather well for a first date. Pleasant. Diego's in no rush to leave. Maybe we'll do it again next week. Then I can't hold it in any longer. I have to ask. When Frank leaves for the bathroom, I ask him about *her*. "So how did it go?"

"How did what go?" Diego orders another Red Tail Ale.

"You know," I say close to his ear, "breaking it off with her."

He cocks his head and sighs, "Barbara, I told you I'm trying." His expression reminds me of a boy struggling with his homework. I squeeze his hand. I don't know what else to do. Saying, "Shit or get off the pot," would dampen the mood. After an hour more of bar chat we're ready for the ride home. Since I'm sober, bars aren't really my favorite places, especially after five. We walk toward the exit side by side.

"Diego. Oh, Diego," chime two girls from a booth. They look about fifteen. He stops and greets them with, "Wassup?" The awkward moment lasts only seconds and we're out the door into the chilly November night air. But I'm thinking, that's a first. Diego didn't introduce me.

"This is Barbara, my wife," he always says with impeccable manners. *Always.* Standing behind him like a roll-away piece of junk luggage, not being introduced, was a cold slap in the face.

I straighten up against the cold wind coming off the Bay. Hear this, you skinny, pubescent-brained, no-moral-compass bitches.

It ain't over 'til the fat lady sings.

# CHAPTER EIGHT
## BLESSED ARE THE PEACEMAKERS

"I can't go, Mom. I want to go Christmas shopping while Deanna is at Kyle's house." Maya, barefoot in sweats, loads a mountain of clothes in the wash.

"Can't go where?"

"To that thing tomorrow. Sara's thing. You know, the blessing of the retards."

"It's a Mass, we should all go, and don't say retards."

"Mom, you know I don't mean David. We love David."

I'm expecting Diego will show. The ceremony is important to Sara and Bill. We've known their son David since he was two, even before his autistic diagnosis. I'm already imagining Diego and I taking communion together like we always did on church holidays. And tomorrow's Mass isn't led by any ol' Tom, Dick, or Jorge priest either. Bishop Cummings is presiding, the bishop of the entire Oakland diocese.

Maya lugs her laundry basket past the living room and I follow her, picking up droppings: a stray sock, hair ties, and fallen panties—a lacy G-string.

Deanna pops up from the sofa like a jack-in-the-box, surprising me. "Gramma, Daddy says he's not sending his presents here this time. He's putting all my Christmas presents under his tree."

I'm shocked. "Maya, you can't go to Seattle!" I tell her in her room. "I'm inviting Dad for Christmas, he'll expect you and Deanna to be here." I place the sock and G-string in her basket on her bed.

"We're leaving Christmas afternoon. We'll do presents in the morning," she says flatly.

Deanna enters. "We're going, Gramma. *End of story*," she says, imitating her grandfather.

Her backtalk irks me, but I've got bigger fish to fry. Whenever Maya visits Jesse, it isn't a question of *if* she'll have a fight with him, it's *how bad*. Broken nose bad? Police calls bad? And now that Deanna has started smarting off, I'm worried she'll be his next target.

Later in the kitchen Maya's loading the washer. While Deanna is in the bath, out of earshot, I try to persuade Maya.

"Look, Beanzo [her nickname], with you and Jesse fighting Deanna is not fine. Yesterday she told me, 'Gramma, it's not a tele-phone, it's a fight-a-phone.' She's only eight years old."

"But Deanna *wants* to go to Washington. Jesse's parents are there. Jesse lives downstairs. Don't worry about it. And Nicki *does* Christmas. She decorates the whole house."

That's a low blow. As if having presents and a tree isn't enough.

"But you two fight in front of Deanna. It damages the child. Maya, remember Lola's dog training class?"

"The one you said she flunked."

*Don't engage.* "See, Maya, a raging man in the house is like a snarling, vicious dog. Saying, 'Nice doggy, be good now,' doesn't work. If you stay in the same room with an angry dog, he'll attack and chew you to pieces. And that's what you do, Maya. You argue with an angry dog."

The sound of Deanna blowing bubbles in the tub travels down the hall.

"Deanna, time to get out," Maya calls out.

"Every dog trainer knows this. When dogs snap, you have to walk away from them and close the door."

Maya shakes her head and walks to the dryer and fills the basket with warm towels. I'm following her.

"You learn to detach. That's the key. That's how they learn to behave."

"Jesse's not a dog, Mom."

She heads down the hall to the bathroom humming, "White Christmas."

Sigh. A failed analogy. I called after her, "Look Beans, it doesn't matter if the teacup hits the wall, or if the wall hits the teacup, it's always worse for the teacup."

. . .

I ENTER ALONE THROUGH the tall, heavy double doors of the Oakland Cathedral. I expect Diego will arrive late. It's his family tradition. The cathedral is massive and the many pews are full; I don't know how I'll find Sara and Bill, or Diego. I walk down the right aisle, dwarfed by white pillars ascending toward a magnificent stained glass dome. It's a tight squeeze between wheelchairs and gurneys occupied with kids and the attendants and walkers parked against the wall. The parishioners boom out "Amazing Grace." Hearing these kids singing out a smiling, enthusiastic, drooling version of "Amazing Grace" spreads comfort all through me.

On the right side, I spot Bill's lanky, dark-suited frame and shorter, proud Sara with her unmistakable thick black hair. David, nearly as tall as Bill now, stands between them with the two girls flanking their parents. But I don't see Diego anywhere.

I'm able to squeeze into the end of the row behind my friends. David spots me first, then pushes past his mom and Annalisa. "Baaab–ra," he says loudly. He wedges himself between strangers, leans over the pew, places his hands gently on both my shoulders and kisses me. For a second he stands back gazing at me, smiles and says, "I love you, Baaab-ra."

I'm with family.

The procession begins. Smiling parents and children assisted by wheelchairs, gurneys, and crutches walk down the center aisle toward Bishop Cummings in his red vestments and high hat. The bishop acknowledges each child and traces the sign of the cross in blessing on each forehead, while a choir sings the words of the beatitudes.

David walks in the line between Sara and Bill toward the altar. He bows his head and the bishop's fingers trace the cross on his forehead. Each tiny hair on my arm stands at attention.

*Blessed are the poor in spirit for theirs is the kingdom of Heaven.*

My vision blurs with tears. I sense Diego here with me. I'll be okay.

*Blessed are they who mourn, for they shall be comforted.*

Most children don't bow before the bishop like David did, but even those most egregiously afflicted with jerks, tics, and involuntary speech became still at the moment of blessing. They know.

The mass ends and Sara leans across the middle of the pew to me at the end. In the cacophony of chatter and hymnals closing, I can't make out what she's saying.

"Barb, did you see him behind us?" she asks.

"He came?" I ask. I search the back of the church but Diego is nowhere to be seen. As the pew empties Sara comes closer. "Barb, it's so darling of him to come. So sweet to bring his girlfriend with him."

*Oh my God!* He brought *her*? To church? I feel dizzy and hold on to the back of the pew for balance.

"She's a lovely girl," Sara says.

I have to leave. I feel sick.

"What's her name again?"

An unforgivable sacrilege.

"Oh yes, Erika," she bubbles.

*Erika? Miguel's Erika?*

"Barb, you okay? You look whiter than white people white."

"Miguel came to mass? With Erika?" I can't believe it.

"So sweet of him," she crows.

I look over the crowd searching for Miguel.

I haven't seen my son for six months. Not since that day he screamed at me to get out of his hospital room.

"Erika said they couldn't stay for the reception. Don't be upset with him, Barb. So darling that they came. It means so much to David."

A happy tear slides down my cheek.


The cathedral basement matches all church basement receptions with their long tables, a giant silver coffee urn, and a white bakery sheet cake thick with pink and blue frosting roses. Sheet cakes are a Catholic tradition, as much as the host and wine.

Sitting alone at a table with Sara is the perfect opportunity to find out what she knows. Has she seen Diego with *her*?

"Oh no, Barb!" Sara says surprised, "We've never seen his other woman."

*His other woman.* That hits like a knife in the gut.

"Men stray, Barbarita. That's what they do." Like they're a herd of goats. "This *girl*, she looks up to him, laughs at his jokes," she continues, mimicking. "Oh Diego, you're so smart, so funny, so good-looking.'"

"But he told me he's trying to break it off with her."

"You know Barb, with your posters and books, and your picture in the newspaper, maybe you made him feel less important."

Not fair. Why can't I have a successful career and stay married? "So what am I supposed to do? Grovel?" I take a big bite of cake and suck the frosting off the plastic fork.

"Keep cooking for him. And you have to forgive him, Barb. He won't come back if you make him feel guilty, ashamed."

She reaches across the table and holds my hand. "You still love him, right?"

"Yes," I say, wondering if it's a curse.

"Make him feel more like a man, Barbarita. Fight for him. Pray for *la voluntad de Dios*. God will help." She crosses herself and pats my hand. Her soft brown eyes look into mine.

"You know, Barb, he did this to us, too."

My hands fold over my heart, holding it inside my chest. "Oh, Sara. That's the kindest thing anyone has ever said to me."

It had been five months since Sara's daughter Analisa spotted Diego with his girlfriend. But that November I was still trying to convince myself that she was a fling. A sideline relationship that would soon disappear and he would come home. But the evidence against my fantasy kept piling up. He had told me she was his student friend. Same age as his daughter Rena. It didn't matter to me that she was black, I thought. But of course it did.

· · ·

"BARRRR-BADA, YOU'RE NOT protecting what's yours. You've let her take over," Pabla tells me over her beef enchiladas and homemade banana pepper salsa. Pabla is my kind, loving, adopted Mexican mother. She's second only to Grandma Buehler, who took care of me as a baby during Mom's long sanitarium visits. I hired Pabla as a babysitter after Maya was born and we've remained close for twenty-five years. She taught me Spanish, how to swaddle an infant, and how to create *salsas autenticas* from blackened peppers mashed in a *molcajete*. Pabla is caramel-skinned, diabetic, a bit overweight, speaks little English, but she is the hardest working, most efficient caretaker I've ever seen. I'd come home from my job as the art director for *The Berkeley Monthly* and the three kids were clean and happy to eat Mexican rice and the candy bars that she bought for them at the corner store. Miraculously, floors were mopped, windows gleamed, and the light fixtures were polished. I don't know how she did it.

When Pabla arrived each morning, I'd have to cajole her to sit at the table and join me for a cup of coffee before doing dishes. In our morning chats over the decades, we shared births, weddings, grandchildren, her son's conversion to Mormonism, and tragedies, like her son Chewie's death.

In the seventies Tacho, her husband, left her and their five boys in Zacatecas, Mexico, to find work in California (Pabla birthed seven boys total; two died young). Tacho had been gone for two years when Pabla decided to head across the border to find her wayward husband. She packed up her boys—Arturo, the youngest, was a toddler then—and headed to the Bay Area. She found Tacho living in a house in Richmond with another woman. "I swept her out, *como una mosca*. Like a fly." she said, demonstrating with a whisk of the broom.

I miss Pabla. Her foot infections were getting worse and she's always been difficult to contact. Her phone number changed frequently because her adult sons racked up huge long-distance bills calling Mexico. If I hadn't been driving on San Pablo Dam Road last July and by accident spied Pabla coming out her front door next to the Goodwill store, she would not have known that Diego moved out.

"*Es tu espouso!*" she insisted. He's your husband! Bring him home.

MY HISPANIC FRIENDS HAVE a very different perspective than my Anglo friends. Latinas regard "husband retrieval" as marital duty. And they generously share their methods even with gringas like me. Enchilada verde dinners, rosaries, prayers to the Virgin de Guadalupe, and if all else fails, witchcraft. I tried them all. Placing a written wish in the manger of Baby Jesus at church didn't bring results, and burning Diego's photograph at midnight with wood shavings from a *Botanica* resulted in my hair catching fire from the candle flame, A Cuban *santero* instructed me to write the name of my adversary on a piece of paper and place her name face down inside my shoe. Left shoe, to be precise. A "sure thing" method of girlfriend disposal, he said. I wrote her name on a yellow Post-it and put it sticky/name side down in a closed-toe shoe. I wanted no serious harm to come to her, no disfiguring fires, accidental drownings, or electric hair straighteners slipping into bathtubs. I only wanted her to go away, to disappear out of our lives, and maybe get fat.

The Post-it didn't work. But I don't blame the *santero.* It was my fault. I believed the fake name that Diego gave me.

· · ·

WHEN THANKSGIVING WEEK arrives, I don't have the heart to cook a bird. The girls and I gratefully accept an invitation to Sara's house. This first Thanksgiving with only Maya and Deanna feels achingly brutal, but the girls don't seem to mind where they get their turkey and stuffing. In December I decide to up my game. Diego's five-month deadline, by my calculation, will run out on December twenty-eighth. Tick tock.

Last week Diego came over when I wasn't home and set up an eight-foot Christmas tree. The tallest one we've ever had. Enough of this pussyfooting around. We need an answer now.

This morning Deanna asks me again, "Gramma, is Papa coming home for Christmas?"

I'm going to suggest that he spend a trial period in the house over Christmas. Mimi's coming in from San Diego on Christmas Eve and my brother, who Diego likes, arrives the same night from LA. We need to move forward. Enough midlife crisis extensions.

That Thursday Diego informs me that he's having his tires rotated at Big O Tires downtown in Lafayette.

"We'll stop by the tire place," I tell Deanna on the drive home from Safeway, "and Sweetie, you can ask Papa yourself if he's coming home for Christmas." I tell myself that I'm not using Deanna to manipulate the situation ... well kinda, sorta. But it's for the good of us. Maybe we'll all go to Squirrel's Café for breakfast afterward.

After leaving Safeway, Deanna spots Diego's silver Nissan Quest in the Big O Tire parking lot. "There's his van, Gramma." She bounces up and down in the passenger seat with glee. The van outside means it's ready for pickup. Bay Area weather has turned bitter cold, a thick sweater and corduroy pants kind of day, so we wait for Diego inside the Big O reception area with smells of pungent deep-tread rubber and burnt coffee.

Deanna in a puffy pink jacket watches out the sheet glass window between towering stacks of tires for her Papa.

"You'll see Papa walking up any minute." He's very prompt. She loves to surprise him. I look out alongside Deanna watching the sidewalk for his unmistakable quick hiking gate.

The surprise is mine.

A white sedan rolls in that I barely notice at first. *Oh my God*, that's Diego in the passenger seat. The driver, a small woman in a red scarf, stops the car in the driveway to let him out.

JOLT. *That's her.*

Diego steps out of the car. I fly out the entrance doors hurtling toward the sedan—"*Stay here, Deanna!*"—bypass Diego, and swoop down into the vacant passenger seat—a hawk with talons spread. My hands flail and slap at her red scarf and shoulders over and over again.

"You fucking black bitch!" She ducks, the scarf askew. I grab a tuft of spongy black hair, yanking it hard, shaking it. A tan arm shields against the flying fist of my free hand. The one with a ring on it.

"Who is this woman?" she yells.

"Uh, that's my wife," Diego stands beside the car, his arms hanging limp. Now she yanks my hair and SLAM! my head hits the dash. Our entwined arms, clutching hair, snarl into a flailing knot in the front seat. My head is shoved between my knees, jammed against a knob. From upside down I see her face. Smooth, wrinkle-less tawny skin. I can't move. My dash-level vision twists toward the window and makes out the jackets of onlookers and two approaching Big O Tire employees—one on his cell, the other with a hairy belly roll hanging beneath his monogrammed blue shirt. Diego's bearded face bends down into the car window.

"Barbara, you better stop this. He's calling the police." He sounds annoyed.

"The dispatcher wants to know if they have any guns?" Mr. Big O asks him.

My scalp is stretched like she's pulling my brains out, but my fist, clenched around a puffy hair tuft refuses to open.

"Are you sleeping with him?" I demand.

"Yes, are you?"

"Yes," I lie. It had been six months, last Mother's Day. My head aches. I don't want bald spots. A crowd of coats and jackets has appeared. My fist lets go. Then she slowly, hesitantly releases her grip, as if another attack is coming any second. I step out of her car and spit a string of expletives to leave no doubt about her moral character to the onlookers. Standing tall, I straighten my cardigan. Blonde strands lie scattered below on her black upholstery like tossed tinsel. I hope she finds them for years.

In seconds tires screech and the white sedan peals out of the parking lot. I'm disgusted. I'm dazed. Shell shocked.

"Barbara, the police are on their way." Diego says. "She can press charges.

You assaulted her." *As if he is so innocent.* "She's the victim here." Diego keeps repeating this.

"Oh, just shut the hell up!"

"There was no need Barbara, she's just a friend," he says. I can't look at him. This time I don't believe him. Within minutes police arrive. I'm grateful it's two officers I haven't met yet. Officer Hernandez patiently listens to every detail of my story, nodding frequently, and occasionally he reprimands Diego to stop interrupting. He gives Diego a pathetic look. "I'm not filing a report," he says. Shaking his head at Diego, he walks back to the squad car.

"I'm never going to Big O Tires again." Diego sulks and walks off to his freshly rotated tires. I head toward my blue Ford Escort and suddenly, *Oh my god, Deanna!*

Deanna stands alone, staring wide-eyed against the glass. She looks so small, glued to the spot where I told her to wait. A small nymph statue frozen between two towering stacks of deep-tread tires. *What do I say to her?*

On the drive back home we're as mute as the bags of groceries in the trunk. I should have handled meeting Papa's *friend* with more tact. Fights, much less matronly hair pulling, catfights simply don't happen in our zip code. Not in downtown Lafayette, with five shops in a two-block radius where you can buy a peppermint latté. I'm stunned and don't know how to explain what Deanna just witnessed.

*That was her.* I wasn't prepared to see her in the flesh—I wanted her to disappear with a Santeria Post-it in my shoe, not actually exist. *That was her.* The thief in my home. She doesn't know my dresser drawer holds a twenty-seventh anniversary card from Diego where he wrote, "Let's have twenty-seven more." That woman stole my twenty-seven more years. My future.


Diego told me her name was Kathy Grant. But it wasn't. It was LaShondra Jackson. The same LaShondra Jackson who put Diego on her cell phone account, the same LaShondra Jackson with the same address and phone given to me by Intellius.com last July. Diego kept her a secret from me and the kids, presumably because I was a dangerous, insane, and jealous wife—which, I admit, that day at Big O Tires was sorta true. Yet it would be another four years before Diego finally let the kids meet her. But I also admit that may have been because LaShondra is a caring, patient woman who honored the time and process it took for my marriage to finally end.

That day she won. She got the prize. Still, seeing Diego's gaping, ashen face as she high-tailed out of the parking lot, I felt as if I at least had fought the noble fight. And I did apologize to her briefly before she left, but that was so I wouldn't have to hear Joanna tell me I owed her an amends. But I wasn't completely sorry for having slapped, clawed and pulled hair in one last Big O ditch effort to keep my family together.

My real regret, and the amends I needed to make, weren't to LaShondra Jackson but to Deanna. The little girl face in the Big O Tire window who watched her grandma attack an innocent stranger and call her bad names. The same grandma who goes to Mass, who says we give time-outs, not spankings, who says, "Every act of violence needs to be reported." It was Deanna's wide-eyed innocent face against the glass that shamed me.

A few days later I found a yellow Post-it on the refrigerator. In Deanna's eight-year-old handwriting it read, "Love sucks."

# CHAPTER NINE
## TWAS THE WEEK BEFORE CHRISTMAS

The doorbell rings. Carrie is prompt. I have to listen mindfully because our bell doesn't actually chime, it sort of thuds. Rather than a ding-dong, it's more of a dull ding-thud. Like an old dog that groans and raises his head when he hears someone approach, then thinks, "Why bother?"

My plan is to give Carrie an hour of sponsoring time because I have papers to grade for my new afternoon high school teaching job. I reserve mornings to read student writing. Surprisingly, I'm finding communication with teenagers, who are not my own, enjoyable and stimulating. Also I figure Carrie will soon figure out she made a mistake asking me to be her sponsor anyway. She deserves a real sponsor who actually can make a marriage work. A sponsor with a husband who doesn't have a girlfriend.

Carrie arrives in a new SUV, looking well put together, but stiff and edgy. She changed to a pink purse, maybe to match her baseball cap. Her long, silky blonde ponytail threads through the hole in the back. The morning is warm for mid-December and we sit out on the patio where the chairs rock, the bird's chirp, and the morning sun dapples the patio stones. Carrie tells me she's originally from Texas, where her parents still live. She describes a perfect suburban lifestyle, married ten years, two kids, good schools, good paycheck, and good adoring dad who takes the kids dirt biking. She talks a lot, but doles out eye contact sparingly.

"Wow Barbara, you stayed married thirty years. What's your secret?"

"Denial," I say, straight-faced.

I appreciate her laugh. "Yeah, and I just beat up his girlfriend at Big O Tires," Carrie's blue eyes pop open wide in surprise. "But today let's talk about you." Any excuse to get my mind off of what happened in the Big O Tire parking lot is a blessing.

"Jay's drinking isn't that bad, really, he certainly doesn't think it is. I know that's what the meetings are about, the alcohol, but ... maybe I don't belong at the meetings." She sighs and gazes into the East Bay hills turning green with winter rain. "Caylee and Tyler love their dad. He bought them each Tyke Bike motorcycles," she says. "Maybe I'm the one with the problem, like he says."

"Oh no, Carrie." I tell her when Miguel smoked pot in high school, I didn't feel like I belonged in the alcohol-focused meetings either.

"But I feel really guilty. I shouldn't be hiding his stuff."

"You hide his booze?"

" I'm so ashamed." Despite her youth and makeup, her face appears tired. "No. I hid his money."

"Okay, so you hid money, no biggie."

"Uh, I've never told this to anyone." Her blue eyes leave me again. "But I've been taking money out of the food budget and hiding it in a box in my closet. Not much, just five or ten dollars a week." Her words are hushed as if my patio is a confessional. "I lied to Jay about what I spent on Caylee's shoes and what the soccer game snacks cost."

"Squirreling away dollars from the food budget isn't a sin. I did that too when my kids were little."

Carrie sighs. "Barbara, I'm probably wasting your time."

"Not at all. Go on." No rush. Student papers can wait.

"I saved close to two hundred dollars in a box in the closet," she says. "You know, just to have a nest egg if the kids need something, you know, like swim team fees. I hate asking Jay for money." Her eyes drift over the fence again. "Then two weeks ago Jay found the box in the closet and ..."

"And?"

"He blew up at me. He said it was *his* money. And he took the box."

Bullet tears streak her eyeliner. I give the Kleenex box a little shove in her direction.

"After that, I couldn't ask Jay for money. This is all I have to last 'til the end of the month." She opens a monogrammed leather wallet. One crinkled five-dollar bill. "I hate having to call my mother."

"You're married, it's your money too, sweetie." I give Carrie a Mama-bear hug.

"I shouldn't complain about his going out after work. He's a good provider. He needs to unwind. He's not one of those falling-down drunks. He's a good person." *Same things I always say about Diego.* Still on a first meeting I've learned to just listen. She dabs her eyes.

"So where does he go?"

"That club on San Pablo Avenue, I think," she says.

I know nothing about the Bay Area club scene. Diego doesn't troll for young women in clubs; he seems to find ample volunteers in his classrooms.

"I wonder if there's someone else involved?"

"Oh no, no, no. Jay's not seeing anyone." She surprised I suggested it.

"Barbara, with Jay, it's not another woman, or even drinking. It's ...."

"What, Carrie?"

"Please don't tell anyone."

"Of course."

"Gambling," she says in a whisper.

Carrie looks past me at the pool. The bottom is dark with rotted leaves from not being cleaned in months. So I'm not perfect. I tell her my story, going through the list of family I had to let go of: Miguel, my mother, Maya and her pregnancy, and now Diego. The more I confess my situations, the more relaxed she looks.

We agree to meet the same time next week, before Christmas. After Carrie leaves I'm surprised that two and a half hours sped by so quickly. My crumble-bumble-ending marriage was no elephant in the room; it stood there in full view not just for Carrie, but for me too. Carrie didn't judge me for it. One good thing about sponsoring; it allows me to act like a better person than I actually am. For a few hours anyway. And afterwards I feel lighter, like a basket of Christmas spirit has arrived on my doorstep.

· · ·

DAYS BEFORE CHRISTMAS, December temperatures turn cold again, plummeting below freezing, and I'm back in bed cuddling between Lola and Tigger for warmth under the comforter. I kind of miss the hot flashes and my lost menopausal fat, which provided me with an internal electric blanket during previous winters. Staying in bed puts me more behind schedule. The outdoor lights still haven't been hung under the eaves. I worry about what our neighbors, Bunny and Steve, are thinking. Their house sparkles with Christmas cheer and ours looks like we're in a blackout, expecting an air raid. It's an awful feeling knowing that you're the weak link in the neighborhood. Still, keeping tradition, I have to give the kids a big, candle-scented, tinsel-tossed, gift-wrapped Christmas. Maya, Deanna, and I hang bulbs and string tinsel on the damn tree Diego had set up, accompanied by a *Christmas with Conniff* album playing on Diego's damn turntable. I sing along for their sake. At least we have a large, gaudy, bulb-saturated, tree blinking in the living room.

I decide Lorraine is right. I shouldn't see Diego or even talk to him on the phone. Cut off all contact. Empty myself of stupid hope. Void him. Erase him. The kids can have Christmas with their dad on their own time, at his place. He's not setting one cheating big foot in my house. Hell with his coming over to water his lemon trees too. But how do I tell the kids their Dad's not coming over on Christmas?

I went through the motions: buying gifts for the grandkids, baking the crescent cookies, setting up our nativity crèche with Deanna. I unwrapped the plastic baby Jesus from the brittle yellow newspaper and pretended to be happy that Christ was born. I brought all this Christmas crap on myself. Long ago I had signed the mommy contract to "do Christmas" and my kids expected it. But that Christmas held no "Joy to the World." Still, Christmas *had* to unfold as scheduled. Our Christmas tradition meant attending Christmas Eve Mass, opening presents in the morning after nine (one at a time with photographs), and I'd serve a brunch with curried eggs, sausage, and croissants. This is what we've always done. I'll push through this, I thought.

That entire week, after having to face Diego with *his woman*, I failed to realize I was running on empty. I was whipping a dead, yet holiday-decorated, horse with bells on. Legally I was an adult, married, fifty-year-old woman, but emotionally I was an orphan.

Still I couldn't allow myself to let go. Not over Christmas. On Christmas Eve the facade finally caught up with me. I dropped the reins.

But then it was too late.

Before the six p.m. Christmas Eve mass, I knock on Maya's door carrying two more unwrapped presents for Deanna: a map of the world puzzle and a Tickle Me Elmo. I haven't told her yet that I changed plans. I'm dis-inviting her father for Christmas and I expect a fight.

Maya is a gift wrapper. I've heard in every family there's a "giving tree."

Maya is our giving tree. She not only wraps her own bounteous gifts, but when she found me paralyzed and teary yesterday holding a Candy Land Game and an unopened roll of Sponge Bob wrapping paper, she offered to wrap my few meager gifts as well.

When I enter her room the bed is no longer hidden under boxes and wrapping paper. All the brightly wrapped boxes are stacked in her closet hidden under towels. The bed is covered with folded sweaters, underwear, hair products, and her large wheelie suitcase.

I move a hair dryer and plop down on the edge of her unmade bed, my gifts beside me. It's too late to keep Maya from taking Deanna to Seattle tomorrow. No use arguing. She already bought the tickets. I'll get only half a Christmas day with Maya and Deanna. It feels like I'm being punished.

"We have to leave the house at one, Mom, so tell Dad to come by ten."

I haven't told Diego either that he can't come. "Promise you'll call me when you get there?" It's an inconvenience to have to drive them to the Oakland airport tomorrow on Christmas day, especially with Mimi and my brother from LA arriving tonight. I sigh signaling my disappointment.

"We need to go tomorrow, Mom. Jesse's surgery is scheduled for Tuesday."

"What surgery?"

Maya pulls out two pairs of jeans from under her bed. Then kicks a stray sock back under.

"The lump, Mom. Miguel's bite lump." She half-smiles when she says it.

"Oh. Jesse's famous lump."

Maya suppresses a laugh and adjusts her expression to reflect the seriousness of a medical procedure. She pulls back her dark locks and taps her forehead. "It's a big hard walnut, right here. It looks like he's got another eyeball popping out of his forehead. Really disgusting. Nicki hates it. She's paying for the surgery. Actually I think he likes it." She shakes a few dust balls off of her jeans, folds them, and places them in her already stuffed suitcase.

"He could cover it up with hair or wear a hat, but no, he has to make it look ten times worse by shaving his head."

I suspect he uses a nasty, cancerous-looking lump on his head as a good excuse to not look for a job. We've all heard about the lump from Maya. I've grown sort of a fond affection for Jesse's legendary lump—the battle scar that marks Miguel's victory and Jesse's retreat to Seattle two years ago. It's become part of our family history. Hearing news of the lump's demise feels a tad disappointing. "Could you take a before picture?" I ask.

"Shut up, Mom." She's stifling a smile.

"Maya, about tomorrow, I decided it would be better—"

"Mom, have you seen my blue ski jacket? I can't find it."

"Sweetheart, I decided that it's better if your Dad doesn't come over tomorrow."

"What?" She sets down a gallon-size freezer bag stuffed with perfumes and glares at me. "You can't tell dad he can't come for Christmas! This is his house too! Deanna wants him to come."

"Sorry, Maya. I have to take care of myself."

"That is *so* selfish. Look, Mom, if you don't want to take us to the airport tomorrow, Dad will drive me."

"No. I don't mind driving you. Really."

"I can't believe you're doing this. Ruining everyone's Christmas. Does Mimi know? She's driving twelve hours after work tonight just to be here. With us *and* Dad. You can't decide for the whole family."

I slip off Maya's bed. Does she really care or does she just want the check from her dad before she leaves? I place the Candy Land game, the puzzle, and Tickle Me Elmo in her closet, covering them with a fallen bathrobe.

"Thanks, Maya, for wrapping the presents for me." She doesn't answer.

"Wrap your own presents!"

I cower out the door feeling like Mama Grinch who just stole Christmas.

. . .

MAYA AND DEANNA LEAVE to visit friends after we attend the six p.m. Mass. I've put off phoning Diego to say he can't come over tomorrow until the girls are gone. Am I being too harsh? Before my brother Bob arrives at the airport I sew a sagging hem on the guest bedroom curtain and mull over the decision to uninvite Diego for Christmas. Erika calls saying she and Miguel are coming with Miguel's two kids from Utah. That means they'll expect to see Diego. The room is too dim to thread the needle and I remember an unused black gooseneck lamp on Diego's desk in the garage. Entering into his garage/gym space twists my gut, not because it's empty, just the opposite, it's still so full: his dresser, his desk, books in his bookcase, an impressive array of leather jackets still in his cedar closet, and his Don Quixote figurines from Cuba on the windowsill. I pick up the wood figure and in a sudden impulse smash it on the cement floor. Nothing breaks but an arm. With a shaking hand I pick up the one-armed Don Quixote and put him back on the sill. I'll glue it later. I unplug the lamp and walk from the garage through the kitchen. An eerie darkness descends on the empty house. Bob calls to say his eight p.m. plane has been delayed till midnight.

I turn on the Christmas tree lights and play "Oh Holy Night" on Diego's stereo system. But the night doesn't feel holy. It feels plagued and lonely. If I were superstitious I might even say haunted.

I place the lamp on the guest bedroom desk. I'll just borrow Diego's lamp for a few days. In the bulb's glare my hands deftly thread the needle, knot the end, and hem-stitch the yellow checked curtain with stitches one quarter-inch apart. But the square weight sewn into the hem corner tugs at the fabric like a nagging toddler, sliding the curtain off my lap.

I stop stitching. I can get through this. I slowly pull the thread through two more stitches. But my will drains. The coal-black night out the window waits in sickly silence. A downward spiraling force, not exactly panic or evil, tugs at me. My hand rises to my neck to protect it from invisible choking fingers. Stories of women alone in dark houses flood my imagination.

I must call Diego. To hear his voice. To tell me I'm okay. I dial the desk phone. He answers. I don't know why, but I hear myself asking him to come over. Just for a few minutes.

"No, Barbara, I can't come over," he says. "I'm going out."

I'm pacing. The curtain is crumbled on the floor.

"Please, Diego." I'm begging.

Silence.

"I, I, I really need to see you right now. Please, Diego. Just for a few minutes. I'm all alone and—"

"No Barbara, I can't. I'm go—I can't right now." His voice flat. Cold. The window's blackness seeps into the room, sucking my strength. I'm scared.

"Diego, please!"

"I have to go." He hangs up.

I sit down watching the endless black night through the naked window. What an idiot I am. A pathetic, stupid old woman. Someone no one will ever want. I gather the fallen fabric lying at my feet. My fingers search for the needle tucked through the hem. Its metal glints at me in the lamp light.

Then it jabs my finger. Once, twice, again. A red pinhole at the tip of my index finger balloons into a ruby droplet that rivers down my palm. Still I poke. Again and again. And again. Until emptied and disgusted with myself. *How sick you are. How immature.* I suck the blood off my finger and fish a tissue from the Kleenex box I had newly placed on the desk.

*You're mentally ill, like Mom says.*

The desk phone rings, startling me. It won't be him. I stuff the bloodied Kleenex into my sweater pocket and lift the receiver.

"Barbara, oh my God, I'm so glad you're home."

It's Carrie. She sounds blubbery.

"What's wrong?" My voice pretends that I'm not a self-mutilating thirteen-year-old cutter.

"Barbara, I have to whisper because my kids are in the living room."

I locate the needle by its curled thread tail, wipe the crimson tip, and pin it safely into the hem. I'm relieved not to be alone. I listen. Carrie's voice grounds me.

"It's Jay. He's at the police station."

"Jay's at the police station? A DUI?"

"No. Worse." What can be worse? Carrie is crying.

"What is it?" With the phone tucked under my chin, I shake the cotton curtain and fold it so it won't wrinkle.

"Barbara, Jay was picked up for prostitution."

"What? Jay is a prostitute?"

"No, he was seeing someone. Barb, you're the only person I can call."

"He's seeing a prostitute?" *Jay? Suit and tie, good-father-tyke-bike Jay?*

"The police stopped him going into some house, and they arrested him. I don't know what to believe." She sounds frantic. "He says he didn't do anything. And I have to go right now and pick him up at the station. Post bail, that's what he's telling me."

"Carrie, do you want to pick him up tonight?"

"I don't know what to do, Barbara. The kids expect him here tomorrow morning to open presents. I'm so confused. Damn him! Why does he do this to the kids on Christmas Eve?"

"Carrie, listen to me. Come over now."

"I can't believe this is happening! This isn't Jay." Carrie is sobbing. The ugly cry. The cry that makes me want to hold her.

"Carrie, this is not your fault."

I recognize denial. So much easier to see in someone else than yourself. I know how we defend them. We create a fantasy ideal husband and when they hurt us, we don't blame them. We blame ourselves and beat ourselves up over it. I have a bloody tissue in my pocket to prove it.

Carrie arrived in twelve minutes and we talked for two hours. She talked and I listened and hemstitched, giving me the faint closeness of my seamstress grandmother, who sat on the floor and talked to me with pins between her teeth while she hemmed my plaid skirts.

I said good-bye to a sad but stronger Carrie at the front door. She decided not to pick Jay up at the police station, not that night anyway. She never saw the bloody tissue in my pocket, nor did she understand the extent of my gratitude for her presence. I thought I could get through Christmas by myself. I planned to visit my sister Patsy in Wisconsin over New Years and I thought having an upcoming trip would pull me through. Not true. We don't all fall down on the same day, and on that day I buckled. I needed support.

I picked up Bob from the airport. My younger brother is six foot four, handsome, a computer genius, and he carries his own luggage. I finally got to bed around two a.m., too tired to wait up for Mimi to arrive, but she would be here by morning. And tomorrow Miguel and the kids were coming. I had a family again.

That Christmas Eve became an "Oh Holy Night" after all.


Christmas morning the vast terrain of gifts, including my own thanks to Maya's late-night wrapping, blanket the living room floor awaiting the late sleepers to rise. Deanna is up early under the tree making a pile of all the presents with her name. But even with all the kids here, I'm nervous about Diego coming. I backed down for the kids' sake. We're going with the original plan—Diego agreed to stop by the house in the morning for only an hour. Today he gets limited access to home and family. There's still some Mama Grinch left in me and I intend for him to spend the rest of Christmas Day as lonely as possible.

This original negotiated one-hour plan was Lorraine's idea. She had me create a cue that would signal to Diego his time to leave. I told him when I go into my bedroom and don't come out, that will be your cue to leave. He agreed. I didn't want any whispering or touching cues. At least I'm setting boundaries.

After driving all night from San Diego, Mimi is up, sitting in jammie bottoms on the couch with her sister. She's been away since graduating from high school and I can't believe how grown-up she looks. As a child she was pudgy, slow to mature, and fiercely independent. At five she decided she was a vegetarian and ate fruit off our backyard trees—an impish, tanned monk in a berry-stained T-shirt. But today she's Jennifer Aniston in cowboy pajama bottoms, a filled-out tank top, and new blonde streaks. Mimi and Maya are inseparable, talking boyfriends, birth control, and hair care products.

Out the kitchen window, my lookout, I see Erika coming down the drive carrying two shopping bags of gifts. She's followed by Miguel holding hands with little Michaela and Michael. It breaks open my heart with joy to have my brother, all my kids, and three grandkids for Christmas. I can do this.

"Hi, Miguel." I wrap my arms around my big handsome baby boy, perhaps holding on a tad longer than he likes. Diego shows up next, looking, well, just like Diego, a little sheepish. No mention of last night's phone call. I stand back as he hugs Miguel. "Hi, guy," he says, doing the patting thing. I notice both their eyes are watering. I'm guessing it's been months since they've seen each other too. Diego hands out checks to the kids and places a wrapped box of See's dark chocolates with nuts under the tree. We all gather 'round Miguel in the kitchen to admire the impressive three-inch scar on the top of his head. He lets me touch it. A thin knotted rope parting his thick, short, auburn hair. Invisible to all of us except my tall brother, because the top of Miguel's head reaches six feet.

"The doc pulled all the head skin upwards to close the hole," he says. "Remember those creases I used to have on my forehead? Gone. I got a free facelift." He says this with a wry, straight face. But we're all bursting with laughter. He flashes me his wide gap-toothed grin.

My son is back.

The gifts are open, carols play on Diego's stereo, and our oak living room floor is covered with wrapping paper and tissues, like a fall of large, crinkly, colored leaves. Diego and Miguel build a crackling fire and Bob turns the TV to *Yule Log* and Christmas carols. Deanna and her cousins play with Barbie, a Brat doll, and talking Elmo. Maya, Mimi, and Erika, all with long blonde-streaked hair, are huddled on the couch chatting.

After an hour of my smiling and picture-taking, Diego's presence in the living room is far too normal. My ache returns. I take my scheduled leave into my bedroom, sit on the end of the bed, and wait to hear the screen door close. And wait. And wait. No metal door slam comes. In fact no one even seems to notice I'm gone. Sitting alone in the bedroom feels like a punishment. I've given myself a timeout. Dumb cue, Barbara.

I walk into the living room and see Diego deep in conversation with Bob. Sigh.

"Uh, Diego." He turns his head. I surreptitiously point to my watch.

"Oh," he says abruptly, and stands up to take his leave.

Miguel quickly picks up on what's happening. "Hey, Dad doesn't have to leave so soon."

"Yes, he does." Of course Maya and Mimi have to weigh in on Diego's side. Everyone is begging him to stay. Great, now I'm the bad guy. But the firm, mock half-smile on my face stands its ground. I will not cry.

Diego doesn't argue. He hugs everyone goodbye. I back into the kitchen. I don't want a hug; I can't handle the patting thing. When the screen door does its little clang, I'm grateful.

I reach for my good friend—my cast iron fry pan—then I melt the butter, add the chopped onion and ginger, turmeric and cumin and one-half serrano chile. I'm frying sausages, warming the croissants, and stirring the curried scrambled eggs when Maya walks in. She holds out the box of chocolates.

"Aren't you going to unwrap it, Mom?"

"Honey, I can't." I stir in the beaten eggs slowly with a wooden spoon. "You open it; it's for everyone."

"Read the label, Mom. It's dark chocolate with nuts. You're the only one who likes dark chocolate. Dad bought this for you." My eyes are on the curried scrambled eggs, careful not to let them cook too fast and become lumpy instead of creamy. Opening that red gift-wrapped box of chocolate-covered pecans and walnuts—my favorites—would hurt. The naked, raw kind of hurt that squeezes up from your heart and into your tear ducts. Not today. Not on Christmas.

It's not only loaded with calories, it's loaded with a hope I can't afford to indulge in. Dark chocolate-covered hope. He always bought me See's candy on Valentine's and Mother's Day. Mays stands there waiting, holding out the box to me.

I take it. "Thank you, Maya." She smiles, hesitates, then joins the chatter in the next room. I stash the box high in the cupboard above the good china so I don't have to look at it. When Maya isn't around, I'll throw the whole friggin' box in the trash. In fifteen quick minutes the croissants are golden in the oven, the sausages browned and juicy in the frying pan, the curried eggs are smooth and fragrant with spice and ginger, accented with green cilantro. The fresh-squeezed OJ and Fatapple's olallieberry jam are on the table awaiting the guests.

Our Flores Christmas day, though dark and bittersweet, still had its good points. For a while we were a family again. I watched my three grandchildren play together. Maya, Mimi, and Erika were inseparable like triplets, and the very best part, I got to kiss my son's healed scar. He and Erika gave me a special gift too—a high gloss, over-color-saturated plaque of the Virgin de Guadalupe. I was so moved. One can never have too many Guadalupes.

And those dark chocolate-covered nuts? Over the next week I ate the whole box.

PART II

# CHAPTER TEN
## NORTHWOOD'S NEW YEAR

When I arrive in Northern Wisconsin, it's encased in ice. The two-hour ride from the Central Wisconsin airport takes my sister Patsy twice as long—four hours—because of the ice storm. She pulls her new blue minivan into her garage. Tree branches spread overhead like sculptures of blown glass and fences of dense pine trees shield us from neighbors. Patsy's lakefront home looks like a Christmas card.

"Barbara, I'll park your suitcase in the boot room." She tugs my heavy suitcase up the two stairs in her garage. I tell her that I'll be in in a minute. There's always a boot room in Wisconsin between the back door and the kitchen—a purgatory for dripping boots and soggy woolen mittens that smell like dog. It's been over two decades since I visited Wisconsin in the winter. The last time was when we baptized Mimi at St. Anne's, Grandma Buehler's church—my godmother's church.

I thought I was escaping to Patsy's home in the Northwoods to forget, but what my soul really needed was to remember. There was a time over a half century ago, before a steady stream of boyfriends, before depression diagnoses, when once I was a contented little kid who popped out of bed on a winter day eager to play in the snow. Now I ache to remember what that felt like. Patsy, my little sister following me on her two-wheeler, crossing the river, cracking ice, getting soakers. When school was out, we had long summer days with no homework, no lessons, only a bike ride to Maude Shunk Library or the high school swimming pool if we felt like it. Mom would set bologna sandwiches and Kool-Aid out on the picnic table for lunch, so she had the afternoon to nap undisturbed until six when she called us in for supper. Free as roaming cattle we explored Menomonee River, the water falls, construction sites, cornfields and the woods vast enough to get lost in. It all belonged to us.

At night when I felt scared like after a scary movie like *The Tingler*, I'd listen for Patsy's breath softly exhaling in the twin bed beside me. This was before fifteen, before boyfriends, before husbands, when having a sister was enough. My pictures of that childhood in Menomonee Falls were easy to access, but in Wisconsin that December, I couldn't find the matching feelings. I was numb, the joy and freedom of our green-grass Wisconsin backyard lost to me. Buried under layers of years and ice.

I stand alone in Patsy's driveway. This is real winter. An honest, simple, cheek-reddening cold. The kind I grew up with. My breath greets the air in small white clouds. I scoop up a glove of crunchy white crystals just to smell its snowness. My front teeth ache in the icy air in a good Wisconsin way. Clean. Jolting. Listerine air.

"Heal me," I ask.

Patsy and I don't look like sisters. We're two years apart but she's fair with blue eyes and dark brunette curls like Mom. I have straight dark-blonde hair, hazel eyes, and darker olive skin like Dad. But we are exactly the same height, five foot eight and three-quarters; or we *were* until Patsy's recent hip surgery, which made her three-eighths of an inch shorter, but only on her right side. Patsy is called the easy-going one, which makes me the not-so-easy-going one. She's a dentist, like Dad, and a Packer fan like everyone in our family except for me, and she doesn't take antidepressants. My favorite photo shows her wearing a Packers ski jacket and a Cheesehead hat. Patsy shared her first dental office with her first husband Greg until he left with Cindy, the assistant. But now they are all buddies and Patsy, Cindy, and Greg all sit together and cheer my nephew at his basketball games. Patsy and Cindy are even in the same trio singing group. I can't even imagine it. She dumped husband number three, Gerard, whom I call the highbrow Jewish art collector of the Northwoods, she sent her kids away to college, and ever since she's been paddling swimmingly in her lakeside empty nest.

For dinner that first night I prepare venison chili. Patsy's van hit the deer last October and the deer ended up in her freezer. "No sense wasting the meat," she says. I cube and brown it like a chuck roast, add charred, oven-roasted peppers, and simmer the pot for three hours until the meat is dark, rich, and falling off the deer bone.

"Bambi stew," Patsy calls it. Oddly, I find her joke hilarious—and the chili is so delicious, I forget that it's road kill.

"We'll have fun at the casino on New Year's," she says. The Chippewa reservation is a half hour away and I'm really not in a party mood. "Won't the roads be iced?"

"They've salted the roads by now."

"Well, we have three days to decide."

After dinner, Patsy pecks on her computer. I sprawl out on her plaid couch, well fed, relaxed, and wrapped in an afghan that Mom knitted during one of her good spells. Patsy's living room feels familiar: a matchy-matchy palette of burgundy, blue-gray, and custard walls accented with a church portrait of Mom and Dad, a framed tomato poster I designed for chef Alice Waters, and a mounted deer head shot by Uncle Harold. I click the remote and every channel is showing coverage of the 2004 tsunami. Patsy's wide screen of CNN replays a monster wave engulfing a hotel over and over again. I stare, numb, under my mother's knit afghan. The shot zooms in on churning black water roiling with wood beams, palm fronds, chairs, and dark blurry arms caught in a blender. Nothing to grasp, nothing to hold on to. No *terra firma*, solid ground.

I stare mesmerized, finding it surreal, yet perversely calming.

While I read the *The Lakeland Times* weekly, with ads for bear bait, my sister is on her computer. She calls me to her desk to check out eHarmony. A page pops up with rows of male head shots like in a high school yearbook, only older.

"The guys with baseball caps are bald," she says. "Hey, check out this guy. Nice smile. Good teeth."

I pull up a chair and peer at this clean-shaven, grinning fiftyish man in a dark suit and tie.

"Fifty-two, divorced, doesn't want children, a doctor from Minneapolis," she reads.

"Patsy, isn't five hours too far to drive for a date?"

"I expanded my radius," she says keeping her eyes on the screen.

The faces she brings up look too polished, too barbered, too Sharper Image, and too white—like rows of stiff, eraser-head pencils.

"Look at this guy. Wants to meet a woman from thirty to fifty-five."

"I bet he really wants the thirty-year-old." I say with a bitter twang.

Patsy sighs. "Barbara, not all men are like that."

I don't get it. How can Diego at sixty-four be attracted to some thirty-year-old as young as his first daughter? What do they talk about? She doesn't remember Bob Dylan, or Janis, or Carlos Castañeda, or Vietnam. Does she remember when Dow chemical meant napalm, not their new advertising slogan, "The Human Element"? What is it? Smooth, firm flesh? No neck or underarm waddle? No cellulite? Or her big brown goo-goo eyes that slobber all over her brilliant Econ professor? Or is it the erections that come easily with someone who's not the same ol' tired wife? Dammit, Diego, that's so cliché, so high school. So perverted, so ick.

"Barb, you're not the only woman to be dumped for a younger woman, ya know. You don't have to dwell on him. What you think about is a choice. Think positive."

"I can't help it."

I hate her new age sermons that sound outdated by West Coast standards. She reminds me of Joanna, who prescribed me a bedtime gratitude list from A to Z. I try but it's hard to get past "A is for Asshole."

"You know you can control your thoughts," Patsy says. Now she's giving me Eckhart Tolle bullshit.

"Stop telling me that!" I snap. "Don't you think I've been *trying* not to think about him for the last six months? That Tolle, Wayne Dwyer, Deepak Chopra bull doesn't work. I tried it. I'm sick of that 'control your mind' crap!"

Patsy stares at me, hurt. We never yell at each. Ever.

I don't really mean it—well, not about Deepak. But I feel too raw, too confused, and too angry to put on some fake positive mask. And I have tried to control my thoughts. Last summer for three whole days every time Diego came into my head, I mind-blocked him with the Serenity Prayer.

*God, grant me the serenity to accept the things I cannot change ...*

It took too much effort to catch myself every minute and it gave me a headache, but it did work. During waking hours, that is. At night dreams of Diego came back. He's sleeping beside me. His arm around me. My head on his chest where my fingers brush those few gray hairs above his abs. The warmth of him bathes me. I'm safe now.

Then I wake up.

The right side of the bed empty. Cold. And I have to relive the crucifying abandonment all over again. So I gave up on thought control, the Serenity Prayer, and the Catholic Church. I've lost more than a husband—I've lost my entire belief system. Like those tsunami floaters, I've lost my *terra firma*.

· · ·

MAYA AND DEANNA ARE cheerful on the phone. Deanna tells me about every gift that awaited her under her grandparents' tree. I feign, "Oh wow," hoping it's not another stuffed animal to join the overcrowded zoo on her top bunk, or another Lite Brite set that ended up spilled in her closet like a million glass beads. I still find them stuck in the soles of my bare feet.

Maya says she's decided to stay a few days longer with Jesse in Washington. I object because school starts on Monday; Deanna shouldn't be missing third grade. Especially fractions. How important is it? Joanna would ask. Very important.

. . .

I CAN'T SLEEP. JOANNA advised me to write gratitude lists. In Patsy's upstairs bedroom, I sit up in bed and dutifully write "Gratitude List No. 168" in a notebook. Between my sister and Joanna I feel like squashy meat sandwiched in new age hell. A hell, I imagine, where ungrateful sinners chained to a school desk have to write gratitude lists into eternity. FYI: Squashy meat was our childhood name for liverwurst.

Didn't I do enough gratitude lists? Before Diego left I subscribed to the covenant of gratitude. I practiced the doctrine and preached it to my kids and sponsees. I was grateful for a teenage pregnancy that turned into a blessing. Grateful that my bipolar, addicted son found a good woman who loves and adores him. Last Thanksgiving I professed to friends my gratitude for having a good-looking husband over sixty who recently installed a new tile roof over our heads with a fifty-year guarantee. I don't deserve to be dumped. God owes me, damn it. I quit my friggin' job as an art director to do volunteer work with Central American refugees—for five years! Diego was proud of me then— proud to call me his wife, and he never objected when I took in a homeless Margarita or a husband-abused Lydia to live with us. And every day that I picked up recently arrived immigrants at the BART station, I risked arrest for transporting illegals. So God, since I committed hundreds of felonies for you and your people, couldn't you at least cut me a little slack? And I know those that I helped, helped me too. Big time. And I have gratitude, goddammit, tons of it. What good did it do me? How could a man leave a wife with this much gratitude?

This isn't supposed to happen. After you stop trying to fix your kids and you stop trying to change your husband into a TV dad, and you work the steps and truly feel grateful for your whole family, warts, felonies and all, then it should be all downhill after that, right? I was a twelve step poster child for gratitude, so how could my whole friggin' life explode in my face? This doesn't happen on Oprah.

And now I'm supposed to write one more friggin' gratitude list. No way. Gratitude bit me in the butt. Gratitude betrayed me. I look at my heading: Gratitude List No. 168. But all I can think about is the crappy shit I'm not particularly grateful for. Little annoying stuff, like gnats. Just for spite I write:

ANTI-GRATITUDE LIST NO. 1.

#1. Prime-time commercials about erections lasting more than four hours.

#2. Conversations with people who use the word "paradigm."

#3. Married men who don't wear wedding rings.

#4. Coed bathrooms with urinals.

#5. Any man who says, "Guns don't kill people, people do."

#6. Wrinkle creams that cost eighty dollars.

#7. Face lifts that make women my age look like extra-terrestrials.

#8. Men over six foot five who spread their legs into my plane seat.

#9. Any Latina who calls me "la gringa."

#10. The kids' friends who refer to me as "dude."

#11. Men who don't believe in global warming. Strike that. Anyone who doesn't believe in global warming.

#12. Newspaper columnists who write four consecutive columns about their cat.

#13. Women who wear jewelry that requires batteries.

#14. Road-hogging bicyclists who flaunt their ball-revealing Spandex shorts.

#15. Anyone who talks to me for over four minutes about wheatgrass.

As I continued to write that night, I thought that no one, especially Joanna, needed to know how pissed off I was at gratitude. It felt sacrilegious. If I ever read an anti-gratitude list at a meeting I imagine Doris dropping over in horror. Yet once my pen got started on anti-gratitude, it was on a roll, spitting out spite like Joan Rivers. Soon I fell asleep.

I highly recommend it.

. . .

IT'S DECEMBER THIRTY-FIRST. We're standing side by side in front of Patsy's bathroom mirror putting on makeup together like we did as teenagers. Patsy wears a navy crew-neck shift with a matching sweater, an outfit I might wear to church. I'm in strapless tea length chiffon.

"Barbara, you've lost weight. A lot of weight."

"I know. I cried it off in buckets." We're always jockeying to be the thinnest. Until recently, she was winning. That new person in the mirror, missing her jowls and neck flab, isn't the me I'm familiar with. But I like the way my beaded spaghetti straps crisscross over my back, showing off bare shoulders and a waning tan. What I love most about my new dress isn't the flattering bias-cut drape or the beadwork, it's the small white tag inside that reads, "size eight." When you've worn a twelve or fourteen your whole life, a tiny size-eight tag becomes a trophy.

Snowflakes drift outside Patsy's bedroom window in no hurry to reach her deck. Her white-blanketed lawn, the glazed pines, and the frozen mirror-like lake beyond look like the holiday cards I bought but never sent. Patsy's rosy face, framed in graying brown curls, glows in the bathroom's natural light. Mine, however, appears dull and grim by comparison. It's the lighting, I tell myself. As a photo art director, working with fashion photographers, we'd use metallic umbrellas, or makeshift cardboard covered in tinfoil, to reflect light onto a model's face. To soften focus we'd smear Vaseline on the lens, or use a dab of spit.

One winter Dad built an igloo for us out of a snowdrift on the front lawn. Patsy was about six that winter, a head shorter than I, and the igloo became our private sister playhouse, a child-sized house of snow. Patsy's little girl cheeks glowed pink in the soft snow-filtered light, and her brown curls, glazed in ice, bounced when she giggled. Patsy always giggled. The memory strikes me now as clear as glass. She stood bundled in her snowsuit and her cherubic face glowed like an angel in a dome of pure, reflected light. To an eight-year-old, it felt like heaven.

Her same face in the mirror, only aged with lines and lengthened features, brings up a fuzzy *déjà vu*. As if that lost igloo memory had been had been there all along buried in the snowdrifts of my mind, just waiting for a thaw. I long to glow like that too.

Patsy's phone rings just as we're about to leave for the party, and my heart leaps. Diego said he'd call. Of course he'll call. It's New Year's Eve. I decided my month of not talking to Diego, which I promised Lorraine, would start on New Year's. Tomorrow,

"It's him," Patsy says clamping her palm over her kitchen cordless. "Want me to say you're not here?"

"No. I'll take it." I need to hear him say, "Happy New Year." I deserve that. The phone cradles against my perfumed ear. "Happy New Year," I say, feigning a casual friendship. I go into the boot room to talk.

"Hi Barbara, I said I would call you, and I did." His familiar voice is tinged with duty and a sharp enunciation that I'd never noticed before. Still, I hang on his words and thank him again for the Christmas tree, the money he left the kids, and the box of See's chocolates. The charade continues until he mentions "settling things."

"Settling things? You mean you want to end it?"

"Well, Barbara, you are legally entitled to forty percent of my retirement and half the tax shelters; that's something, but we don't want to get lawyers involved. That's not necessary. "You're a strong woman, independent ...."

I can't speak. My head somersaults into outer space. Of course he wants to settle things, what did I expect? Crying feels so redundant, so useless, and so unavoidable. I leave the boot room feeling, well, booted.

"What did he want?" Patsy asks, barely hiding her annoyance.

"A divorce."

Now I have to redo my eyeliner.

. . .

MY HIGH-HEELED BLACK leather boots, perfect for a damp San Francisco winter, slip and side on the ice-coated parking lot of the Lake of the Torches casino.

"Careful, Barbara, it's a skating rink out here," Patsy warns. My sensible sister wears clear plastic galoshes over her pumps. My high heels slip on every third step, and my loose left shoe (my left foot is two sizes smaller than my right) makes balance even worse. I manage to stay upright with an arm firmly attached to Patsy.

The casino on the Chippewa reservation holds the biggest New Year's Eve party in Northern Wisconsin. I'm determined to have a good time without thinking about Diego wanting a divorce, or Maya being attacked by Jesse in Washington. Inside the glitzy entryway, a hand-drawn "party" sign leads us into a cavernous hall as dark as a movie theater. When my eyes adjust, large round crowded tables appear in front of dark dancing silhouettes. Songs from the sixties blast from a three-man band on a makeshift wooden stage. I don't drink, but I can get high singing along to the schmaltzy oldies. A club in northern Wisconsin is very different, and very gringo white, compared to the Latin clubs Diego and I loved to dance at in San Francisco's Mission district.

"I see my friends." Patsy points to a table up front with three men and a woman. The hall smells of beer and vibrates with guitar and Wisconsin accents. I'm surprised they're mostly dressed in jeans, T-shirts and plaid jackets—lots of green and gold—Packers' fans. A necktie is nowhere in sight. In strapless chiffon, I'm way overdressed.

"No one cares what you wear in the casino." Patsy reads my mind. "People don't dress here." *Obviously.* Her navy shift and matching sweater is simple and high-necked, but that's who my sister is. Simple and high-necked. By comparison, my beaded skinny straps and floaty summer-peach chiffon look gaudy, out of season, and, well, slutty. My bare shoulders would have been *de rigueur* on a New Year's Eve in San Francisco, but in the Torch Casino, I feel like I've walked in wearing a wedding dress with no groom. I drape my wool coat over my bare shoulders like a cape.

Patsy introduces her friends Bob and Herb who both sport graying mustaches and plaid flannel shirts. "Hey, we got live music!" Herb's uneven teeth flash under his beer-foamed mustache. The three-man band is not the big-band Cuban orchestras I'm used to. But at least they're not wearing lederhosen and playing accordions.

Herb leans in so close I can smell his Schlitz breath.

"So-oo, ya want a be-eer, aye?" Herb speaks in the local nasal dialect that stretches one-syllable words into two.

"Just a soda water with lime, please. I don't drink." Patsy whispers that they say "aye" (rhymes with hay) because they're U-pers—from nearby Upper Peninsula Michigan bordering Canada.

"Barbara's not really an alcoholic," Patsy adds. "She gave it up for her kids." For the last fifteen years my sister won't give me the credit of being a real alcoholic. It's mildly annoying. Patsy asks Herb to bring her a red wine.

"Sa-ay, Bar-rrb, you like the tables?" Herb points to the two double doors.

"No, I don't gamble." Watching the lake freeze would be more fun. Herb is harmless, uncomplicated, and familiar, like most white Wisconsin men. But he's also large, beer-bellied, and looks like he shoots deer. When Herb returns with drinks, he makes small talk about his booming septic tank business and the Chippewa Indians who shot more than their quota of ducks. Ho-hum. I nod, twisting the wedding ring that I had moved to my right hand. I can't recall ever spending a New Year's Eve without a man before. The wall clock, between the antlers of a large moose head, moves its hands slowly toward ten, then eleven. More and more beer bottles gather like an assembling militia on the round white tablecloth. I can't help thinking about Diego's call. I need to dance, to move to a rock 'n roll beat pounding in my brain, because I can't get smashed like a normal woman who's shot out of the saddle.

Patsy chats up the other woman at the end of the table, a local I guess based on her short brown hair and polyester blue dress with a lace collar, like one my Grandma Buehler would wear. I consider asking her if it's vintage, but I think I'd better not. The chair next to her is unoccupied except for a plaid sports coat. The only other member of our table is a younger man with his back to me, watching the band.

Patsy, the U-per twins, and the blue lace lady are deep into planning a Super Bowl party. *Thank God I don't live here.*

"Wanna dance?" I shout to Patsy.

She doesn't hear me. The lone young man turns around. He pushes his glasses up his straight aquiline nose, and a shock of straight black hair falls loose on his forehead like this Clark Kent. He smiles at me. Or I think he does; he could be cleaning his teeth with his upper lip—I have fuzzy vision without my glasses. I half-smile back.

"Dance?" I ask. "Twist and Shout" is playing. He grins at me and nods. Before realizing what I just did, I'm following this tall young man to the dance floor. The banter between Patsy and the blue lace lady stops. I know we're being watched. He's taller than I, over six feet. Nice. We move with simple side-to-side steps, one-two, one-two, throw in a few twists, and I allow my bare shoulders to match his beat. We stand far enough apart on the Casino dance floor for a moose to pass between us. My body feels good in sync with a man again, even though we're dancing with all the grace of two refrigerators.

"I'm Eric," he calls out over the pounding music.

"Barbara," I shout back. I glance briefly up into green eyes. Dancing with a light-eyed stranger feels odd, even exotic. Direct eye contact is too scary, and the band, doing a Led Zeppelin imitation, is too loud for conversation. When our eyes meet, we exchange tentative smiles. I relax enough to add in salsa hips—a move not native to Wisconsinites. The music ends and I expect we'll walk back to our table. Why would he want to keep dancing with an older woman? I'll graciously give him an out. But Eric remains on the floor. He tells me he works for Krausman's, as if I should know the place. Probably a local cheese maker, or a bratwurst factory. Before I know it, we're dancing again. At the table, Patsy is laughing with the mustached U-per twins. Now the only one watching us is the blue lace lady. During the next break Eric confides that he's getting over a breakup.

"So how long were you and your girlfriend together?"

"Two years." His face drops as if this was the first and only love of his life. Maybe it was. We start dancing again, standing close now to talk.

"I know. I'm going through a breakup myself." I shout loud enough that the couple beside us turn to look.

"How long for you, Bar-rb?"

How do I say thirty-one years to Eric? What if he hasn't even lived that long? I don't want to embarrass him, or worse, sound really old.

"It was a very long time," I shout back, cupping my hand to my mouth. I'm feeling a bit winded, and ready to sit and offer a bare shoulder for Eric to cry on. But the next number is "Hold Me, Thrill Me, Kiss me," a slow dance.

"C'mon." Eric smiles and opens his arms for me to move into them. I've never been a slow-dance person since my little left foot in a shoe stuffed with Kleenex gives me balance problems. I worry about losing a shoe that could be kicked around the polished casino floor like a hockey puck.

What the hell? This is no different than dancing with my son. I place my right hand in his and my left on his back. His flesh is warm and firm beneath a soft cotton shirt; his hand firmly guides my bare back. I melt into his move and we glide across the floor. The rough stubble of Eric's beard brushes my cheek and a whiff of his scent makes my knees go limp—Aramis, familiar and mature, old-school. Faster and faster we turn, centrifugal force presses my breasts up against his chest. I'm feeling light. In his arms, I'm flying. I breathe this man into me, taking him into me. Oh my God, this is no mother/son dance. This is ... something else.

"You're a good dancer," he whispers in my ear.

I smile, feeling sexy, slightly drunk, and suddenly very single in the dim light of the dance floor. Another slow dance. I close my eyes and surrender. An ecstatic shiver pulses through me. Maybe we'll meet tomorrow for coffee or a hot chocolate—a Wisconsin thing. Just to talk.

"You play sports?" I ask.

"Just track in high school."

"Did you go to college here?"

"Two years at Stout, a few years ago," he grins pulling me in closer. My head rests gently on Eric's shoulder, like it belongs there. But two years at Stout, only a few years ago? That doesn't make sense; he looks in his thirties.

"Eric, if you don't mind me asking, how old are you?"

"Twenty-two." He keeps dancing.

*Holy moly!* Twenty-two? My son is twenty-eight.

"I like older women," Eric brushes his curl back. "Now it's your turn, you tell me?" he whispers. *Holy shit.*

"Tell you what?" I know what's coming.

"How old are you, Barbara?"

"Uh, guess."

Eric looks into my face with wide innocent eyes. "Uh, thirty-five."

"You're kidding!" I stop dancing and burst out laughing. "You're joking."

"No."

"Thirty-five, really?" This is hysterical, but Eric doesn't think it's funny. "It's not you, Eric." I chuckle. "I'm fifty-six."

Abruptly Eric stops swaying dead in his dancing tracks. Stone silence. Eric stares dumbstruck, like a deer caught in Patsy's headlights.

Instantly I'm a Cinderella in a peach chiffon dress who's suddenly a rotting pumpkin. And it isn't even midnight. I want to say, it's all right; we just had fun. I take it back. "I'm sorry, Eric."

"You're older than my mother," he says with a frozen face. I'm a serpent-headed Medusa who changes young men into stone. He mumbles something about having to find his father for Texas Hold 'Em and walks off the floor, stopping at our table to speak briefly with the woman in the blue dress. He kisses her on the cheek and leaves. *Jesus, that's his mother?* She's been watching us the whole time. The tall lanky silhouette of a boy lumbers toward the bells and bright lights beyond the double doors. *What was I thinking?*

I plop down at the table, ignoring the glare of the blue lace lady. Patsy walks back from the dance floor with Bob. "Looks like you were having fun," she teases, then they head toward the bar. I feel stupid and ashamed. Eric isn't coming back. I'm too old to even be a friend. No consoling hugs, no coffee, no hot chocolate. Now the lady across the table hates me. Suddenly I'm a cougar who stuck my nail-polished talons into her boy. Was it obvious to her that I found myself attracted to a much younger man? I wanted to erase that illicit feeling. But I couldn't deny the arousal, to myself anyway. Is this what Diego feels with LaShondra?

Head down, I pat my sweaty neck and face with a soggy napkin that sponges off the last of my concealer. When I look up, the woman in the blue lace turns away from me. We're not so different, I think. I too know what it's like to sit alone on New Year's Eve.

"Ya know, you have a very fine son there," I say to the blue lace woman facing the gambling room doors. "You should be proud of your son. He obviously cares about his mother."

"Thank you," she says and offers a weak smile. I hope she thinks I'm human.

Herb suddenly appears and places a glass of iced soda water in front of me. "Thought you could use this, aye."

"Yah, you betcha, aye," I'm grateful he can't tell I'm mimicking. And the cold sparkling soda revives me from the inside, like watering wilted lettuce.

Patsy and Bob rush to join us for the countdown. "Ten, nine, eight, seven, six ..." Our voices join the booming chant echoing in the cavernous room. A tall, balding middle-aged version of Eric scuttles to the chair draped with a plaid sports jacket. He reaches for the hand of the blue lace lady. I'm happy she's not alone.

Patsy grabs my hand and we twirl in a downpour of multi-colored balloons. I notice Patsy's sleeveless sheath. Without the matchy-matchy sweater she looks stylish, shapely, even elegant. Not so backwoods after all. Eric doesn't return to the dance hall, but Patsy and I chatter and giggle about him during the car ride home.

"Barb, so what? He obviously was attracted to you."

"Maybe he needs a new optical prescription."

She laughs.

"C'mon. Thirty-five?" This embarrassing moment with a twenty-two-year-old kid begins to sound like a gag on *The Golden Girls*. Patsy and I can't stop joking about it.

Going to bed that night in Patsy's Northwood's home encased in ice, the chuckling in my head slips into a dream. We're in our boots and snowsuits lying side-by-side on a blanket of snow gazing into a bowl of skim milk sky. Our arms and legs wave furiously in the powder. Then, holding hands, we, oh so carefully, help each other release from our molds. Standing side by side in padded snowsuits, we admire what we made.

Twin angels in the snow.

# CHAPTER ELEVEN
## SINGLE LIFE

It's February. California's wettest winter on record since some date back in the Ice Age. I set my produce bags on the table and add Diego's mail to his paper mailbag. Why after living in his apartment for eight months is he still getting his mail here? One of the envelopes in his mail is from the college where he teaches. I shove it into the full bag on the greenhouse window. I used to call him when an envelope looked important but now I don't bother.

Still that grocery bag full of his mail makes me wonder if he still wants to come home. I've talked to him only twice in the last six weeks. I'm doing good in my goal to go a whole month. Last week we did talk about the high January PG&E bill but Lorraine said brief conversations over the house and kids don't count.

Then I fudged over the line when I asked him for the truth. When did it start? He said last year in February. That jives with a year ago when he stopped wanting sex. Diego's refractory period went from thirty minutes to thirty days. But Diego's timing doesn't fit with Maya overhearing him on the phone two years ago.

"You shouldn't ask questions," he said. "It's my private life."

But Dr. Phil says you need full disclosure to heal.

"Your *friend* knows who I am," I said. "So I want to know the same about her."

"Barbara, I don't want you making trouble for her at her work."

I don't know why I asked. It makes me feel like a nut cracked open, with all its flesh and inner crevices exposed. Mimi said I should have made him take a lie detector test when he was still home, but it's too late for that. However, I did learn something from that phone conversation. He said she works as a midwife. That's problematic for me because I never met a midwife that I didn't like.

· · ·

MAYA AND DEANNA ARE in the kitchen eating Eggo waffles at four in the afternoon. Leona, our mountain lion puppet, is lying on the kitchen table too close to the syrup bottle. I check Leona's fur for sticky spots.

A tug at my sweater sleeve. "Gramma, I want my Daddy to stay here with us."

"Maya?"

"We won't fight, I promise," Maya says with a pleading look. "Jesse's driving to the Bay Area next week and I told him he could stay here."

"What? No way, Maya." *Abso-friggin-lutely no way!*

"Please, please, please, best Gramma in the world." Deanna jumps up and down, taking my sweater sleeve along with her.

Jesse coming here? Nose-breaking Jesse? Not in my house.

"Mom, Chuck and Nicki won't allow me to stay there any more."

"Oh, now I get it, now because Chuck had to call the police over Christmas and you're banned from visiting, now you want your violent, abusive boyfriend to stay in *my* house." I could call him worse, but Deanna is right here. "Was his coming your idea? You're paying his gas money, right?"

She doesn't answer. I ask Deanna to go watch cartoons and slide the kitchen door closed behind her.

"Legally, Jesse does have joint custody. Mom, would you rather I send Deanna to Washington alone?" The thought sends quivers down my spine.

"He's getting therapy, Mom. You have to give him a chance."

"I don't think a guy who broke your nose deserves another chance!" Forgiveness is not my long suit.

"Please please, please please, please, please, please, please!" Deanna calls from behind the living room door.

"Stop it, Deanna," I snap. Eight-year-olds can be very annoying. "Your daddy has his own money and he can visit you, but he's a big man and he can stay with one of his friends or at a motel."

"Mom, he doesn't have friends here anymore. They're like all in jail or rehab."

"He's not staying here, Maya."

"Please, please, best Gramma in the world." Now Leona's puppet face peeks through the door. "Leona wants daddy to stay here too, right, Leona?" Leona, on Deanna's hand, nods her furry mountain lion head. I'm outnumbered but I stand my ground. Jesse is definitely not staying here. You don't invite the person who threatened to kill us into the house. That's against program principles.

·   ·   ·

AFTER RECORD-BREAKING RAIN comes record-breaking February cold. The front page of the *San Francisco Chronicle* shows snow in Berkeley. Coldest temperatures in thirty years. Both Mt. Tam (Tamalpias) and Mt. Diablo are peaked in white. Diego's going to complain about the PG&E bill.

"Barbara, I can't afford two houses," he says.

"Well, you're the one who moved out," I remind him.

After I told Diego I called a lawyer, he hasn't brought up divorce. His idea is to "settle things" without lawyers. My idea is to stay separated and let's see where the cards land. I'm careful how I use our joint checkbook but Diego's nagging about not being able to afford the house scares me. He destroyed the family and now he wants to take away our home too?

I love my home. My happiest times are cooking on my new gas range, backyard barbecue parties, and playing "baby" with Deanna in the pool. I pretend to be Deanna's baby who she carries around. The baby always drowns. It's more fun than it sounds.

To fight the cold and the threatening February high gas bills, I join a gym. There I girdle my flab into sports bras and leggings (with panty lines), take yoga classes, pump the bike, and measure my body fat index. Darn, I'm three percentage points higher than Diego's 19%.

The best part of my gym days is the steam room. I slump, in a good way, on a clean white towel in a steamy pine-scented cloud. In the wet heat I sweat. And sweat. Drops on my forehead turn into trickles that flow into a steady stream. A river of sweat pours out of my aching flesh onto the blond wooden planks. Like being able to cry out of every open pore. After twelve minutes of allowing muscles to melt, I relax into a fifty-seven-year-old wet noodle. In my steam room sanctuary, the dark tangled root mass of my mind melts and lightens. I'm drained. Clean. Refreshed. Content.

I decide I can be happy without Diego.

. . .

LAST FAMILY DAY AT THE gym Deanna and I had so much fun playing crazy-moon-shot racquetball that I forgot we're a broken family. On the ride home Deanna begged me to let her Daddy stay with us again. Something changed.

I don't know if it was the soothing hot tub or an unexpected discovery I made on laundry day. A puzzle piece from our United States puzzle had been missing for months. Drove me crazy having one state piece missing out of fifty and I searched all over the house. This week I was checking clothing pockets prior to washing when I found something hard and flat in Deanna's jacket. There it was. Washingston State, where her Daddy lives. A small wood puzzle square that would fit in the palm of her hand. The only part of him she could hang onto.

The day we arrived home from the gym her begging continued. "Please Gramma, best Gramma in the world ...." I softened and caved like butter. I couldn't say no. Thrilled, she monkey-wrapped around me so tight, that I wasn't sure where I ended and Deanna began.

. . .

JESSE ARRIVES. A SKINNY gangly boy, taller than Miguel, with a long face. Deanna says he looks like SpongeBob's friend Squidward. No tattoos, but there's a small line scar above his right eyebrow. Since my bedroom is past the kitchen/laundry/garage door side of the house and the other three bedrooms are past the living room down the hall, I rarely see Jesse. I hardly know he's here. He's quiet and polite and the only sound he makes is his shower, which goes on—and on—and on. Like his showers, his visit is extending too. Somehow his one-week stay has expanded into three. Too long. But I can't find the right words or the right time to talk to him about it. Asking Maya to tell him to leave is pointless. Like telling a drug addict to throw out his stash. But his long showers mean I'll have to explain an astronomical water bill to Diego. And he's complaining about last month's $500 PG&E heating bill— that's equal to a mortgage payment in Wisconsin.

"How long does Jesse need to be in the shower, Maya?" I ask one morning.

"An hour," she says as if his dirt needs a Turbo dishwashing cycle. "Mom, It's an OCD thing."

OCD (Obsessive Compulsive Disorder) has become an epidemic around here since Maya first "caught it" from Jesse's sister Paige in high school. Paige had it, then Maya had it, Jesse has it, and Maya claims her dad has OCD too. Diego's superstitions are a milder form of OCD, she says. If he sees a dog pooping he says it's good luck, but if a black cat crosses your path it's bad luck and Diego will do a U-turn to avoid it, unless, however, we own the black cat (like dear departed Figaro). In that case, a black cat becomes good luck. Go figure. I really do sympathize with Maya's constant battle with her thoughts. But other than offering her the best therapy and meds we can, I can't fix it. Fixing our water bill, however, is another matter.

Saturday night during Jesse's visit I'm startled out of bed by screaming. Jesse's idea of evening family entertainment is watching slasher films. Not high on my list of family fun. I slog my tired self into the living room. Deanna is wide awake, well past her bedtime, sitting between Maya and Jesse on the couch, watching gory murders on TV. Both her parents look straight ahead twitching their bare feet at an identical rapid rate. *This has got to stop.*

"You guys need to turn it down, and Deanna needs to be in bed, Maya." I say firmly. Although we bend weekend bedtime rules sometimes, Deanna isn't ever allowed to watch R-rated movies and this film looks like torture training for terrorists.

"Go to bed," Maya tells Deanna. A blood spray splatters the inside of the TV glass. Yuck. I shiver.

"But I want to stay up with you and Daddy."

"Go to bed," Jesse tells her with his eyeballs glued to the set.

"Right now, Deanna!" Maya points to her daughter's bedroom. I'm on standby ready to walk Deanna down the dark hall, which she says has spiders.

"But I don't want to go to bed." She snuggles into her Dad's arm but Jesse pulls back and mimics her in a whining voice. "I don't waaaanna go to bed. Waaa, waaa, waaa." Then he laughs at her.

Deanna's face is blank, her eyes blinking. She releases her father's arm and takes hold of my outstretched hand. I'm stunned. I never heard him speak that way to Deanna before. Maya doesn't say anything and everything he had said to me that night two years ago comes flooding back in a huge thundercloud of resentment. Deanna, at eight, is too big for me to carry but I pick her up anyway. She clings to me like an overgrown chimp in a pink nightgown.

That night Jesse's video pick curdled blood, but his demeaning mimicking of my granddaughter (mimicking is listed in the book *The Verbally Abusive Relationship*) curdled my last drop of tolerance. The next morning I told him it was time to go back to Washington. And he did.

Maya didn't fight me about it.

. . .

IN TRADER JOE'S I'M RUFFLING through my purse for my shopping list— I always lose it. If it's not in my purse, then it's in the sweet potatoes. I look up over the balloon and flower display. I'm paralyzed. There *he* is heading to checkout.

Diego sees me before I can duck behind a candy rack. "Hi, Barbara." He grins and approaches with his little basket hooked on his arm like the wolf dressed as Little Red Riding Hood. I walk over casually and glance at his basket. Cashews, unfiltered grape juice, pickled okra, French bread, feta, and a cabernet. A cab? Since when did Mr. Micro-Brewery drink cabernet? The same items we bought in the eighties for a day at Stinson Beach.

"Yep, yep, yep. Just stocking up." His happy, carefree tone irks me. From the looks of his basket, he thinks our separation is a real picnic. Lorraine told me I shouldn't be talking to Diego on the phone, but she gave me no instructions of what to do in person at Trader Joe's.

"How's Kathy?" I ask, not realizing the name he gave me at Big O Tires was fake.

He looks confused for a second, then smiles. "She's fine."

I have to wing it. "She's very pretty," I add.

His face lights up. The smile in his eyes kills me. Why grin and drool about it? Why rub it in? Oh, fa-la-la-la-la, aren't we so friggin' happy partying with your new canoodle, shopping at Lafayette Trader Joe's. Dammit, Diego. Use your own TJ's in Walnut Creek. This is my Trader Joe's.

"Well, good to see you, Barbara." He glances toward checkout.

"So are you going to move in with her?"

"Shhhhh."

He doesn't want a scene. Diego hates scenes.

"I told you, she's just a friend," he whispers.

"Diego," I call out. "Don't you ever come in here again. This is my Trader Joe's." Some woman with two kids in her cart quickly wheels away from me. I spin my little red cart around to the cereal aisle and peer at him behind the display boxes of Gorilla Crunch. He puts the wine, French baguette, and feta on the counter.

I was the one who turned him on to French feta.

. . .

THIS WEDNESDAY I'M DRIVING through Walnut Creek to get to Lorraine's office. We're meeting every other week now. Through the rain-streaked windows, I imagine Diego will pop out at me from behind Nordstrom's in the Broadway Plaza shopping district—the same area where Maya's friend Angela reported a sighting. I'm imagining his unmistakable gray beard, rose-colored glasses, his arm around *her.* The image grabs my throat. Whenever I'm within a mile radius of his apartment I'm shadowed by low-grade panic. Paranoia.

*What's wrong with me?*

Lorraine's office on the third floor of the Kaiser mental health building is dinky. Walk-in closet size. Just room enough for a desk, two chairs, and a bookshelf. From the first time I met Lorraine, my Kaiser-assigned post-hospitalization therapist, I liked her. Instead of suits and heels, she dresses in what I call Berkeley chic, long flowy skirts in muted burgundies and navies. Non-intimidating colors. My same style, except my mixed patterns and bright colors are more arty-farty than her safe matchy-matchy. And she's more polished, adding a scarf and simple jewelry beneath her chin-length, sculpture-cut auburn hair. Lorraine's toned-down wardrobe matches her patience, which works perfectly for me. Many single women I know have long deal-breaker lists for men; but being over-therapied in my life, I've written my own short deal-breaker list for therapists.

#1. Therapists who keep the *Diagnostic and Statistical Manual of Mental Disorders* in their purse.

#2. Therapists who say my problem stems from dad being half German.

#3. Female therapists who allow yelling during marriage counseling.

#4. Therapists who say I'm not allowed back unless I've seen a divorce lawyer.

#5. Male counselors who say teenage boys are damaged by their mother's short nightgown (we're talking Target, not Victoria's Secret).

Lorraine, however, never shows any frustration with me, even though, month after month, I enter her cubicle office with clear, without-a-doubt evidence that proves Diego must be outgrowing his late-midlife crisis.

"Well, it's been nine months now," I crow, "and he obviously has no interest in moving in with her."

"Every couple has their own separation process," she says patiently. She gently steers me past my post-mortem marital fantasies and puts the focus back on me.

"Lorraine, he lives just a few blocks from here. I dread driving here thinking I'll run into him, or them," I confess. "I hate going to Squirrels, our brunch spot, or the Butterfly Café, where he got his morning mochas. And I hate going to parties alone; really I'd rather stay home and watch Benji movies with Deanna." I sigh, longing for a safe place where my mind won't incessantly think that I'm seeing him walk down the street or his van drive by. Lorraine nods, expecting me to go on. I tell her what Sara told me last month. "Diego took his *friend* to a New Year's party at Frank's house. All our friends were there." Lorraine nods again and waits for me to exhale.

Then she patiently explains the five stages of grief: denial, bargaining, anger, depression, and acceptance. I'm kinda disappointed that paranoia isn't one of them.

"I think you're angry, Barbara."

"No, no, no. I'm not. I'm over anger."

"Don't you think that someone who stabs herself with a needle may be angry? Angry at herself?"

She would have to bring that up. I'm still pissed at Diego, yeah, but not fist-slamming-the-car-seat angry, not Don-Quixote-figurine-smashing angry, well, not today. And I'm sure as hell not angry *at myself.*

"Barb, two months ago you attacked a stranger sitting in a car." She gently states the fact, no accusation in her voice. I'm not sure what to say. I wasn't myself? Uh, the devil made me do it? But I don't believe in the devil. Maybe I should; he could be handy in this situation.

Lorraine explains that the stages of grief don't come in any set order. You will move back and forth between denial, bargaining, anger, depression, and acceptance, she says. But none of those places ring true. Finding my own stage of grief feels like I'm shopping for a dress in a hardware store. The selection ain't that good. Yet it feels important for me to find out which stage I'm in.

I'm past raging anger, but at times I do feel like I'm backsliding, but into what? Nostalgia? *No.* Regret? *Fuck him.* Depression? *Not really.* I know real depression and how it takes a team of six horses just to walk a few feet to the mailbox. So, I'm not sure what I'm feeling.

Lorraine ends our session suggesting that Diego and I cut off all communication. I think she's figured out that keeping our conversations purely business isn't working.

"Communicate only by email," she says. I balk because we're still partners with a family, home, cars, and lemon trees that require upkeep. We've worked out an operable division of labor that worked for three decades, I explain. I handle the food, kids, clothes, and school expenses. He takes care of bills, cars, income taxes, watering, and jail visits.

"Besides," I tell Lorraine, "he's still coming over to get his mail."

Her mouth opens to reply, then closes. A pause. She looks at me with soft brown eyes. "Every couple has their own process, Barbara," she says. "Some couples separate very slowly."


When "restricted" calls that week, I ask Diego not to phone but to use email. He says he doesn't use email. How can a college professor not use email? This baffles me. I use email every day with my high school teaching job. I'm annoyed but simultaneously it's a relief. Now I can tell Lorraine he doesn't use email. That takes care of that. I tried. He must want to keep talking to me. And vice versa.

Swinging back on the reconciliation track I tell him not to take his "friend" to any parties with our mutual friends. "It puts Sara and Bill in an awkward position," I say, trying not to sound manipulative.

"Okay," he says. "I'm sorry." I'm surprised to get an apology. It feels like I won one. But won what? He still won't even admit to having one girlfriend although every sighting spots him with the same short, light-skinned, young, thirtyish black woman. I may have won his "sorry" but still I'm the wallflower on the gym bleachers watching him on the dance floor. I know the world wants me to say, "F-you, good riddance, have a nice life," and march my petticoated ass out the gym double doors, but my butt isn't moving. I know I'm living a charade of a marriage. But does he hold out the carrot? When I told him not to bring *her* to our friends' parties, why did he say, "sorry"? Shouldn't he be saying, "Barbara, it's none of your business"? Is he just telling me what I want to hear? Why? Why not email me and get his snail mail at his own damn mailbox? And for God's sake take his furniture so I don't have to look at it?

Maybe this annoyance is the anger Lorraine talks about, but it's a tired anger, with no more flame to it. No momentum—it smolders and spins in memories and regret. Not much anger left in my tedious conversations with him either. Just bitterness. Damn right. Hey, I am bitter, that's the right word. *Bitter.* It has just the right acid, pepper, and slow burn to it. Yes, bitter works quite nicely for me even if it isn't one of Lorraine's official five stages of grief.

My mom was bitter, off and on. As a child I would get up and sit with her late at night in a haze of Salem Menthols and keep her and her bitter complaints company. Then bitterness wasn't so bad. It had a tender, soft, warm center when Mom served it with hot cocoa and Ritz crackers on the living room couch at two a.m.

"You mean you *choose* to be bitter," Joanna said over the phone.

"Uh, not really."

She isn't nearly as thrilled about me being bitter as I am. I'm confused. I didn't choose to be bitter. As if a waiter is holding an emotional dessert tray under my nose: happy, sad, grateful, *joie de vivre*, bliss, bitter. "Gee, I'll take bitter."

"Victims never get better, they get bitter," Joanna said.

"I'm just being honest. Can't I be bitter?"

"No."

"But honesty is part of the program."

"Barb, the way to heal is to find gratitude."

"But after a thirty-one year marriage, don't you think I have a reason to feel—"

"No."

So now I'm the bitter-victim-loser sponsee. No one in program admits to being bitter. It means you're a newcomer and you still have the magnifying glass on *him*, your qualifier, not on yourself, and you haven't accepted step three yet, where you give your bitterness over to God. All the program literature about bitterness is negative. Being bitter means I'm stuck in the quicksand of my resentments and I have a pouting emotional age of six.

Another thing that's really annoying: I still see Carrie every Wednesday morning so I know she no longer believes that Jay's Christmas Eve fling with a prostitute was a one-time deal. She told him to move out while she gets her head together. "Our focus is being the best parents we can be," she says. "I'm okay." How did Carrie get it together and start taking care of herself so quickly? But me, I'm the wrinkled eggplant turned bitter in the crisper who's headed for the garbage bin.

Okay, I resolve to get past bitterness. Because everyone knows bitterness is unhealthy, immature, selfish, and most of all it's unattractive. An emotional purgatory for old crones with taut, hairy upper lips. I can feel the tingling in my upper lip already—those budding black hairs waiting to pop out.

. . .

AT OUR NEXT LUNCH I tell Joanna about my new resolve to think positive and write more gratitude lists. "Fake it till you make it."

"There you go!" she says in approval.

"I've got lots to be grateful for. My family and my sister, and I'm still close to Diego's family too. His family is on my side. Partly, I bet, because they don't approve of Diego dating a black woman." I douse my salad with extra splashes of vinegar and extra virgin olive oil.

"Barb, you never said his girlfriend was black."

"I didn't?" I shrug as though it doesn't matter. But I know it matters. Her color wasn't in the foreground of my resentments against her, like her age and being pretty. Yet when I first learned her race, I made an issue out of it, like my mother would, making racist slurs to Diego like "your black whore." But with Joanna I quickly change the uncomfortable subject.

"I *am* moving on, I did an intake form with that shark divorce lawyer Gail referred me to."

I knew my calling a lawyer would make Joanna happy, her and a lot of other folks. But I didn't tell her I couldn't go any further than to place his card in my Rolodex. I wasn't ready to make the first move. Too many unanswered questions. Too many what-ifs. What if they break up? What if some tragedy pulls us back together? That's what happens in books and movies. Like the parents in *Bridgette Jones's Diary, High Fidelity*, and *Love Actually*. Those separated couples married over thirty years always reconcile in the end. Of course I don't want anything really terrible happening to my family or some horrible tragedy that kills people. Maybe a little tragedy. A little 7.0 earthquake, or Diego could have a heart attack—a little scare.

But that's just wishful thinking.

# CHAPTER TWELVE
## DROP DEAD ED

The phone rings. I set aside my high-school kids' essays on personal quirks. It's Rena, Diego's daughter in El Paso. She tells me she's driving to the hospital. I panic. Something terrible has happened to Diego's family, and it's obviously my fault for having bad thoughts.

"Barbara, Helen's in the hospital." Rena's voice sounds tired, strained, not her usual enthusiastic self. "She's dying." I tell her I appreciate the call; she could have let her father call. I call Diego and he tells me he's flying out to El Paso the next day. I tell him if his mother passes, I'd like to attend the funeral. I expect to hear, "Of course. You and the girls *should* be there."

"I'll let you know," he says. "Barbara, thank you for your prayers." He's sounds sincere. And so sad. I tell him that Helen is a beautiful woman, a real lady, and she's been a positive influence in my life. All true. Even in her nineties Diego's mother is still attractive, with perfect alabaster skin, and her once jet-black hair is still thick and stylishly coiffed in a blue-grey bubble. We share a common interest in cooking, and after I asked Helen for her recipes for enchiladas *suizas*, egg foo yung, and *menudo* (the tripe dish that cures hangovers), I think she started to like me. By 1990, after she gave up drinking and became my sobriety role model, I told her, "If you can give up booze, so can I."

Helen's grand ninety-second birthday bash, hosted by Diego's sister Charleen, was held just over two years ago. Yet it seems like yesterday that Diego and I stepped off the elevator at that elegant top-floor restaurant overlooking the El Paso city skyline against majestic red mountains. We were greeted by a life-size cardboard cutout of Helen in a 1920s flapper chemise — a photo from her reign as Miss El Paso. At ninety-two, Helen hadn't lost her looks or her sassiness. At the head of the dinner table of fifty guests she quipped in grand Mae West style, "I've outlived my three husbands and their whores." She was still a pistol, all right. I loved her for that. The morning after the party I remember well how the clear West Texas sun lit our hotel bed like a Vermeer painting. After making love, Diego held out his forearm for me to examine his skin.

"See this crinkled skin. This is old skin," he tells me, seriously concerned. I laugh and make a joke about pushing him around in a wheelchair when he's ninety-two. At that time Diego chasing his youth struck me as funny. Not any more.

Diego calls two days later. "Mother has passed." He's crying.

I sit on my comforter prepared to listen. "How are you doing, Diego?"

I hear him sniffling. "Not so good. You only have one mother."

My chest aches thinking about my mother-in-law. I still care. He's the only man I've ever known who cries with me. And he's never been annoyed at my tears. Just the opposite. Tears soften him. He's unlike most men I've known, like my father, who live in a buck-up, John Wayne world. When a woman cries, they walk away, hiding disgust. "Get a grip. Don't be a baby." Even my mom considers tears to be a weak feminine trait. But not Diego.

They don't spell weakness to him; they mean *corazón*. Having a heart. When I cried over losing our cat, or a baby bird, or a phone commercial, he'd remind me I was a sensitive, sympathetic, compassionate person. I had *corazón*, he said. He was my alchemist, who took the emotions my parents labeled sick and he turned them into normal. It takes a man with *corazón* to appreciate it in others. With him gone, I can do without the sex and his great in-shape body (though I do miss those biceps), maybe even let go of his intellect I so admire — those parts I can give to God—but I can't let go of his *corazón*. I don't know how. That's why I know I still love him, and probably always will.

As our phone call lapses into longer silences, I'm thinking don't tell him, Don't say those three words, Barbara. He'll stab thorns in me. But the tongue betrays me.

"I miss you." I say aloud.

There's silence. Then ...

"I know," he mumbles. His voice so heartfelt and reassuring that I'm reminded this separation is painful for him too. I want to tell him that I'm coming for the funeral. Then I wonder, am I going really? Am I trying to force something? Am I using Helen's death to manipulate him? Shafts of afternoon light pour two diamond swaths across a new tropical print comforter I purchased in Florida. Seated on the end of my bed, I scootch across it to allow the sun's warm hand to caress my face and shoulder.

No, the truth is I do care about Helen. I'd want to attend her funeral, even if Diego weren't there. Tears roll down my cheek. This sentiment belongs to the mother, not the son.

"Diego, I truly want to be there."

He pauses. "Uh, I don't think it's a good idea, Barbara. It will send the wrong message." He means about us. "Barbara, it's just better this way. I'll tell everyone you called. Tita, Charleen, Rena, they'll appreciate it. I'll call you after the funeral from the house," he says. We say goodbyes, and our "say-hi-to-so-and-sos," and we're at the conversation's end point, where we always said, "I love you," and "I love you too." The words rise up in my throat, but they're stuck. I refuse to let them out. Still, they flutter alive like trapped birds.

I put down the phone and reach into my nightstand drawer. I need something to calm myself. My fingers grope through spools of thread and various orange vials in the drawer's recesses. Finally they find what they're looking for. The familiar touch of smooth, round, threaded beads.

My rosary.

Under the circumstances it was understandable that Diego didn't want me to fly to El Paso. It felt okay. But why was I okay with not being wanted? That felt odd. Foreign. Feeling unwanted is familiar. Being outside the flock. Abandonment and not belonging have haunted me since before kindergarten, perhaps since I was six months old, when Mom's sanitarium visits began. Even well into my fifties these "I'm not wanted" feelings persisted, I'm ashamed to say. I'm well practiced in feeling excluded.

But for some reason the days following Helen's death felt different. I was granted a reprieve from self-pity, betrayal, and abandonment. An emotional truce descended, a ceasefire from firing guilt bombs at Diego. And at myself. Letting Diego exclude me not only felt acceptable, but even made me feel lighter somehow. And although he was four states away in Texas, I felt connected to him in a new, non-physical way. Diego was where he was supposed to be. And I was where I was supposed to be. And so was Helen.

She was free.

• • •

IF DIEGO DIDN'T COME HOME, I reasoned that first year after he left, then I'd have to face getting on with my life. But I had no idea how to do that. I assumed that getting on with one's life meant finding a new husband or at least a boyfriend. Yet the thought of some strange man holding my hand or his whiskey breath on my neck gave me the creeps. But in three short years I'd be turning sixty. A dating expiration date. I'd be alone and single the rest of my life. As Isadora Duncan wrote, "a phantom ship on a phantom ocean." Since Diego was drifting further and further away, I needed a Plan B. Quick.

Even dating at fifty-seven sounded age-inappropriate—like auditioning for a Cameron Diaz ingénue role when I was better suited to a Kathy Bates part in a Stephen King movie. But if online dating was working for Patsy in the Wisconsin Northwoods, then finding romance in San Francisco should be a breeze. The Bay Area, the birthplace of Apple, Google, and Stanford Business School start-ups, swarmed with dot-commers in Dockers and Bluetooth headsets. But back in 2005, I was unaware that match.com men weren't searching for an accomplished, artistic, Julia Child-type résumé—they were rating headshots and evaluating the potential benefits of online relationships. When I wrote my online profile, I didn't realize that "mature cookbook author" translates as fat.

. . .

THIS WEDNESDAY I ARRIVE for my therapist appointment with men other than Diego on my mind—namely the men whose profiles I viewed on match.com.

"You're making progress, Barbara," Lorraine says as a compliment.

While scanning the dating site, I noticed the online male profiles have a disturbing similarity. It seems a fitting topic for a therapy session. "Men my age all want younger women. What's up with that?"

"Women date up in age and men date down," Lorraine explains from behind her clean, polished desktop.

"So, you're saying I had more men to chose from in my twenties, but now the advantage has switched. After fifty, the men have the big advantage."

"True." Lorraine nods. "Now it's men who have the bigger playing field. That's their option." Lorraine shrugs.

*That sounds blatantly unfair.* "So am I too old to date men my own age?"

If men my age want women ten years younger, that means the only guys who would want me are close to seventy. Dating prospects suddenly look bleak. I notice Lorraine is wearing a ring on the third finger of her left hand. A tiny diamond on a plain silver band. Looks like it's been there a long time. In other words, she doesn't get it.

"Barbara, go for it. Get your feet wet." Lorraine nudges me out into the dating pool—or at my age what amounts to an evaporating puddle. "Relax, have fun. When you're relaxed, you attract others," she says. "If it feels good, do it."

A good first online date would be a walk around the Lafayette reservoir. But I'm appalled at how many men on match.com can't spell reservoir. After spending half my life with a professor husband, how can I date a guy who can't spell reservoir, whether he wants to walk around it or not?

Then I meet Ed online. Ed can spell reservoir.

We buy coffee at Peet's, then hike. He looks as handsome, tall, and trim as his online photo and he sounds as educated and professional as his techie profile. On our hike Ed tells me about his four-year-old daughter Natasha, and I talk about Deanna. We're talking like two simpatico moms at playgroup. We wave goodbye. No hug. I suspect that this will be the last I'll see of Ed. For one, he's six years younger than I. And two, from his profile he looks like Richard Gere. I don't need a number three.

So I'm surprised when Ed calls. He invites me to go with him to a baseball game at the new San Francisco Giants stadium. My smile is so wide it shoves my cheeks clear up into my eyeballs. This is no big deal, I tell Maya; I'm just going out with a friend. But when Ed's car pulls up Maya and Deanna are both staring out the kitchen window.

"He's getting out of the car. I think it's a BMW," Maya calls out. Over the girls' heads I see Ed walking down the driveway in a taupe Burberry trench coat. A tad dressy for baseball.

"Mom, that guy's gay."

"Move over, Mama. I want to see too." Deanna stands on her tiptoes, then she rushes to the front door before me. I should have met Ed at the BART station.

"Come in. Come in." Deanna says. "This is our house." She greets Ed like an eight-year-old real estate agent. *Jesus.*

I make introductions and Ed sits on the couch while I go to my room for my coat. When I return I see Deanna drawing the curtains to the living room—curtains to section off the living room from the kitchen when I taught writing classes at home.

"For privacy so you two can be alone," she says.

Ed glances around the room. "Wow, these are nice antiques."

"The leaded glass bookcases and the poker table, they're antiques from El Paso. They belong to my husband."

"Really?" *He wants to know why they're still here.*

"He moved out nine months ago." We hear whispering, the refrigerator door closing, and glasses clinking behind the curtain. Then Deanna swings open the curtain and enters with two wine glasses filled with orange juice.

"Something to drink, Madame." She hands us each a glass, bows, and leaves. Deanna's watched too many date movies. We hear Maya cracking up behind the curtain. This is embarrassing.

"I'm sorry, Ed. We can go. They aren't used to—"

"No, actually this is delicious. Mmmmmm." He downs half the glass. "I've been running around all day."

I'm suddenly disoriented. I have no more idea how to act on a date than little Deanna does. And this eight-year-old is making matters worse. Ed says he thinks Deanna is cute. He says he could see his daughter doing that in five years. What a disastrous start for a second date. I'm going to kill Maya when I get home.

At the stadium we take an elevator up to a top floor, where we're shown to box seats in a private room with catering. This stadium overlooking the Bay Bridge is nothing like watching a Braves game in Milwaukee in the fifties. We get an instant photo taken of us for free. I'm surprised how attractive the photo with Ed makes me look with no glasses and a longer hairstyle. Everything feels so elegant. So un-baseball. Instead of beer and hot dogs, we snack on salmon and caviar in the room and I meet Ed's coworkers from his tech company— something to do with FICA credit scores. Amy is recently divorced and inebriated.

"Dirty rats. Life is better without 'em, right? " Her hand whisks the air. "We don't need 'em. If they wanna come back, they'll just cheat on you again, believe you me!" She pours more pinot into her wine glass. "Once a cheat, always a cheat."

I only nod. I've been hearing that a lot lately. Ed pulls alongside of me and circles his arm around my waist, which feels, well, sexy. We sit in cushy leather seats to watch the game beneath us through the wide glass. My soda and his red wine rest in cup holders. Turning to look at Ed, I'm astonished that this man wants to date me. Lorraine said men in their fifties date down. He did mention that he told his ex about my books and posters and she replied, "Not too shabby, Ed." So maybe I'm not too old and shabby after all.

However I'm feeling horribly guilty about lying about my age online. I said I was a year younger, fifty-five, so my profile would pop up in more searches. Now a huge guilt is gnawing at me. How do I tell Ed?

"Ed, I have to confess something." I know he'll probably never want to go out with me again.

Ed puts his glass of cab in the cup holder and turns his swivel box seat towards me.

"I have to tell you. There's something I just don't feel right about."

A look of concern spreads across his clean-shaven face.

"Uh, Ed. I'm sorry about this but I'm not really fifty-five. I'm fifty-six. I lied." I hold my breath.

Ed looks surprised, then he laughs out loud. I can't imagine why he thinks this is funny. "Barbara, don't you know, everybody lies online." Then he glances over at Amy, who is gabbing with another co-worker. "Just don't tell that to the women here." He smiles and squeezes my hand and says, "Look, Kevin Correia is up to bat." He watches the field beneath us intently. His profile melts me. Oh my god. I'm dating Richard Gere. And the best part comes later, at the door when Richard Gere kisses me goodnight. It isn't icky. He tastes like cabernet.

It's been fifteen years since I tasted a good cabernet.

. . .

I SPEND MUCH OF WEDNESDAY night working on my marriage break-up fourth step for Joanna. Thursday morning the first thing I see on my windowsill is the five-by-seven color photo of Ed and me taken at the stadium. The woman smiling in the photo looks thin and young and even happy.

Joanna and I are waiting at our rough-hewn wood table at Cherubini's. After the Thursday meeting, I'm starving. Our sandwiches are late in coming. It's a delightful, yellow daffodil, sunny spring morning and the café is busy. I can't stop talking to Joanna about Ed. Just thinking about handsome Ed makes me grin all over from my empty stomach to the top of my ponytail. We scheduled a third date; I invited him to the house for a barbecue. Maybe after that I'll offer to cook dinner in his North Bay apartment. He says it overlooks the Bay. I don't tell Joanna that lately I've been dreaming about men other than Diego, men with water views. Dreams are a real sign I'm moving on. Doing my fourth step on Diego is just burial work. Emotional cleanup. I expect Joanna, who listens intently, will congratulate me.

Joanna picks up the end of her long braid and tosses it over her shoulder. "Barbara, can't you see that Ed is a diversion?" She sounds disappointed.

"But part of recovery is to have fun, right?" And as Lorraine said, "If it feels good, do it."

"Of course we're supposed to have fun. But Barbara, for you men are slippery. You know that Diego is your addiction, right?"

"I'm getting past that. I don't dream about him anymore, well, not every night."

"Just like having to drink, you don't need a man to have fun, do you?"

Well, it helps, but I can't say that. There isn't much in our program literature about dating. Dating almost seems to be regarded as suspicious, an iffy slip activity—like an AA member who drinks Nyquil. Even dating people within the program (called thirteenth stepping) is highly ill advised for newcomers.

Maybe Joanna isn't the best person to talk to about match.com. She's been married her whole adult life. Why argue with her about what Lorraine told me? After all, Joanna is the one who says, "Barb, you don't have to go to every argument you're invited to."

I open my spiral notebook journal to "My Diego fourth step" and ready myself to read to her. Joanna's eyes brighten, regaining their impish fairy godmother interest. After all, the fourth step is the meat of the Twelve Step Program. This is the step where we pull up our big girl panties and separate the girls from the women. Do the work. The path to feeling happy, joyous, and free. And one of Joanna's quips proves to be true: "Everything we let go of has claw marks all over it."

WHY THE PHILANDERER LEFT ME: MY PART

#1. My drinking in the early days added to our fighting, several broken windshields on Diego's van and one broken bookcase window. (my anger)

#2. I was always busy—working until seven at my studio when Diego was home with the kids. (I was selfish)

#3. I dragged the whole family into therapy. (controlling)

#4. I always got to choose our restaurants, vacation spots, and therapists. (sense of entitlement ... arrogant maybe?)

#5. Sometimes I snuck lard into the beans. (all of the above)

#6. My nighttime acting, theatre rehearsals, and writing classes took away family time. (selfish again)

#7. After CPS took baby Deanna away from Maya and Jesse, I coerced Diego into allowing Maya and the baby to move in with us against his wishes in spite of his diaper allergy. (critical, judgmental, and controlling)

#8. I blamed him entirely for the break-up. (blaming, controlling)

#9. I made Diego feel responsible and guilty for breaking up the family (controlling again).


Joanna scans my character defect list. Angry, selfish, high expectations, controlling, guilty, critical, judgmental, maybe arrogant. "This is good," she says.

I'm feeling quite proud of it.

"So ...?" Joanna gives me one of her "how do you feel about that?" looks as our sandwiches arrive.

"Well, I can see my part. I was always busy with work and, well, I wonder if Diego could have felt abandoned too." Was Sara right? Did my achievements make Diego feel like less of a man?

"Did he say that?" Joanna lifts her hefty sandwich with two hands.

"He never said it outright."

"We all have some selfish motives. But aren't you entitled to pursue a career and do what you love? What makes you happy? You're entitled to your own life, right?"

I realize that those are the exact same words that Diego used to defend his leaving. "I'm entitled to my own life. To be happy."

*Makes me sick.*

"Good fourth step. Now keep adding to your character defect list. We can't ask HP to remove what we're not aware of."

A new worry arises. If HP, what Joanna calls Higher Power, removes my blame, control, judgment, selfishness, arrogance and entitlement ... then what is left? Who am I?

• • •

I'M IN THE CANNED MEAT aisle at Safeway with Maya, scanning my shopping list for the Easter barbecue. Sara and Bill are coming. Ed says he'll drop by around five. Miguel is going to barbecue tri-tip. It feels like a real family holiday again. But Maya is trailing behind my shopping cart complaining.

"But Mom, why did you have to invite Ed for Easter? He's not part of the family."

"He's my friend, Maya. I always let you invite your friends to our parties." Maya invited Paige, Quinton, Fish, and even Trey for Easter. Taser-gun Trey, who last time brought his pit bull, which he claimed killed a cat. I hoped it wasn't true. Still I always welcome all of the kids' friends as long as they don't bring alcohol, drugs, and pit bulls into the house.

"Tray and Quinton are Miguel's friends too." That makes them even more questionable, but I keep my mouth zipped. Truthfully I'm relieved to see that my son Miguel is friends with Trey, who's black. Some years back when jail time turned our son into a racist, Diego and I became outraged. Not our son. Like us, he always had black friends, and he looked up to his Godfather Frank.

When Miguel was in a Berkeley grade school we were thrilled to learn he was friends with Black Panther Eldridge Cleaver's son. After Miguel spent the night at the Cleavers', the next day Diego and I couldn't wait to hear about it. "So did you meet his father? Mr. Cleaver? What was he like?"

Miguel looked at us funny and said, "He was just an old man in a bathrobe."

At ten he didn't see color, but ten years later, after six months in jail, he came home saying the N-word and "raghead." Racist slurs made me cringe, but they pushed Diego into a tirade. "Not in my house!" he bellowed. It took time, not threats, for Miguel's racism to wear off. Now Miguel has returned to his humorous, quick-witted, openhearted self. Except since 9/11 he's become fiercely patriotic, to Diego's disappointment. On holidays Miguel insists on displaying a large American flag on the garage flag support in front of our house. He'd put it up and Diego would promptly remove it. Then, when his dad wasn't looking, Miguel would fly Old Glory again for all Glenside Drive to see. I stayed quiet, but every time I peeked through the kitchen window and saw the flag, my heart would fire a fifty-one-gun salute. It's one of those bittersweet family memories that pushes through grief and makes the corners of my mouth turn up.

"Ed isn't your type, Mom." Maya means that Ed is not like her father. Diego is funny, politically radically liberal, emotional, and more pro-Mexican than most full-blooded Mexicans I know. Ed is serious, high-tech, factual, and more, well, metrosexual.

"Miguel won't like him."

"Does Miguel like your father's girlfriend?"

"He's never met her. None of us have. He keeps her a secret."

Good, I'm not the only one in the dark.

. . .

AT MY NEXT MEETING WITH Joanna she's talking about my fourth step work.

"There's a pattern here, Barb. And before you start dating again it's better to understand the pattern so you don't repeat it."

"What pattern?"

"Hasn't it dawned on you that both Diego and your mother are narcissists?"

"Well, so what?"

Joanna lets out a deep breath as if I'm trying her patience. She stacks up our finished plates and speaks in her calm doctor voice. "Barb, look back at your childhood." She taps the notebook where I wrote my parent resentments. She took a keen interest in my childhood surgeries: the club foot surgery at eight, an operation for lazy eye at nine, and the tonsillectomy at ten that Mom called "preventative."

"I suspect your mother suffered from Munchausen's syndrome by proxy, as well as being bipolar. These mothers tell docs that their kids are sick to get attention for themselves." Joanna writes the diagnosis name, abbreviated MsbP, in my notebook. "Barb, do some research."

But Joanna never met my mother. Or Diego for that matter. And what does my past have to do with dating Ed? I bet she'd give him a diagnosis too, like "addicted to electronics." She's too quick to label people. And this Munch-what-ever-you-call-it syndrome is way over the top. My mother wouldn't admit me to hospitals for unnecessary operations. And I went willingly. Besides, by sixth grade I bragged about having six doctors and three operations. Other kids only brought their puny gray tonsils to school in a jar. Having three operations was something. I felt like a war hero.

"Barb, all I'm suggesting is to look at the pattern. There's a pattern of abandonment and mistreatment here."

"You don't understand. My mom volunteered in hospitals and visited sick children. She was just very proactive about my health. And Diego, he knew he had a problem with anger and dealt with it; he went to his men's anger group for five years. You don't see that—"

"I see that you defend the very people who mistreat you the most. Barbara, you don't want to make another man your higher power, do you?" Joanna writes "dishonest?" next to "selfish" on my character defect list.

"I'm not dishonest."

"Barbara, when you accept mistreatment from others, you're not being honest with yourself."

Cyndi Lauper's song "Girl's Just Wanna Have Fun" is playing in the background. Our song. The girls and I used to dance to it, holding hands, hopping, twirling ourselves silly round and round in the living room. This is our happy song. I let it play in my head while Joanna's lips move and her pen taps on the notebook.

*"I wanna be the one to walk in the sun. Girls just wanna ..."*

I like Ed. Talking about our girls, baseball, his new iPhone. Not disorders and character defects. I'm tired of being defective.

*Girls just wanna, they just wanna ...*

. . .

ON SUNDAY OUR BARBECUE is on track. I potted the impatiens, cleaned the pool and deck, and filled three trash bags with soggy pine needles and palm fronds. I pre-made the salsas and chocolate pie. Ed called and asked what should he bring, and I suggested a few NA beers for me. Erika called to tell me that she and Miguel were coming at four and would it be all right if she brought her nephew Wyatt. "Of course, the more family the merrier." As long as *family* doesn't include Diego. He said he made other plans. *Good.*

He called this week about our taxes and I promised him the 2004 figures from my ledger before leaving for Florida over spring break, and I added, "Please move your furniture and your other belongings out of the garage while I am gone." He agreed. *Double good.*

· · ·

EASTER SUNDAY FEELS MONUMENTAL. The last time Miguel stayed to eat dinner with us was over a year ago when his Dad was still here. Then we were all sitting around the dinner table when Miguel's head suddenly dropped face down in the spaghetti. Deanna stared at her uncle's hair in the tomato sauce. He looked like a Mafia victim.

"Mama! Miguel's asleep."

"Let's just let him sleep." Diego shrugged. "He hasn't been sleeping well." So we twirled our spaghetti and passed the fresh-grated parmesan as if this were a normal dinner. What we didn't tell Deanna was that someone with bipolar disorder could stay up for days in a manic episode.

At our Easter barbecue I take a break from the kitchen and sit at the patio table where Maya narrates Jesse horror stories to Sara and my friend Wendy. Stories I've heard a hundred times. I hope she finishes her Jesse-did-it-to-me stories before Ed arrives. Please God, for one day let my family look normal.

"Another time Jesse started choking me, and he even dragged me by the hair in front of his mother. He was going to throw me down the stairs."

"Oh my goodness." Sara, who just came from Easter Mass, looks appropriately shocked. Maya exhales cigarette smoke through the side of her mouth. *Disgusting habit.*

"Why don't we talk about something more pleasant?" I suggest. Now I sound like Mom. My hand waves the smoke away from my guacamole.

Although my Mom smokes, it's different when it's your daughter.

"Mom, Bill smokes too." Maya shrugs. Yes, Bill is smoking too but he's a proper, shameful smoker who holds his cigarette down and behind him like a concealed weapon. And he uses a flowerpot ashtray, not the patio stones. His smoke drifts away from us while he keeps a watchful eye on Deanna and David riding the blow-up dolphin in the pool.

"Did Mom ever tell you about the time Jesse dented the front of Dad's van with a pipe? Two years ago when Deanna was six; she was in the front seat, scared to death."

"Deanita was in the car?" Sara asks, incredulous. "You deserve so much better, Maya." Sara pats Maya's hand and Maya soaks it up. She plays the crowd for sympathy like a newcomer at a meeting. Some newbies come and spill all the abusive stuff their guy does to them, and when the focus turns back on their own behavior, they disappear. It cheats us, really, like having to watch the first half of a bad romance movie where all the bad crap happens over and over again, but we never get to the end where the heroine learns to value herself and leaves the schmuck.

"But Maya, why would you send Deanna to Washington alone?" Wendy asks.

*Whoa. Did I miss something?* "Maya, I thought you said you couldn't visit Jesse any more."

"Nicki didn't say I couldn't send Deanna. Nicki would love to have her."

Sara looks deeply concerned. "Maya, you don't want to expose Deanita to his temper," Sara says.

*Darn tootin'.*

"Oh, Jesse would never hurt her. He comes after me. Deanna protects me. When I went to Washington over Christmas, Deanna hid me in a closet."

This is shocking news to me. Maya told me after her Christmas altercation with Jesse that his father tried to hold him back, but when he couldn't, he called the police. She never said anything about Deanna having to hide her in the closet. "You would let Deanna go there alone?"

"Deanna's almost nine, Mom. She can go to Seattle by herself."

*Over my dead body.*

I pick up three squashed cigarette butts left at the foot of Maya's empty chair.

Twenty minutes later I'm browning sourdough croutons in the kitchen when I hear a chorus of cheers coming from the patio.

"Ahhh, you came? Sara, look who's here." It's Bill's voice. I put the assembled Caesar in the fridge (sans dressing) and rush to look out the sliding glass doors. I hope it's who I think it is.

Out the windows I see my son is pouring coals into the barbecue grill. For a sec I stand back and admire him lighting the coals, the new man of the house. Flames shoot up and he steps back, with a wide grin across his face. Since he was a little tyke, Miguel always loved fire. He lowers the lid, adjusts the vent, while talking to Bill. He looks so tall and a new wispy beard has appeared on his chin—a goatee like his dad's. I ache to wrap my arms around his waist and hold him tight, but I'd embarrass him, so I wipe a tear on my apron hem and walk out on the patio.

Bills raises his brewski. "Barb, look at Miguel. He's a regular barbie-meister."

"Hi, Mom." Miguel salutes me by raising off his baseball cap like a ship captain.

"Happy Easter, Miguel." I hug him and close my eyes to treasure the few quick seconds he hugs me back. A real hug. Then I kiss Erika, who has a grocery bag in one hand and her nephew in the other. She's chatting with Maya.

"Here, let me take the bag."

"Mom, the tri-tip's in there. Put it in the fridge," Miguel instructs. "I'm marinating it." Bill pops open a Dos Equis and hands it to Miguel. "Your dad likes this brand." Miguel guzzles down half the bottle and burps. Maya knows what I'm thinking.

"Mom, Miguel can have one beer," she snaps. "He's doing the cooking."

"Okay." I let it go. After all, he's almost thirty.

The kids' friends arrive and they form their own clique sitting on the steps leading down to the pool. I postpone an argument with Maya about sending Deanna to Washington. It never occurred to me that she would even consider sending Deanna alone into the lion's den.

During dinner Ed arrives, still wearing his trench coat, which makes him look very FBI. He carries a six-pack of Buckler NA. "For you, Barbara."

I'm so touched—Diego never bought me a whole six-pack of imported NA beer before. I'm happy Ed is here to eat with us, even though I know that we're just a convenient stop on the way to his daughter's house in nearby Walnut Creek. It's a good day to be single. I roll the thought over in my mind, like wiggling into a new shoe.

I'm making progress too, allowing Diego and the kids to lead their own lives. But I do notice, after Ed's arrival, that Miguel and Quinton retreat to the side yard, Diego's orchard, which is hidden from the house and street by tall trees. I don't follow the boys, but still I feel queasy about Diego's side yard. That's where Diego hid a plastic bag stash under a patio rock, and that's where Maya overheard Diego's secret phone conversation with his girlfriend. Seeing my son disappear with Quinton brings back days, before Erika, when I'd find his broken pens missing the shaft, strange black burn marks on my pans, and missing baggies. Quinton's shaggy sandy hair and plaid jacket look familiar. He's younger than Miguel, in Mimi's class, I think, and his slightly hooded eyes make me wary. I have suspicions but I'm not playing Mother Narc. Not today.

By dark, after company has left and I've loaded the dishwasher and picked up all the beer bottles on the patio, I'm thinking, wow, I actually had a great time. Talking to Sam and Wendy, and Bill and Ed really hit it off; they both share similar techie jobs. And everybody raved over Miguel's tri-tip and my chocolate butter cream pie. Amazingly, Easter all happened without

Diego. And gratitude seems to have returned on its own like a lost cat that shows up at the back door.

. . .

EVERYTHING IS FALLING INTO place just before my Easter break trip to Florida. But then my father calls.

"Your mother's stopped talking," he says calmly, as if Tiger Woods had lost a match.

"She's depressed again?"

"No, she can't get out the words, Barbara. She stutters. I wanted to warn you, before you come. It just happened a week ago. She woke up that morning and couldn't talk."

"Well, what did the doctor say?"

"But she's sleeping well." My mother's medical condition has always been evaluated by family by her ability to sleep through the night—like a three-month-old.

"Did they do tests?"

"She hasn't been to a doctor yet, Barb. I'm waiting until you get here."

"But Dad, she could have had a stroke!" My mind is racing. What if there was brain damage?

"Your mother's in good spirits."

"I think she should be seen. Immediately. Strokes can recur. And they're worse the second time—"

"Okay, Dr. Barbara," he says sarcastically.

"Can I talk to her?"

"She's sleeping now. She sleeps most of the day now."

There's no point in arguing with Dad about her seeing a doctor immediately. However, he does agree to get a referral to a neurologist so we'd have an appointment scheduled when I arrive.

I call my sister, but she hasn't heard from Dad. "I guess he didn't want to bother me," she says.

# CHAPTER THIRTEEN
## FLORIDA

Before saying goodbye to Ed that Easter I went along with him when he stopped at his daughter's Walnut Creek home to drop off a jacket she'd left behind. I should not have been snooping. When he left me in his black Beemer, I found a computer printout in the back seat from the match.com site. Another woman. Directions to her house. Maybe it's old, from before he met me, I thought. I checked the date but it was last week. Of course I put the papers back in the seat pocket where I found them and said nothing.

But it was something.

I wasn't online with other people, checking out other options, so why was Ed? I wanted to be enough, but obviously I wasn't.

It's a hot and muggy April evening when Dad picks me up at the Palm Beach airport. "Ahhh! I love this air." It feels like a warm blanket wrapped around me. Dad drives the fifteen minutes to the condo. He tells me Mom can still walk and stand but she prefers her new wheelchair. Figures. "Medicare pays for it," Dad gloats. "She's very content." Dad pulls my suitcase over a newly installed ramp and into my parents' first-floor condo. Mom sits in a wheelchair wearing a snap-front housecoat watching *Golden Girls*. Her hair is freshly lacquered into a webbed, translucent dome that reveals her pink scalp. So she's keeping her weekly hair appointments.

"How you doing, Mom?"

"Ffff-fine." She grins.

"She can't get the words out." Dad states the obvious.

I make small talk about the flight and Deanna's upcoming birthday. Mom nods and smiles, acting oddly comfortable with being a mute in a wheelchair. I hope the doctor will say she had a small stroke and she'll recover her speech with a speech therapist. But I know how Dad thinks, considering my mother's awful bouts with depression. If it's not broke, let's not fix it.

Mom points a shaky white finger at her orange chair. "Bbbbbbab-ra, ggg-get my ...." She takes a deep breath, as though getting words out is like climbing a steep flight of stairs.

"Get what, Mom?"

"Mmmm ..." Her eyes dart like two bluebirds in a cage. "Pu-pu-pu-"

"Purse," Dad says. Mom's eyes brighten.

I catch sight of the yellow flowered purse behind Mom's orange chair. It smells faintly of baby powder and diapers. I hand it to her. She unzips it and pulls out a half-smoked cigarette. The silver lighter in her hand wavers back and forth under the white stick as if she was searing meat with a blowtorch.

"Dad, you're still buying cigarettes?"

"Don't know where she finds them." He shrugs, keeping his eyes on the TV.

Mom smiles, takes a deep inhale, and raises her eyebrows impishly at me. She's still here.

"You can sleep here on the hide-a-bed, Barbara. Your mother stays in bed all night now."

"Okay."

Mom nods. I study her face but find no trace of annoyance, despair, or sarcasm. Nine months ago she was walking and chatty, telling jokes and complaining about Dad's golf outings. I suspect she's over-medicated and both Mom and Dad act quite happy about it. But would that explain her speech problems? I count the burn marks on her housedress, over twenty now, half of them covered with iron-on alligator patches.

"Tiger's on the green," Dad calls out. Mom doesn't respond. Her eyes are half closed and a half-inch of quivering ash dangles at the end of her lit cigarette like a sagging gray caterpillar.

"Dad, I think Mom's falling asleep." He picks up a section of newspaper and tosses it on her lap as an ashtray. "But Dad—"

"Yes!" Dad leaps off the couch as Tiger sinks the putt. Mom jerks awake, and the smoldering ash lands on the newspaper. Dad, glued to the set, doesn't notice.

A curl of smoke rises from the newspaper on Mom's lap. "Dad, this is dangerous!" I snatch the newspaper and fold it tight, smothering the lit ash.

"Barbara, that's the sports section," Dad objects.

I shake the folded paper at him. "Dad, this paper is kindling. So why don't you throw some lighter fluid on her too?" True to his unconfrontational nature, he smiles sheepishly. That irresistible Johnny Carson grin that always melts me.

In the kitchen I poke around looking for a better lap-size ashtray. Both my parents are glued to the expansive green on TV, neither concerned with Mom being a fire hazard. I'm relieved we're seeing a neurologist in three days. Could the tranquilizers that Mom's been consuming for over fifty years have reached critical mass? And boom! A spontaneous lobotomy. And why am I the only one in the family who seems concerned? I need to call Patsy.

I finally find a pewter tray, less flammable than the sports page, and place it on Mom's lap as a two-foot ashtray.

"Barbara, w-w-what time is it?" Mom tries to push the chair around but her arms lack the strength to move it.

I glance up at the clock above the sink. "Five after four."

"Good," she grins. "Kkk-Ken, it's happy hour."

. . .

THE NEXT MORNING I head across A1A to sit by the sea before the midday rays become too intense. From the Barbican, my parents' condo, it's only a hop, a skip, and a flip-flop jump over the top of the grassy dune to the sea. Today the water is calm as an aqua mirror, merely ruffled by a lacy foam washing up on the sand. The beach calls me, as always, with its vertical clouds on the horizon standing up like puppies saying, "Look at me!"

My grandma Miller, Mom's mother, moved here when I was twelve, Since then I've been both mesmerized and terrified at the ocean's power. I've watched waves twenty feet high rise and collapse like falling glaciers, turning wood stairways into toothpicks. Not long ago, plastic chairs, used for a beach AA meeting, had been chained together under the Imperial deck. But after last year's storms, not a chair, a chain link, or even a wood deck support—thick as a tree trunk—remained. The entire back deck was carried off into oblivion.

Today the Imperial's beach entrance is still blocked off with yellow tape, so I slip down the dune on my butt to the beach. The sand beach where I spread my towel seems to have shrunk since last year's hurricanes, Frances and Jeanne, and the Lake Worth pier visible two miles south is still broken into three sections. The missing Imperial deck was replaced by large boulders that were trucked in and stacked against a remaining scratch of lawn to keep the four-story condo from tumbling into the sea in future storms. Behind a chicken-wire fence and yellow tape, planks of gold lumber are stacked on the condo's ocean front property. Likely for a new staircase.

Since the millennium, I've noticed we've had more violent, coast-collapsing storms and hurricanes than I can remember in the last three previous decades put together. Once a year, it seems, residents gather to watch monster waves from the high deck of the Hawaiian Motel; it's like watching a natural disaster movie. We leave for cover, however, before hurricane-strength winds hit or our unprotected limbs will be sandblasted—as painful as the biting pepper spray I remember from protests in Madison. Life here in South Palm Beach means constant yellow tape and new wood in a changing milieu of rebirth and impending doom. The stacked, pine-scented yellow wood for the new staircase may not even be granted a season to bleach white in the sun before it's swept off to sea.

After a restful nap on the sand, I sit up noticing how crowded the beach has become in thirty minutes. The sun is bright and hot. I'm glad I got rid of my saggy black one-piece and bought a new "tankini" the clerk called it. "Better for hiding stomach pooch." I look for my sunscreen and catch sight of a Will Smith lookalike on a beach towel a few yards away. He's applying sunscreen but misses the middle of his dark, toned, tattoo-less back.

"Want help?" I offer in my mom voice. He turns around, grins with straight white teeth and taps the free space behind him on his large towel. I get up (less gracefully I'm sure than a woman his own age) and kneel behind him. He hands me his tube.

"Dark skin still burns," I say, rubbing the chalky white cream into his smooth back and firm roux-brown deltoids. We start talking and I'm thinking, so what if I'm flirting, this hunk is way too young for me anyway. Still, chatting with an attractive, obviously educated, thirtyish man is an improvement on what I usually do at the beach—stare at every man with skinny ankles walking on the shore, thinking he looks like Diego. And my new friend is quite willing to listen to my thirty-year marital woes.

"But I'm over him," I tell Will, not totally believing myself.

"Barbara, you should try the Dariana Bran," he suggests.

It sounds fattening. "What is it?"

"Girl, it's a tiki bar in Boynton. On the Intracoastal. Ten minutes from here." I love that he called me girl.

"I warn you. It's an older crowd. A woman like you, you'll get hit on."

That's no warning. That's an invite.

. . .

MAYA CALLS ME ON my laptop while I'm doing pre-appointment stroke research in Dad's room. "Mom, when are you coming home?"

"I put my itinerary on the fridge, Beans."

"I can't find it and I need you here next week. Deanna doesn't have school—"

"Maya, get your Dad to watch her. He's five minutes away."

"He says he's moving to Castro Valley. That's like an hour away."

Castro Valley? I remember that Intellius.com reported a LaShondra Jackson who lived in Castro Valley. I can't think.

"Mom? Mom are you still there?"

After Maya's call I'm more lured than ever to the Banana Boat. I need to get my mind off Diego. Everyone seems to know that he has a new love in his life but me. Some sick part of me is still waiting for it to end. It hurts to think about it. So why not check out the Banana Boat—just for the music, I'll tell Mom. And its major attraction, I've never been there before with Diego. I begin daydreaming of calypso, sailboats, and single white-bearded Hemingway men who smell like the sea, beer, and Coppertone.

On Saturday I'm hesitant to tell Mom I'm going out by myself to hear music at happy hour. Even if she can't talk, she can still raise a thinning eyebrow. I could lie and say I'm going to Boynton Beach Mall, but I'm a lousy liar. Ask Maya.

"Y-y-y-you're going to a bar?" she asks when I tell her. "But you don't d-d-d-drink." Years ago Mom would count my drinks, but after I stopped drinking, now she thinks that not drinking is antisocial. She doesn't like the dishtowel I put over the booze bottles displayed in the kitchen either. No way can I get around it. If I go to a bar alone, she'll disapprove. I admit it, at fifty-six, it sounds a bit trashy.

I leaf through the Palm Beach Post TGIF section looking for a Sunday music listing at the Banana Boat. I find it: Sunday 4 p.m. Reggae. Wonderful! I love reggae.

The Banana Boat is just as I'd imagined. The bar is open on three sides with the sunlit Intracoastal waters glistening beneath the boat dock. Paddle ceiling fans hang from a high tiki roof, and a two-member band, keyboard and guitar, is doing a song about drinking tequila. The circular bar is crowded with all ages, but mostly hard-hat types over forty. I notice they dress their beer cans in brightly colored little foam sweaters. Apparently, the super-handsome Hemingway boat captains are still out at sea, but I only want a little friendly, intelligent conversation spiced with some flirty eye contact, like my beach meeting with Will. I have to be back at the condo at six to cook dinner.

I claim a lone free bar stool, in a short jean skirt and cami, hoping to conjure up some of the nerve of my old college spring-break self—the Barb who had the nerve to go to a bar alone, but rarely left that way. With my glasses tucked in my purse, I focus my blurred eyes on the reggae band playing in the corner. I take a deep breath, inhaling the smells of fried chicken wings, cigarettes, and boat gasoline. *I can do this.*

However, sitting alone feels dangerously close to my worst nightmare— ending up an overly tan prune drunk on a barstool. I tell myself, listening to reggae on a barstool for a half hour won't kill me. I can try to appear approachable, thin, and less married. Besides, I can't feel any lonelier than I do already. Truth is I don't know how to sit at a bar without imagining Diego walking in. A thirty-one-year habit.

I picture Diego, my vacation companion, in his gray beard and black fanny pack, walking up the wood plank ramp to the bar any minute. It hurts. Sitting on that swivel stool, after five agonizing minutes of staring at the band, I consider leaving. Being fifty-six and single feels like a terminal disease. Then a round-bellied, balding, mildly sotted-looking gentleman saddles up to an adjacent bar stool.

"Whatcha drinkin', honey?"

*I'm not your honey.* I point to my soda water and smile, not knowing what else to do. His bloodshot eyes shoot down to my bare lower thighs. He lights up a cigarette, coughs, then offers me one. *Yuck! If I ignore him, he'll leave, right?*

"Sure you don't want nothing, doll?" *Doll? At fifty-six I'm a doll?*

"No thanks. I don't drink." My tongue, on auto-pilot, is ready to say, "I'm waiting for my husband."

"You don't drink?" He looks astonished. "You in one of them recovered programs?"

"Sort of." I hope saying "sort of" combines enough honesty, anonymity, and vagueness to dodge further questions.

"I'm fine with soda water, thank you." *Please go away.*

I forgot the old adage, "To meet a prince, you have to go through a lot of frogs." Why am I here? I'd rather go home and watch spaghetti boil.

I turn to go and a clean-shaven man one stool away throws me a smile. He has a tan, rugged, age-appropriate face. And doesn't appear to have any missing teeth. Collared white shirt, no stains. A body that does not appear to be horribly misshapen, hair in all the right places. Nothing wrong with him. So I smile back.

Before I know it he offers his hand to dance.

I head to the makeshift wood plank dance floor, then turn to face him. Oh dear, I'm a good three inches taller than he is.

"I'm Jerry," he says, not in the least bothered by my towering height. And I have to admit, he's a good dancer for a white guy. Back in the day (circa 1970s) women didn't dance with shorter men, because we embarrassed them. So what happened? I think it was Tom Cruise.

After three dances we've joined a conga line snaking around the bar singing, "Olay-Olaaay. Olay-Olaaay," and "Hot! Hot! Hot!" Though I'm not sure what I'm singing, this is fun. And two hours slip by with Jerry. We talk at a waterside table about his roofing business, his two teen kids, and his wife who died in a car accident.

"When we moved into the big house in Boca," he says, "I think my teenagers scared the neighbors." So nice to have delinquent kids in common. "It's a big, four-bedroom with a large tile entryway. That's where we put the pool table."

There's something boyish, self-effacing, and shy about Jerry and I like the way his gray-blue eyes look at me as though he thinks I'm attractive. Then Jerry leans over and kisses me. I'm surprised but I don't pull away. My Tropicana Rose lipstick smudges his thin lips and makes him look like a little boy who was playing with his mother's makeup. I touch the left side of my mouth and he swipes his, smearing the lipstick even more. He shrugs and grins impishly, which makes me want to kiss him again—a sweet, innocent, thank-you-for being-here kiss.

As I drive away from the Banana Boat, I'm certain I'll never see Jerry again. He probably lost the yellow Post-it with my phone number that I stuck to his forehead. Just as well, I wouldn't know what to do if he invited me to his Boca home anyway. Ed felt like seeing a friend and I haven't read the *Dating for Dummies* handbook yet. I can't imagine sex with another man—a man who puts a pool table in the entryway. Definitely bad feng shui.

Diego and I had been separated for ten months but we were still legally married with no divorce papers in the works due to my reticence and Diego's fear of lawyers. So technically, I thought, if I was with another man, then wouldn't I be cheating on Diego? But what's the point of cheating on him in Florida if he'd never know about it? I suspected that I only dated Ed to leave his picture in my bedroom window to make Diego jealous.

Face it, I'm a one-man woman, Diego's woman—never had an orgasm with anyone else—and I'll likely stay that way. I just want a man to buy me dinner, look into my eyes and tell me I'm beautiful. Is that so wrong? Joanna would say yes.

. . .

MOM HAS A BATTERY OF tests on Monday, but now we have to wait a week for the results. I'm convinced that she had a small stroke and her chatty self will come back. But worries about Mom are interrupted by thoughts of Jerry's light gray-blue eyes and his lip smudged with Tropicana-rose lipstick. I'm aroused in a way I don't expect. Sensations rise from deep within me like purple crocus heads pushing their way through spring's damp earth.

The following Wednesday I've just finished swimming thirty laps, and Dad appears at the sliding glass door. He holds out the phone. "It's for you."

*Jerry.*

Friday night Jerry takes me to dinner at Two Georges restaurant, across the waterway from the Banana Boat. This time I wear flats. We sit at a pier table surrounded by sparkly moonlit water while the thrum of reggae drifts over the canal. Dining outside with Jerry on a warm April night feels like a luxurious dream come true. My skirt rises to mid-thigh, and my bare legs stretch out long, tan and smooth under the linen tablecloth. Feeling this pretty feels unreal, as if I've entered some strange time warp and I'm twenty-five again.

Jerry looks handsome across from me with his thick sandy hair, a ruddy tan, and a clean-shaven but sun-weathered face. I want to drink in the blue of his eyes, but with my glasses in my purse, I have to settle for a blurred twinkle. Jerry wears shorts and his shirt is worn Florida style, not tucked in. Here I am, seated across from a man without a beard, and I feel like I want him to kiss me. We're laughing through dinner about silly things. He's telling me that he thought he lost my phone number the morning after we met.

"I felt like such an idiot," he says, "when my friend tells me the next morning I'm walking around with a Post-It on my head."

I have to chuckle. After dinner, Jerry drives to the Key Lime House for drinks. He's so open I'm learning more about him. He's fifty-four, recently widowed, and he drives barefoot. His roofing business is booming after the previous year's hurricanes. At the bar, his cell rings. He glances at it but doesn't pick up.

"It's Tiffany," he says and turns off his phone. He tells me she's engaged — to someone other than Jerry. "We just get together for sex," he says casually as if it's his dry cleaner calling for a shirt pick-up. I'm shocked, not sure if I'm shocked more at Tiffany's behavior or at Jerry for telling me. Men never said that in 1970. Another new rule? The *friends with benefits* rule?

"I'm so sorry about your wife," I say changing the subject. Jerry pushes his empty vodka and grapefruit to the barmaid for a refill. "How long ago, exactly?"

"Four years." He half-smiles but his soft, blurry eyes still look sad.

Four years seems like an eternity. Certainly in four years I'll be over Diego, won't I? But then I have the disadvantage of having a living, breathing husband.

After a few more rounds, soda water and lime for me, I picture myself in Jerry's house, making dinner for him in his new granite counter-topped kitchen — a Cobb salad maybe or a Niçoise, baked potatoes, whipped chocolate mousse for dessert, and he'll barbecue a marinated mahi or chicken.

Maybe I'll come to Florida when school lets out and we can barbecue on his pool patio all summer long. Maybe he'll fall in love with me and he'll want me to move in with him. A blended bicoastal family—our kids bonding over their rebel attitudes and pot-smoking.

Since I asked Jerry his age, I feel like I owe him mine. Being three years older isn't that awful, is it? "You want to know how old I am?" I tilt my head to look flirty.

"Age isn't important," he says, watching football on the overhead screen. *What a sweet gentleman.* I look into his blue eyes. What is it like to make love to a blue-eyed man, I wonder. To be in the arms of a blue-eyed man, to feel loved, adored, and filled up by him. And—just at that moment of release—to open my eyes, look up, and sink into a deep sea of adoring blue. And let go.

I realize I'm falling for this funny guy who measures my height in flats.

We drive home to my parents' condo and we're standing outside the front door when Jerry makes his move. My lips feel stiff as hard clay at first, then soften to his touch. The intrusion of a wet tongue, an unfamiliar tongue, not Diego's tongue, takes some getting used to, but gradually I stop thinking about an invasive wet, foreign object in my mouth, and focus on other sensations going on below my neck. *Not bad. Not awful.*

I invite him inside the condo knowing it's well past my parents' bedtime. I'm not desperate to have sex. But I am desperate to have feelings for a man again.

When we enter the dimly lit condo, the hide-a-bed has already been unfolded in the center of the living room. I know Dad, sweetheart that he is, pulled it out for me. The inviting bed is a logical place to lie back and continue. The touch of Jerry's hands in my hair and on my bare back feels magnified a hundred times over. I ache to lie next to a man and to be held again. I'm a starving woman and Jerry is one big gourmet cheeseburger in paradise.

He lifts my hair off the nape of my neck and pulls it back slightly so that my lips lift to his. My body yields to him; I'm being handled, clothes pulled off, and lifted into position—a bit rougher than the old routine—but I like it.

*Don't stop.*

We're rolled together like two half-clothed enchiladas. I'm on my back, topless when I notice my breasts have fallen off the sides of my chest. *When did that happen?* I quickly turn over to my side to shape them into some semblance of cleavage.

Jerry whispers, "Just a minute." He gets up as the mattress squeaks. In the window light I watch him pull out a small square wrapper from his pants pocket. Diego didn't use condoms. With his back to me, I witness this strange new male ritual. This plastic square was as foreign to me, as if Jerry had pulled Spock ears out of his pocket. Jerry bites the plastic casing, and fumbles with its contents while I lie back. What if I look a lot older than Tiffany? I should have bought new lacy bikini underwear, but instead I roll down the elastic of my granny panties below my navel. Did he expect a flatter stomach? Are my breasts too small and squishy?

Jerry turns around, still in his open shirt. Then I see it. How could I not look at it? Pale and white like a bratwurst, a tight rubber glove around it and there's this little sack thing hanging at the end of it—like a four-year-old who doesn't know how to put his socks on. Jerry quickly slides under the sheets. I'm still thinking about what's under there. It wasn't a totally erect bratwurst, as I saw it, more halfway between a cooked brat and a miniature slinky. Maybe I don't turn him on enough.

Getting down to business, my hand under the sheet begins to stroke, but I don't want to go near that weird flappy thing at the end. I'm used to Diego's smooth, pink velvety tip with its sweet innocent slit, rounded, clean, and freshly powdered as a baby's bottom. But Jerry's penis feels greasy, as if it had been shrink-wrapped in Saran Wrap and dipped in Crisco.

Jerry's talking in a low voice, joking around, affectionately and inaccurately calling his penis "Peanut." His hand slides into third base. I relax into his hand moves and I'm pleasantly surprised that I feel something. I'm actually turned on. Is my vagina blindfolded and assuming the man touching me is Diego? Is she a lost puppy who will come to any stranger who calls? And he's calling her, c'mon girl, faster and faster, beckoning her and then, amazingly, that puppy comes.

*Oh, my!* And comes again. *Oh, my Lord.*

Three times, I stop counting. I half want him to keep going but I'm on fire down there, out of breath, my legs jerking uncontrollably. I'm going out of my head.

What if this doesn't stop? Like labor pains that come one on top of another. Could that happen with orgasms? A woman could go crazy? Couldn't she?

Squeeeak. Squeeeak-eek.

"Barb, Shhhhh!"

I don't realize how loud the hide-a-bed is squeaking.

"Oh, sorry," Embarrassed, I listen for signs of Mom and Dad stirring. But there's only the hush of waves across A1A coming through a cracked window. Jerry cranes his neck to glance down the hallway.

I whisper that Mom is safely bedridden and Dad can't hear due to the loud pool pump outside his bedroom window. Besides, my Dad sleeps in the nude and it's unlikely he'll come snooping down the hall looking like an octogenarian at a toga party.

Once Jerry is assured, I slide my hand down Jerry's flat abdomen. I want him to finish the job.

"Better not tonight, sweetheart." He moves my hand away.

"I'm fine with that." I grin feeling gratified and fulfilled. I'm already relaxing into a perfectly content cool-down. *Nice. Real nice.*

"Next time," he says, "we'll stay at my house. Stay the night." He kisses my forehead.

He rolls over, removes the rubber, and puts on his pants. Did he put it in his pocket? I hope he didn't toss it in the wastebasket next to the couch where Dad throws his bill envelopes and dental floss.

Jerry climbs back into bed, pants on, and puts his arm around me. His arm hair has been bleached blonde in the sun and I like his maleness wrapped around me. I roll over to face him grinning, looking into his eyes. Without my glasses they're smudgy indigo pools, and, darn it, it's too dark to swim in the blue of them.

"I guess you don't mind me being tall."

"Why should I mind, baby? Lying down you're only nine inches."

I laugh.

"You know," I confess. "That's never happened to me before, not like that. Not that many times." I thought the Big O women talk about meant one big one and that the multiple orgasm thing was a myth. I bet my program friends don't know about this. He listens to my stunned reaction and glowing praise over his Herculean digital performance. He grins up at my parents' popcorn ceiling with his hands behind his thick head of hair, looking rather pleased with himself.

That night I felt like I was nineteen all over again. I had made it past that first-time awkward sex—well, halfway—after all, it was Jerry's decision that "peanut" hadn't been called up for duty. As far as I could tell, there wasn't any equipment problem. And Jerry didn't appear to mind my breasts sliding around like Jell-O. I can only guess that it was the parents-in-the-next-room issue that prevented Jerry from consummating the deal. But really, I didn't miss act two. I felt sublimely satisfied. And very proud of myself.

Perhaps I was so unexpectedly aroused that night because Jerry was new and cute, and I thought he liked me. Or because I had nicknamed my former

Latin lover Speedy Gonzales. Lorraine would say I was on vacation and felt free to let my hair and my granny pants down.

Or maybe it happened with Jerry because I really *was* cheating on Diego, and it felt damn good.

. . .

THE FOLLOWING MONDAY MORNING we see Dr. Aravinda, Mom's assigned neurologist, to discuss her test results.

"There's no evidence in the CAT scan that your mother had a stroke," he tells us. He bends down to Mom's wheelchair. "Jeannette, you must be happy that your daughter's here to take care of you." She looks at him and then up at me.

"Yyyyes." She smiles at me. On my last visit she suggested I stay in a motel.

"But Mr. Buehler, it looks like your wife has some dementia."

My dad, who I feel should be addressed as Dr. Buehler, doesn't react.

"What caused her to suddenly stop talking? Maybe it's the tranquilizers?" I ask.

"There's a lot about the brain that we don't know. But you say she's sleeping well. Are you feeling happy, Jeannette?"

Mom looks at him for a moment, her brain stuck in slow mo.

"Yyyyes." She smiles with the denture Dad made her in place. Mom's always been very gracious in public.

The doctor stands up, signaling the appointment is over. Dad stands too but I remain seated. I tell the doc about Mom sleeping most of the day and he suggests her psychiatrist lower her tranquilizer dosage.

Dad starts to wheel Mom out but I still want answers. Maybe some strokes aren't detected by a CAT scan? Maybe we need a second opinion.

"C'mon, Dr. Barbara. He has other patients to see." I hate when Dad calls me Dr. Barbara. Dad is already out the door. He looks concerned, but not surprised. Reluctantly I follow. I have to follow his lead, after all he's her caretaker, I'm only a visitor here for ten days. And if Mom had an undetectable stroke, then her speech should return slowly. I bet by the time I visit in the summer her normal catty sarcasm will be back. I miss my old mom.


Don't interfere," Patsy tells me over the phone. "If Dad doesn't want a second opinion that's his choice." I call my brother Bob in Los Angeles, who hasn't seen either of our parents in ten years. "Bob, you should really try to make it to Florida to see Mom. She's not doing well." But he says he's been on disability since he lost his Microsoft certification teaching job, and he's having money problems.

To give Dad a break, I take Mom out in the afternoons to the Boynton Beach Mall, the Dune Deck for a chocolate shake, and her weekly appointment at the Neptune hair salon. Yesterday I noticed at the mall that other shoppers would run ahead of us to hold doors open for Mom's chair. "There you go, sweetheart," they'd say, grinning at her.

"Th-th-thank you." Mom smiled and waved as if she were a queen on a prom float. The more time I spend with her, the more I see Dad's point. For the first time in years, Mom seems content, not manic go-go-go happy but serene. I get why he doesn't want to rock the boat. And I have to admit as I wheel Mom in for her salon appointment that we're actually having a good time. The salon girls call her Betty White, because she resembles her. After her comb-out and spray, I go to get Dad's station wagon and Mom waits outside in the shade of the entrance. Watching through the car window, I watch Mom's wheelchair inching down the sidewalk. She's using the heels of her Velcro strap shoes on the concrete to edge forward. *What in the world?*

She glances up and down the walkway to see if anyone is watching, then sidles alongside a tall metal ashtray. I watch as she picks up two half-smoked butts, blows off the sand, and places them inside in her yellow flowered purse. *Ahhh. That's where she gets them.*

As I pull to the curb, she sits demure and proper in her chair, every white curl in place, hands folded over her purse and a slight smile on her lips.

. . .

THE DAY OF MY DEPARTURE I'm finding myself reluctant to leave my parents. Mom's speech hasn't improved and Dad is having trouble with his eyesight. "Sometimes I can't see the ball on the tee. Black spots. Floaters," he says. I suggest that he see an ophthalmologist—I had my own eye surgeon in fifth grade—but I doubt he'll go unless his floaters become a threat to his golf game. And there's Jerry. We never did spend a night at his Boca pool table home but he did say to call him if I come back in the summer.

Dad tries to lift my fifty-pound suitcase into the station wagon; I notice he's wobbling. His balance is off. "A little neuropathy in my legs," he says. I realize now that I took Diego's baggage handling for granted. And airports are suddenly lonely places. All around me travelers are hugging, kissing, or on their phones saying, "I love you. I'll call you tonight." At the curb, women in heels watch as their men hoist their bags. I lift my own bags from the car. I used to be one of those women.

On the plane, as the aqua sea and Palm Beach sand pull away from me, I realize something terrible. In three years Dad will be ninety. And Mom's only a year behind him. None of my grandparents lived to ninety; in fact, both my grandfathers died early in their sixties with heart problems. What if my parents die at ninety? That means, even if I see them twice a year—oh, my Lord—I only have eight visits left. That's impossible. That's totally unacceptable! Why, why, why didn't this occur to me before? Mom always talked about dying, saying she wants "to be with Jesus." But we grew used to it. But this new possibility, this reality of both of them leaving me hits me hard. *Dad can't die.* And if Mom goes too, then I'll be an orphan.

Out the plane window a cotton bed of clouds blankets the central Florida swamps. I vow to visit more often. Up from my usual once or twice a year to three or even four times at least. And why stay only two weeks? That was Diego's rule. He griped, saying, "I'm not going to be stuck at home with the kids while you're out gallivanting on the beach." I don't even know what gallivanting is, but I'm sure I wasn't doing it. But now that he's gone, let the gallivanting begin. Why live by his rules? I vow to return to Florida in a few months when school is out.

# CHAPTER FOURTEEN
## SPILLED MILK

APRIL RAINS CONTINUE IN CALIFORNIA. I walk across the kitchen in my moccasins, making sticky sounds on the linoleum. It has been several weeks since I returned from Florida, and I'm back to the usual morning drudgery: let Lola out, pick up Maya's stuff, and avoid the garage. Diego was supposed to move his furniture out while I was in Florida, but his dresser, with clothes, desk, and cedar closet is just the same as before I left. Part of me is annoyed and another part of me thinks that maybe he's keeping his options open. *Don't think about that.* Remembering Jerry's lipstick-smudged face works as my talisman against plunging into fatal optimism where Diego is concerned. I pick up the house, gathering Maya's jacket, high heels, a hair spray can, hair ties, BART tickets, and a Victoria's Secret bag. I stack the items next to the pile I left at her bedroom door yesterday.

Today, I won't fight with Maya. During my Wednesday therapy session, when I complained about Maya, Lorraine claimed again that I was angry. She says the reason I had a good time over spring break was because I was relaxed and I didn't take my anger with me. I told her, sure I get ruffled at Maya occasionally, but not angry enough to want Maya and Deanna to move out. And I take the antidepressants and Lithium, so why, I wonder, is it so important to Lorraine that I acknowledge feeling angry? Yes, I cut myself (Lorraine says that's anger directed inward) and yes, I attacked a woman at Big O Tires. But that was nearly five months ago.

Maya drags herself into the kitchen dressed in sweats to drive Deanna to school.

"G'morning, Maya." No answer. Deanna, at the table, pours Cheerios into a bowl and some O's spill and roll onto the floor. No big deal. Maya taps my freshly filled coffee pot with her index finger ten times, making her count an even number. Then she dumps my remaining decaf down the sink.

"Sweetheart, I wanted that–"

"Can't I even make a damn cup of coffee in this house?"

I walk my tepid coffee over to the microwave, my moccasins crunching Cheerios.

"I heard you and Jesse yelling on the phone at three a.m." When Diego and I fought, we kept reasonable hours.

"Well, at least I *have* a boyfriend."

I decide to hit back, breaking my rule not to talk about Deanna's father in her presence. "Yeah, a boyfriend who calls you the C word and hasn't paid child support for nine years."

"What's the C word?" Deanna asks.

I can't say the C word. Even Diego, who possesses an impressive bilingual repertoire of swear words, never sank that low. The C-U-N-T word might belong to Maya's generation, but not to mine. And I refuse to allow that word spoken in my house, not even over the phone at three a.m.

"What's the C-word, Mama?" Deanna dribbles milk down her chin onto the table.

"Don't talk with your mouth full," Maya reprimands.

"Coochie," I tell my granddaughter, "and don't you ever say it."

Maya narrows her eyes. "Mo-om, don't tell her that!"

Deanna's eyes widen like she just discovered a contraband beer bottle hidden under the couch. The dishes are piled high in the sink. I search in the cold dishwater for the blue sponge. It feels like the house has become Maya's ashtray—a dump littered with Coke cans, dried ice cream bowls, spilled popcorn, and Taco Bell wrappers.

"Before you leave this morning, put your dishes in the dishwasher, okay?" I wipe the milk spots on the table and Deanna's chin. Maya doesn't answer me.

"Gramma, what's a coochie?" Deanna's round face turns from me to her mother.

"A private part. And I said don't say it."

Deanna grins.

"You're crazy, Mom. You act really crazy."

I'm not *really* angry at Maya, just annoyed. I've weathered worse. She's likely upset that she lost her job. And she fought with Jesse but at least I heard no mention of sending Deanna to Seattle.

"Now I know why Dad left."

Ouch.

She turns on the Grind 'n Brew and its blades screech like knives being sharpened.

*Don't escalate.* I remember when Diego talked about his men's anger group: walk away from a heated confrontation when you reach level three. Remove yourself from the conflict. Take the high road.

I retreat into my room and lock my door. I'm already at a three; okay, maybe a five. But I know how to control my temper. Maya, she sounds like a seven or eight; she's already out of control. Diego needs to tell Maya to respect her mother. It's 8:21 a.m. Diego would be up by now. I reach for the phone and stare at the Rolodex card with Diego's number in it. Though I've used his number often over the last eleven months, I've made a point not to memorize it, because it slows down the process of having to call him. If I call he'll want to know everything that happened: what she said, what I said. And he'd be understanding, trying to help, asking me, "Barbara, what would you like me to do?" in his same comforting voice. Even when he was lying he'd be tender and caring. That's the worst part.

I don't need Diego's help. I can brave this out myself. Maybe Lorraine is right about Maya needing a place of her own.

No noise on the other side of the door. I hope Maya and Deanna have already left for school. Cautiously, I step into the kitchen. The sink, still high with Maya's dinner dishes, is now topped with her coffee cup. Deanna's cereal bowl filled with milk is still on the table. The bowl glares back, mocking me. Deanna appears in the hallway wearing her pink backpack, and Maya is ushering her out the front door.

"Maya, *please* put your dishes in the dishwasher!" Deanna turns and sticks her tongue out at me, siding with her mother. I pick up Deanna's dripping blue Cheerios bowl off the table, and follow them to the doorway.

"Maya, you come back here!" The screen door slams inches from my nose, sending cold milk down my arm into the sleeve of my bathrobe. Outside, the cool air slaps my face, and my moccasins sink in as I cross the muddy soaked grass. Maya and Deanna are already seated in her Sebring in the driveway. I'm holding the quivering cereal bowl.

"Damn it, Maya. I'm not Deanna's mother."

"You're crazy, Mom! No wonder Dad left you for whoever her name is!" The remark squeezes through her closing car window. Maya guns her engine and takes off. The bowl of milk at the end of my shaking arm sloshes like a churning sea.

"And don't come back!" I yell. My arm jerks back, flinging the bowl across the driveway towards the ivy. But milk flies up like a traveling white cloud. My bad aim and a northern breeze causes it to rain down on the hood of my Ford. White tears run down the car door.

The empty spot in the driveway, where Maya parks, is dotted with black spots from a rogue olive tree Diego should have cut down years ago. Those olives splatter the drive like ink pellets. I stand paralyzed, trying not to notice Bunny, my duck-obsessed neighbor, as she watches us from across the street.

I can't look at Bunny. Please just walk away and disappear behind your neatly trimmed hedge. I hope their house, with its For Sale sign, will sell quickly, and a new younger couple will move in—a nice family that doesn't know about us.

For a second my eyes meet Bunny's worried look. but she's kind enough not to offer a single patronizing word. And kind enough to go back inside. I grab the sponge from the kitchen to clean off the milk before it dries.

Outside I wipe the hood, but the small blue dish sponge doesn't cut it. I'm wringing it out repeatedly onto the driveway's black leaves, which have rotted into near dirt after a year's accumulation. I can't use the damn hose either because Diego attached some complicated white box digital timer to water his citrus and I can't figure it out. My efforts only coat the hood of my aqua sedan with a dirty milky film.

This is all Diego's fault. He spoils Maya. He pays for her car and the insurance. Damn it, he's the one who deserted this family and left me without a damn hose. My arm flings the tattered sponge in the air—a lone blue kite against a vast white nothing sky.

"I hate you, God!" I scream at the sky. "Why did you do this to MEEEEE?"

Lorraine was right. I was angry. Not just angry, enraged.


But on that spilled-milk day when I told Maya, "Don't come back," I didn't a hundred percent mean it. Or maybe I did. To me, Maya, at twenty-six, still acted like a sixteen-year-old angry with her mother. I realized she couldn't break up with Deanna's father no matter what he called her over the phone—and her left cheek developed a red rash from having her cell phone plastered on it. And she lost her medical assisting job, a decent paying position, one she had been certified for and had worked hard to keep.

I wasn't the ideal person to live with, either. Even with an exciting new career as a writing teacher in the Oakland school system, fear still rumbled: fear of divorce, fear of being forced to sell the house, fear of Maya leaving and taking Deanna, and at the very bottom of the black pit lurked the fear of never finding another man to love me—fear of being alone forever. Although Joanna prodded, "Have you filed for divorce yet?", I prolonged the separation. Even an unraveled, rat-chewed thread of a marriage was better than none at all.

I don't believe either Maya or I were happy living together then, and I suspect that our conflicts had more to do with our similarities than with our differences. Maya knew Jesse was being abusive. Diego admitted years ago that he was a rage-aholic, a curious admission that combined a mix of embarrassment, pride, and machismo. Yet with five years of work in his men's anger group, I'd always wondered why he skipped remorse and apologies. In program it's called the ninth step.

In retrospect, I see that Maya and I were both under the not-so-nice thumbs of men who didn't live with us any more—and we were both afraid to let go. Two angry bitches lived in the house and we turned on each other viciously, like caged tigers. But fights with Maya, like flash storms, would end quickly.

Within a day, we'd be back in my big bed together watching a two-hour Sunday special on Michael Jackson's nose. And I have to admit that Maya is the caretaker kid. If I end up bedridden like my mother, Maya will be the one to buy the Depends. She's compassionate, but she can also be the most vicious—just like her Dad. Not comfortable, but familiar.

Maya takes an hour to drive Deanna to school on spilled milk day, but then her car pulls into the drive. She enters, squirts soap into her hands, and turns on the sink faucet. I come up behind her and wrap my arms around her shoulders.

"Honey, I'm sorry."

She doesn't turn around.

Maya stares down into the cereal bowl that tops the mound of dishes in the sink. Her streaked gold hair closes around her face like a curtain. "Beanzo, I'm so sorry I said don't come back. I didn't mean it." I bury my nose into the clean apple scent of her hair, kiss the back of her head, and hang on. Finally she says, "Mom, all my friends are dying."

"Now who?" I turn her around. Last year one of Mimi's high school friends was shot.

"Quinton," she sobs. "Miguel's friend. I just heard. He died last night of an overdose."

# CHAPTER FIFTEEN
## MIMI

"Did you hear about that boy that died?" Gail asks at lunch. "You know he was one of our own. Lafayette High School. An overdose. Shame."

"My son knew him," Linda adds somberly. Linda's son Bryon is living under the same Walnut Creek bridge where Miguel lived five years ago.

"He was in Mimi's class." I can't say any more. Not here. I can't tell my friends what Maya told me about Miguel and Quinton.

"Well, we say using leads to jails, institutions, and death," Gail says, then she asks the waiter to tell us the soup *du jour*. "White bean chicken," he says.

I keep seeing Quinton's boyish pink cheeks and hooded eyes in our side yard on Easter. He and Miguel hushed up when they saw me coming. I want to think that they were only hiding a joint from me but I didn't smell any skunky smoke or see any snack-size baggies. But later Maya told me that Miguel had sold him drugs. That scared me. She wasn't sure if he had done it recently. Still, I couldn't stop thinking about it. What if it was my son who sold him the fatal dose? What if I run into Quinton's mother at a meeting?

I try to look happy and recovered at the long wooden table with my friends but my turning stomach doesn't match my face. Miguel will go to Quinton's funeral, I know it. He cares. One Easter when he was only eight, he sat in his top bunk weeping uncontrollably. "Why did Jesus have to die, Mom?" he asked. I don't remember what I said. Probably some sanctioned Catholic answer. I hope I didn't say something blaming like, "He died for your sins."

Miguel will take Quinton's death hard. Real hard. It scares me.

Jails, institutions, and death. AA teaches that's where addictions lead. Miguel already knocked out two out of three. I'm not naïve. I look over at Linda and Ellen thinking that our kids are like war casualties. A drug war is killing our children.

"So Barb, do you want to split the eggplant melt and a Niçoise salad again?" Gail asks.

I decline and order a cup of soup. Maybe Miguel had nothing to do with it. It was likely a combination of things. I may never know the truth.

Carrie pulls some business cards out of her purse. They read CARRIE'S HOME SALON with a roller brush drawing. We each take one.

"I did them myself," she says sheepishly.

"Very professional," I say, complimenting her ingenuity more than the design. These days everyone thinks they're a graphic designer.

. . .

MIMI SHOWS UP AT THE door with three garbage bags stuffed with all her belongings.

"I'm staying, Mom. Costco's letting me transfer to the bakery in Danville."

"Really?" I'm surprised. "You're moving home?" I give her an enthusiastic momma-bear hug.

"Mom, chill."

When Mimi left for San Diego, not long after high school, my youngest seemed barely grown. Mimi was a late bloomer compared to Maya, who *started* at twelve and gave birth at sixteen. But at twenty-three, in summer shorts with blonde streaks in her long curly chestnut hair, Mimi had grown curves in all the right places. After watching her sister grow up too fast and her brother spend his teens in rehab or under a bridge, I think Mimi decided to put off puberty. The box of Kotex I placed under her sink stayed resolutely wrapped in plastic until she was halfway through high school. Then she left home right after graduation, despite her father begging her not to move to San Diego, a twelve-hour drive away. And now she moves back home, leaving her junior college studies and a three-year boyfriend in the dust. That's who Mimi is. Strong-willed. While Maya and I cling to men like pit bulls with lipstick, Mimi packs up and moves on. No regrets.

Mimi drags a stuffed garbage bag down the hall while Maya and Deanna and I parade behind. Lola brings up the rear. I notice Mimi's shortie boy shorts—her backside reads, "Per—fect"—one syllable for each perfectly rounded bun. But I don't dare say anything.

"What about Dan?" Maya asks. Dan is, or was, Mimi's boyfriend, a Marine first responder in Iraq who earned the yellow ribbon I tied to the olive tree in the front yard.

"It's over." Mimi shrugs. She looks at Maya, then at me, and says emphatically, "I don't need a man." A sentence never heard aloud in our house before.

At the end of the hall Mimi pauses to assess her bedroom options. She stares into Maya's room, where she spent nine years. The floor is blanketed with discarded clothing, shopping bags, Taco Bell wrappers, and scattered beauty products. The smaller bedroom on the left has a bunk bed piled on top with Deanna's stuffed animals. The walls are covered with Britney Spears photos. Mimi turns the corner towards the third bedroom down the hall. "I'll stay in Dad's old office," she announces,

"You mean the guest room," I correct.

"Fine."

"Your dad remodeled the garage into his office/gym last year," I remind her.

"Get over it Mom," Mimi says without a trace of compassion.

"That's what I tell her, Mimi." Maya plops on the new guest bedroom comforter I bought when my brother stayed for Christmas. "Mom's still in love with Dad."

"No, I'm not." They're ganging up on me already. Maya and Deanna in the house I can manage. But three girls feels slightly threatening.

"It's wonderful to have you home, Meems. What would you like for dinner? We'll celebrate."

"Sarah and Amber and I are going to kick it. Wanna come, Maya?"

"No thanks."

"So you're going to let that chauvinistic dickwad control you from Seattle. How many years now? Ten?"

"Nine," Maya whispers.

"Douche."

Maya unties Mimi's black plastic bag and peers into it. "Hey, that's my jacket." She pulls out her ice-blue satin jacket. "I wondered what happened to this."

Deanna, unfazed by hearing her father called a dickwad douche, scuttles past me to sit next to her aunt Mimi. Mimi circles her tan arm around the niece that she helped raise for five years and Deanna snuggles in closer.

"I just don't feel like going out tonight, that's all," Maya says as she continues to pick through Mimi's clothes. "Tomorrow is Quinton's funeral."

. . .

THE NEXT DAY MIMI is stretched out in my new pool chair. Her long, curly brown hair is bundled on top in thick knots and the smell of coconut suntan lotion wafts through the warm spring air. I sit down on the bricks circling the fire pit to share some sunshine with Mimi. Through the glass doors I see Deanna sitting with crossed legs on the sofa with Lola. She's eating popcorn and watching *Benji* for the tenth time.

"You're not going to the funeral, Mimi?" I ask. "Maya said Miguel will be there."

"No big whoop. I didn't really hang with Quint in high school."

Maya stands near the patio doors as if she wants us to hear her phone conversation with Jesse. "Why are you saying that to me? Why? ... don't you swear at me ... that's disgusting."

I sigh. "Maybe I should go inside and talk to Maya."

"Just ignore it, Mom. Y'know when I was fifteen, all I wanted in the whole world was to break her and Jesse up. You didn't see the worst of it, Mom. I had to live in the same room with her the whole time I was in high school. Jesse would say this crap to her on the phone and she'd freak out and slap her cheeks and pull out her hair. Made me sick." Mimi shakes her head. "No pride."

"I hate you, Jesse, you know that. I really *really* hate you." Now Maya's shouting behind the glass. Neither Deanna nor Lola appears to notice.

"You and Dad were so worried about Miguel and Maya, you never thought about me, Mom."

"We did what we could, Meems." I know that's no excuse.

Maya's dark silhouette paces behind the sliding door. "I don't care what you say, Jesse. I'm going to the funeral, my friends will be there .... Go ahead. Break up with me. I don't fucking care .... Don't say that to me."

"In high school it was like such a big friggin' deal just to go anywhere with Maya. Once we went to Target and she like always had to wear long pants, and she couldn't wear makeup or shorts. He thought she was going to meet other guys, that's so sick, but we were only going to Target for diapers. But we had to hurry because if we took more than an hour then he'd think she was *cheating on him*. And see, I wanted to look at lip liners. So I stalled. I did it deliberately 'cause I really wanted Jesse to get all pissed off." Mimi chuckles. "They fought for five days over the phone over that."

I realize Maya has left the living room. No noise. Just Benji barking. But I don't go inside, enjoying the silence of Mimi's company and the coolness of the bricks against my thighs. Mimi was the good one. No trouble. It's true, with all Miguel and Maya's drama, Mimi wasn't on our radar.

After some minutes I say, "Meems, I'm sorry." And I'm sorry that she has to come back home and see that nothing has changed with her sister. It's sad that Jesse won't let Maya go places and she puts up with it. She turned down our vacation to Hawaii because Jesse wouldn't allow it. He won't let her go to the funeral either. I don't hear any more yelling so I picture Maya in my bed crying like Cinderella who can't go to the ball.

"I gave up on Maya years ago," Mimi says. "'Go ahead, Maya,' I told her, 'you wanna self-destruct like a crack-head, and go crazy over that douche, and make yourself bald, go right ahead. Cut yourself and be miserable; I don't care anymore.' I just started laughing at her. See, Mom, it's called reverse psychology."

Mimi takes one college psychology course, and now she's Dr. Phil.

Maya slides open the glass door. Mimi's eyebrows arch in surprise. This is not the Maya we know. This Maya looks stately wearing makeup and a black dress that I suspect she borrowed from her friend Paige. Not tight-fitting but sleeveless and sleek. The hem slightly above the knee. Maya hasn't shown knees, or arms, her pretty tan arms, outside the house in years. Nine years.

"Sweetheart, you look gorgeous!"

"I hate him. I hate that scumbag."

Even with eyeliner and mascara I see the redness in her eyes.

"I don't care what he says; I'm going to the funeral! That loser, white bread, troll of the earth!"

Mimi's finger nods at her sister. "You're rockin,' Maya."

. . .

MY PURSE SITS ON MY COMPUTER chair next to the bed. Inside my wallet is the torn piece of cardboard with Jerry's phone number written in pencil. "Call me when you're coming back to Florida," he said after our night on the hide-a-bed. "Probably in July or August," I told him. Setting the phone on my lap, I reach over, pull out the wallet and finger the soft sensual folds of leather, then open them. The scrap of cardboard with his number is still there. But is it kosher to call a man in May to confirm a date for August? I put the phone back on its charger.

I make a decision. The kind of decision that might give me a future.

I've decided to go blonde. Really blonde. All the way blonde. Not just streaks. I visit Annette in Berkeley, who has been my stylist at Peter Thomas for years. She has gone platinum too, and we joke about being the only two blondes in Berkeley. There, in the seat of feminism, being a bleached blonde is practically antisocial. To view blondes en masse, you have to drive through the Caldecott tunnel to the burbs like Lafayette, where I live. There, moms with blonde ponytails poking out of baseball caps can be observed grazing in clusters at Starbucks and Peet's before and after school bells.

After color, cut, and blow-dry I put on my glasses in the dressing room and holy cow! I'm blonde-blonde. Platinum blonde. I squint at myself in the bathroom mirror thinking these glasses have to go too. I could get rid of the glasses with Lasik but then the bags under my eyes would become more obvious. Bags that appeared after months of crying over Diego. At checkout I splurge and add on a private-label conditioner, Boost Light, to my tab, and pick up a new thirty-dollar red maxi-size roller hairbrush.

*I'm worth it.*

I'm nervous about under-eye plastic surgery; after all, I had more surgeries and medical procedures in my childhood than most people have in a lifetime. Why do that to myself? Still, these bags under my eyes from crying have been with me for too long. And Maya gives me an inside tip. Call Dr. Prescott, she says. He's the plastic surgeon all the doctors' wives use.

I call and make an appointment just for a consultation. In the waiting room I can't guess the age of his blonde receptionist; she has one of these wrinkle-less faces that could be anywhere from thirty to fifty. That's a bit scary.

Dr. Prescott, a tall stately middle-aged man with a calm manner, looks old enough for me to trust. He answers my question. "Yes, crying every day for over a year can cause bags under your eyes, but it's also hereditary," he says. I'm watching the mirror as he repositions the skin around my eyes. He suggests removing the sags on both upper and lower lids. Looking at my fifty-something face that looks fifty-something, I'm thinking, yes, the procedure will take years off my face, but how many years? I'm kind of attached to the way my upper lids droop a bit at the outer edge. They soften and wisen my face; they make me look more like Dad. The baggy lower lids, however, make me look like Al Pacino.

"Just the lowers," I say.

The lower lid blepharoplasty is relatively painless. During the few recovery days I have little pain but my eyes itch like crazy—like having poison ivy in your eyes. Maya suggests Benadryl, which helps a lot. Maya has switched careers and found a job at a San Francisco restaurant club.

But to me she'll always be a nurse.

## CHAPTER SIXTEEN
### DEANNA

June is a month of promise. In San Francisco we call it June Gloom because of the heavy fog. But where we live, in Lafayette, on the other side of the Oakland hills, the fog burns off in the morning and the rest of the day is fabulously sunny and warm. No rain in the summer, either, only droughts. It hasn't been bad since the seventies, when water was so scarce you weren't supposed to flush. But this June morning, nearly a year since Diego left, looks promising for a swim in the pool and a bike ride with Deanna through the golden hills.

It's my birthday, the anniversary of Miguel's long forgotten car accident, and today I'm fifty-seven years young. After my bleph–a–whatever-it's-called, the purple moons under my eyes have paled to warm green finger smudges—like I missed with the eye shadow. But even they are disappearing like the stitches did into the smooth, bagless under-eye skin I had in my forties, which in my opinion was my most beautiful decade. It's going to be a good day. Maya will buy a carrot cake from Trader Joe's, I plan to go to a meeting, and Diego will call but I won't answer. And best of all, I'll be in Florida again in a month. Although, Mom's speech has not improved, Dad said she's still content.

I'm in my robe, sipping my morning coffee, paging through the *Chronicle* for any four-star G-rated movies, when I'm surprised by a strange guy with a shaved head lumbering down the hall in low-ride boxers. His upper body is covered in tattoos up to his neck that lace down his arms. He pauses at the refrigerator a few feet from me and adjusts his crotch—a maneuver I'd expect on late night MTV, but not in my kitchen at eight a.m. I suppress a gag reflex.

"Hi, I'm Houston." His pink baby face offers me a chipped-tooth grin.

"Barbara." His smile is disarming, but the rest of his mostly naked self is somewhere between fascinating (like at the circus) and terrifying. At least he wore boxers. I have a phobia of bulging briefs and Speedos, especially with morning coffee. He opens the fridge and slugs from a two-liter bottle of Mountain Dew, then heads down the hall to Maya's room.

Maya has told me little about Houston except that he also was a friend of Quinton and he was recently released from prison (not a good sign). "He's real nice, Mom." I wondered what Deanna thought of her father's replacement. From the looks of him, anybody, say a butch girlfriend, would be an improvement.

Maya wasted no time replacing Jesse. Maybe an hour. She met Houston at Quinton's funeral.

Deanna spends the morning in my bed with me playing war with Leona. Dr. Phil is on, a rerun of a family faced with drug-using kids and teen pregnancy. I consider any family with dysfunctions worse than mine to be entertainment. This morning Leona wins two card games in a row, and in my baby lisp voice she gloats about her wins over Deanna. Leona does her victory dance on the comforter wearing a frilly pink doll dress over her brown fur, and my rhinestone earrings. Leona is into bling. "I'm the best, I'm the best play-ew." Leona has the same lisp I had at four.

Instead of riding downhill on narrow Snake Hill Road, Deanna and I take the flatter bike path through Lafayette. Both paths lead to the staging area at the bottom of the hill. Deanna's a fast peddler and I don't have to slow down anymore for her to keep up. She wears her leggings, a T- shirt, and a helmet. I hate helmets. Both sides of the bike path have backyard fences that protect landscaped lawns, wooden play structures, and turquoise pools. So what can possibly hit me, a flying squirrel?

On our ride Deanna talks about her grandmother's house in Washington.

"Gramma, I have my own room. And there's matching flowers on the bedspread and the curtains. And I have a nightstand and a lamp, and there's a shelf of Grandmother Nicki's antique dolls. They're still in the boxes! And their neighbors have real horses that come up to the fence and you can feed them apples and everything!"

Nicki's a retired decorator who hung wallpaper professionally. "Sticky Nicki," they called her until her knees blew out. I'm embarrassed to say that Deanna's room in my house looks like a dump. It hasn't changed much since Miguel left, except for the recent addition of pictures of Britney Spears. The same bunk beds, wood floor, and a white Goodwill dresser that Deanna recently colored with markers.

"Daddy says if I move to Washington, he'll get me a cell phone."

"You're not moving to Washington, sweetheart." No way.

"If had a cell phone, I could call Mama whenever I wanted."

"You can use our house phone."

"Mimi's always on it talking to Javier. Hav-yerrr! Ick."

"Deanna! Slow down!" Her wheels squeal to a dead stop in the intersection just as a BMW swerves around her. Teenage driver.

"You have to stop at all intersections, Deanna." I point out the small ten-inch stop sign on the path for bikers. She looks both ways down Peacock Court twice and we take off past Stanley Middle School, where both Miguel and Maya began their legendary reputations as what Mimi calls "white wannabe gangsta."

"Gramma, why couldn't I go today to San Francisco with Mama and Houston?"

"They went to Fisherman's Wharf and it's not far from the club where your mama works. She's going to work afterwards." Maya isn't saying much about her restaurant job, except that she gets to dance and she has to buy outfits. I didn't know she could dance. Paige got her the job at a high-class club, she says.

"I liked it better when Mama worked in the daytime."

"Me too, Deanna." I can tell Deanna is missing her time with her mom. Maya has been busy lately with Houston and her friends reliving the teenage years she never had.

Deanna speeds up and I push into high gear to keep up with her. I'm huffing. Out of breath, keeping up. She's enjoying this, beating me. We coast downhill, and I stop in the staging area parking lot for a breather. On the weekend the lot serves hikers and bikers who take the old railway trail.

This is where it all ended.

I avoid this parking lot. When I do drive past it, I never look at it. And here we are in the middle of it. The gravel crunches beneath my feet and my gut clenches at the memory. It replays in vivid, cinematic detail.

I'm crouched behind Diego's van.

"I love you. I'll call you tonight," he says into our gold cell from the front seat.

I fly into the van, arms flailing, fists screaming. "I hate you. I HATE YOU!" His face surprised. Then terror. He ducks and blocks me with his forearms. I keep swinging.

"Now, you know," he says, ducking.

I'm shooting F-bombs, blows, then finally land one, hard on his shoulder. His eyes narrow, and *bam*, he slams my head sideways. Stars explode like fireworks in the black of my brain. Like in cartoons. I'm no match for him, a practiced boxer. My head pulls in like a turtle crouching under crossed arms. I find the door latch and tumble out, fleeing to my car.

It had been years, two decades maybe, since Diego whacked me like that. That day with Deanna in the parking lot brought it all back. I was the shamed, cheated on, battered wife again. Or was he the battered husband? I knew, no matter what they said, I gave as good as I got.

I look at that gravel lot where Diego's van stood a year ago. A deep powerlessness overcomes me. I can't change it, nor can I avoid what looks like a bleak, empty, husbandless future. I heard once that we play both the victim and hero roles of our own lives. I know, only too well, how to play the victim. Now I need, somehow, to find a script for the hero.

Deanna has doubled back to see why I stopped. She looks up at my gaze stuck in the white gravel of the parking lot. She knows what happened here.

"Gramma, you have to make new memories."

I give her a weak smile. "I'm trying, sweetie."

"Right now. That's what we're doing," she says more accurately than any therapist. "We're making new memories. C'mon!" Her two-wheeler slices across the gravel taking a short cut back to the paved bike path. "Try to beat me, Gramma." She races ahead, her little stick legs rotating in a tanned brown blur.

I knew it was time to let go. Those few seconds back in Diego's van had upchucked a backload: years of arguments, name-calling, slapping, kicking, being spit on. Blaming him worked, but only in the short run. Our marriage was like two children in a sandbox who kick and throw sand until they can no longer see each other in a dust cloud of their own making. My biggest problem during those years prior to Diego's anger management group wasn't his violence.

It was I believed I did something to deserve it.

Something else happened during my birthday bike ride with Deanna. I found it scribbled in my journal. One of those kid memories that you lose if they're not written down.

I brushed off a tear and followed Deanna's speedy two wheeler to the east end of the parking lot. The warm dry air felt clean, fresh, lightly scented with jasmine. We stopped at the busy Pleasant Hill Road stoplight and waited for the green light.

"Gramma, can I ask you a personal question?" she asked. She had just turned nine. I didn't know she knew what a personal question was.

"Sure." I expected it was about Houston.

Deanna looked at me very serious. "So when girls get boobs, do they come one at a time like teeth, or both at the same time?"

I laughed. "Same time, baby girl."

That whole day I chuckled over "boobs coming in one at a time," and I couldn't wait to share it with Maya. Funny that she said it right there, in the same haunted, infected parking lot I avoided for a year.

Deanna was right. New memories were born.

. . .

I'M LYING IN BED, THINKING only five more days 'til I leave for Florida. Last night I left the window to smell the freshly cut grass. Miguel actually came over on the weekend and cut the lawn for me. He didn't get to finish the front because he ran over the cord. Maya said she thought he came to see us because he was depressed over Quinton's death, so I didn't get too mad about the cord.

Lola has taken over Diego's pillow, at least until Deanna comes in and claims it. Deanna is supposed to be caring for *her* dog, but somehow dog feeding and walking has become my job. But we don't mind, do we, big girl? She licks my face. I kind of like big wet morning kisses. Usually I turn on CNN first thing to hear Wolf Blitzer talking to me in the bedroom, but today the silence is nice and the coo-coo-coo of the mourning doves fills the space.

Reminds me of how I feel waking up in my parents' condo. In Florida I have a freedom to do what I want. Adventurous things. Maybe cruise the Bahamas; go snorkeling in the Tortuga Islands. Try bungee jumping. I'll invite Jerry.

I'm excited about seeing him again. Especially since the result of Prescott's de-bagging eye work is better than I imagined. Now that I lost the glasses with a simple in-and-out Lasik procedure, I feel ten, no fifteen, years younger. Being able to leave for Florida with new eyes is a start; it makes the possibilities of a bicoastal lifestyle seem endless on a seacoast horizon. I'm suddenly brimming with ideas. I even feel like painting my room yellow. I look around my bedroom and it feels lighter somehow, helium lighter. As if hope comes in molecules.

· · ·

EVER SINCE THE KIDS were babies, I prefer chairs that rock. My favorite is the wicker chair swing that swings from a chain hooked to the patio overhang. It resembles a giant egg. There used to be room for Deanna and me to sit side by side but now that she's nine, we feel too squished.

I rock the chair, doing nothing. Deanna's tennis ball rhythmically thumps the side of the house and a hawk curves lazily across the powder blue sky.

My right palm cradles my grandmother's cross. A silver necklace cross. I hold it the way baby Maya used to walk around the house with her blanket. I've had it over a year now and I still haven't purchased a chain for it. That strange day it arrived seems somehow prophetic.

It was in February, four months before Diego left, when a small brown package mysteriously arrived from some town in Texas. I didn't recognize the sender. I sat here in the egg chair unwrapping the brown paper when Diego came through the patio doors wearing a shocked expression and a bath towel.

"I lost my ring," he said, rubbing his naked ring finger. We had never exchanged wedding rings because Diego always wore his deceased father's onyx ring on his left hand.

"It just slipped down the drain in the shower," he said as if Tigger had been hit by a car, God forbid. I mentioned something about a plumber, then thought no more about it. Looking back, I wonder if I should have done more. Followed him inside to console him, but by then, if I believe Maya, his affair had already begun.

But at the time I was more interested in the mysterious box than in Diego's ring. Under the cardboard flap was tissue paper and inside lay a two-inch engraved silver cross with a clear plastic bubble in the center holding minuscule pink roses. Like they were carved by teeny little fairies. I recognized it immediately. Aunt Ginny had worn it when I met her for the first time in Wisconsin. I admired it and she told me the cross had belonged to Grandma Buehler.

"Barbara, you can have it when I die," she said in a southern accent different from all my other aunts and uncles. Since I didn't really know her, and she lived in Texas and had her own daughter, Sandy, I never expected to see this cross again. That was ten years ago. But I had heard that Aunt Ginny recently passed.

I lifted the cross to my lips, and was taken aback. Stunned. Its scent, "Here's My Heart," the perfume Gramma bought from the Avon lady, was unmistakable. The cross smelled like Gramma. How could that be? She's been dead for thirty years, I thought. I flipped the cross over looking for a latch to open the bubble but it was sealed. For weeks I kept that cross with me and I asked my friends to smell it. They smelled a hint of perfume too but didn't know what it was.

They didn't know it was Gramma. My godmother.

I'm thinking about how it arrived on the very same day Diego lost his father's ring, the ring he had worn for over forty years. Weird. The ring was never recovered. Was it just a coincidence? An ancestral warning? A prophecy? A talisman?

I lift the cross to my nose and hold it to my heart. The scent is fainter now but still with me. It reminds me that I felt loved once, way before I ever met Diego.

· · ·

DEANNA IS ASLEEP ON HER stomach with one arm hanging innocently over the side of the bottom bunk. It's the start of her summer vacation and her regular eight-thirty bedtime has flown out the window. I'm embarrassed her bedroom has the furnishings of an army barrack or a monk's cell—if one imagines a tiny monk who leaves teeny jeans on the floor and tapes photos of Britney Spears on the walls. It's a good room to start redecorating—so much potential. Make it a real girl's room. We'll do it together. Let Deanna pick the colors.

I start by organizing clothes. I fan a stack of clean tiny cotton panties in her top drawer. Sock balls on the right. Tees and jeans in the middle drawer. Dirty clothes go into a pile in the hall since her hamper is filled with toys. I roll out the suitcase that's been in her room since Christmas and the wheels squeak.

Deanna rolls over and one open eye peers at me from under the blanket. "What are you doing in my room, Gramma?"

"I'm putting the suitcase in the garage where it belongs." I whisper so as not to wake Maya. She won't be going to Washington, not with a new boyfriend.

"No, I'm using that." Deanna sits up and rubs her eyes. "Mo-om! Gramma's taking my suitcase!"

"Shhhh. Your mother's sleeping."

Deanna bolts up, grabs the pull handle while I have hold of the strap. "Give me *my* suitcase! I have to pack."

"Where are you going?" We're in a tug of war.

"Gramma, it's mine." She wrenches it out of my hands. I fall backwards and catch myself on the dresser. I raise my hands in defeat. *Strong little bugger.* I can barely pin her down on my bed anymore. "Are you going to Reno with your mom?"

Deanna gives me her none-of-your-business scowl, and pulls the suitcase tight to her little chest. I hate Reno and any dark casino-like places—like Chuck E. Cheese's. But lately Maya is going out at night in tube dresses and shorts. She's thrown out the burqas. Deanna's mom appears at the doorway, looking grumpy and perfectly gorgeous with her long streaked-blonde hair and new C-cup breasts—a present to herself for leaving Jesse. Lola click-clacks her nails down the hall to see what's going on.

"Deanna, I told you to wait until Sunday to pack."

"Gramma's taking my suitcase!" Deanna stands guard in front of her suitcase as if it's her pet baby elephant.

"Where does she think she's going, Maya?"

"You woke me up Mom. I can never sleep in this house." She rolls her big root beer eyes, turns on her bare feet, and heads back to her room. I follow her and close her bedroom door.

"What's going on, Maya?"

"Mom, I didn't want to tell you about Deanna moving to Washington because I knew you'd freak out."

"What do you mean moving? You're done with Jesse—you got implants."

She sighs, exasperated.

Deanna's voice sings out from the crack under the door. "I'm going to live with Daddy, just me."

"What?" I open the door.

Deanna is lying prostrate on the hall floor like a little priest about to be ordained. "Mama's not going, Gramma."

"Deanna, go watch SpongeBob." She obeys her mother.

I stare at my daughter. "You're really sending Deanna to live with him?

You can't be serious? That violent scumbag who broke your nose. I can't believe it." I throw my hands up in the air in pure disgust. I'm pacing now; my eye sockets are so wide it's a wonder my eyeballs don't fall out of my head and roll under the bed with the rest of Maya's junk.

"You're never here, Mom. You said you're going to Florida *again*. I need babysitters at night now and no one does childcare until three in the morning. Nicki searched out the schools and everything."

"I'll only be in Florida a few weeks, no more than a month."

"You were gone two weeks during Christmas and again for spring break and now you're leaving again. I can't rely on you."

*That hurts.* The new me, Bicoastal Woman, couldn't wait to call ship ahoy. But old rusty Barbara felt anchored in the harbor.

"Does your father know about this?" He could get off his flat butt and watch her too.

"He thinks it's a good idea for Deanna to live in Washington. He said it's time I get on my own two feet and get an apartment."

"An apartment? You know why, Maya? He wants to push us all out of the house so he can sell it. That's why. That's his sneaky little plan. To get rid of us. So we don't interfere with his new plum-picking life. 'I sink down on Maya's bed. My anger sinking into hopelessness. Now he's pushing Deanna out of my life too, my baby girl, my pal, my lifeline.

Maya looks up at me, her urgency softening. "Mom, try to understand. What else can I do? It's just temporary."

"I can't believe you're sending this innocent little girl to live with a nose-breaker. A tire-iron assaulter. He threatened to kill us, Maya, all of us. Don't you remember? He said, 'the whole family.'"

"Jesse would never hurt Deanna."

I think about fighting Jesse for custody, but then I'd have to fight Maya too. She turns away staring into her open closet. A teardrop glints off her cheek. Behind her I notice something odd. Collared shirts and pants are hung neatly with all the hangers going the same way. Those aren't Diego's shirts.

"Whose clothes are those?"

"Uh, Houston's."

"What? Houston is living here?" This is all wrong. How did this happen? Deanna's leaving and some tattooed creep I don't even know has moved in?

"Houston thinks it will be a good idea for Deanna to be in Washington."

*Of course he does.*

Then I can work more nights while Houston looks for a job."

"When, Maya?"

"He uses my car before I go to work."

"No, when is Deanna leaving?"

"Day after tomorrow."

I feel suddenly sick.


Deanna's jumbo gray suitcase lies flat and open on the living room rug, her jumbled clothes mounded inside. Beside it rests her ski jacket and one shoe. I cried and prayed and bargained with God about losing Deanna for two long nights. But the Zen proverb says, "If you want something, step aside." I'm not going to blubber in front of Deanna and make her feel guilty.

"I found it, Mom." Deanna sprints down the hall with her other Adidas. She plops down on the rug and puts on one white sock and one blue sock. I stand in the kitchen doorway, still in my morning sweats, cradling a cup of coffee, staring at the suitcase.

Maya and Deanna, with Lola tagging behind, run back and forth down the hall adding more items: Sherman, the stuffed dog that's Leona's boyfriend, hair ties, and her Beanie Babies collection.

"Mama, can Lola go to Washington too?" Deanna calls down the hall.

"No, Deanna." There are coyotes and wolves in the woods behind Nicki's house.

Maya gives packing orders. "Toys in the backpack. Clothes in the suitcase."

"You really think she'll be all right alone on the plane."

"Mom, it's a direct flight from Oakland to Seattle, don't worry. Nicki will pick her up." I know that Nicki is reliable, almost too reliable. *Damn it.* I suddenly resent her for stealing my granddaughter. And I hate her wallpapered house and matching bedroom sets and her basement apartment where they enable their unemployed, pot-smoking son. I even hate the damn neighbor with horses.

Deanna pops up to standing in a leap my knees can no longer accomplish, and she encircles her thin bare arms around my waist. "I'll be fine, Gramma, don't worry. We can talk on the phone. Daddy says he's getting me my very own cell phone."

"That's wonderful, sweetheart." I clap my approval in front of my cheeks so my thumb can discreetly wipe a tear.

"Gramma?"

"What, baby girl?"

"You always told me that we should share the things we love, right?"

"Yes, baby."

"So Gramma, you had me forever, and now it's Gramma Nicki's turn, right?" She bear-hugs me tight, her tangled-haired head presses into my ribs and drops deftly into my heart. I never want to let go.

Maya, in short shorts, closes the top, sits on the suitcase, then bounces up and down—her usual suitcase closing method before zipping.

"One last thing," I tell Deanna.

"No, Mom, we can't fit in anything else."

I return from my room with a drier face and my "one last thing."

Deanna's eyes pop open when I hand Leona to Deanna.

"Are you sure Gramma?"

"I'm sure. Take good care of her."

Deanna twirls around holding Leona by puppet paws. "Leona, you're going to Washington with me!"

Maya is surprised. She knows I never let Leona out of my room.

I stand the suitcase upright, shaking it, then carefully place our little puppet into the wee free space at the top. As they head out to the car, I'm standing by the front door calling out a few last-minute Leona instructions.

"Deanna, don't get her wet, it rains a lot in Seattle, so don't take her outside. And be sure to wash the syrup off your hands before you put her on—Leona doesn't like her insides getting sticky. And never, never take her into the woods, okay?"

"Okay, Gramma." She nods, taking foster puppet care seriously.

Deanna is waving to me while her mother loads the suitcase in the trunk, but suddenly Deanna puts down per backpack, rushes back down the path, and wraps her arms around me one last time. As Maya's Sebring pulls out of the drive, Deanna blows me kisses from the passenger window. I grab the morning air, catching every one.

Watching Maya's car disappear down the hill I feel suddenly dazed.

. . .

DEANNA WAS ONLY TWENTY months, a baby, when they took her. Maya was a teenager trying to balance high school, an apartment with Jesse, her job at Target, and taking care of a baby. I repeatedly told Maya that she needed to move home, she couldn't stay living with Jesse. Her CPS worker said so. Child Protective Services. Mimi, sixteen then, and I were taking care of the baby the afternoon Maya rushed into our house, wearing her red Target shirt, looking terrified.

"Jesse called me at work. They're looking for the baby! They're coming!"

Mimi, who had the baby on her lap, rushed little Deanna into her bedroom and locked the door. I didn't think that was necessary. Surely I can reason with the CPS worker, I thought. I'm the child's grandmother. She's safe with me.

*I was wrong.*

I'll never forget Maya's screams as three police officers held her down trying to muffle her cries in the living room rug. Another officer held Diego, who protested Maya's rough treatment. The sounds of that day play like it was yesterday. The lamp crashing and Diego yelling, "Let her up, she can't breathe!" And Maya.

After a struggle I convinced Mimi to unlock the door because an officer was threatening to break it down. Then I carried Deanna in her diaper. I bounced her up and down and placed her blankie over her head to blind her from the scene in the living room.

"Horsey, horsey," she said, thinking I was playing a game, as I carried her out to the gray unmarked sedan parked on the street. Dianne, the Child Protection worker, closed the front door to drown out Maya's cries.

"No!" I said firmly. It's my door and I want it open." She opened the door a crack.

"Wider." She obliged. She had to hear it too; the screams of a mother when her child is being taken away. Maya's shrill cries grew deeper into long belly whale groans that shattered the silence of our pristine Lafayette neighborhood.

Staying calm for the baby, I buckled little Deanna into a scratched gray car seat that showed its wear. She bounced up and down in the seat. "Horsey, horsey," she said, delighted to go for a car ride. I wrapped her blankie around her bare shoulders and chest to shield her from the biting February cold and handed her her *baa baa*. The milk Mimi had put in the bottle was still warm. I tucked in her blue cloth doll beside her and pulled its string.

"Tickle me again. Tickle me again," it said.

Deanna giggled. "Again, again ...."

The car door slammed. Diane, who was shaking, jumped in and gunned the engine. Her black tires spun and spit gravel at my moccasins. I tapped the window and made faces with thumbs in my ears, wiggling my fingers, running along side the car. Deanna's little face laughs ... until ... I can't keep up. Out of breath ... I watch the gray car turn down Snake Hill Road and disappear.

. . .

AT MY MEETINGS WHENEVER I hear a woman's story, especially a tragic story of a woman who loses her children, I listen. After the meeting, even though I'm a stranger, I'll go up to her and offer a hug. Most often, she lets me hold her. Sometimes she breaks down and cries in my arms. I caress her hair with my palm and hold her head until the weight of it drops like a bowling ball onto my shoulder.

"I know, I know. It's going to be okay."

Same words I told to Maya.

Same words Grandma used to say to me.

"I know." I've been there.

After a newcomer cries with me, sometimes I never see them again. That's fine. For one supreme, beatific moment, we have a connection. I'm blessed.

Blessed to have their precious tears dampen my shirt.

Blessed to hold grief in my arms.

Sometimes these women ask for my number after a meeting; some call, and a few have asked me to sponsor them. Over the last decade I sponsored several women of color. Why they asked me, *white Wisconsin me,* to be their sponsor, I don't know. Two came from the Caribbean, another from urban Baltimore. These women have stories that make my trauma over Diego look like a cakewalk. As we worked together doing the steps, a one- to two-year process, enduring friendships emerged. I learned so much not just about their different lives, but about myself and the invisible racist attitudes I drag along with me. There are the hidden silent ones that lie dormant underneath my white privileged background, and the not so dormant ones that emerged in less-than-kind remarks I made about LaShondra. Still, if there was no LaShondra I might never have experienced what uncomfortable, infected views lie hidden below the surface of my congenial midwest personality. Also I was offered the opportunity to talk about my racism with my new sponsees who have become my dearest friends. For all of these women, who saw my dirt, and liked me anyway, I'm grateful.

Now I believe these women were brought into my life to heal me.

# CHAPTER SEVENTEEN
## BICOASTAL WOMAN

Every Friday afternoon is Serenity Book Club. This Friday, the Friday before I leave for Florida, five of us women, all over fifty (except Carrie), meet in Ellen's study. Sometimes our talking and Ellen's low-calorie lemon parfait take precedence over reading our latest self-help book *du jour*. It isn't true program conference-approved literature, which is why, I suspect, Joanna doesn't attend. I think of the gang in my Friday book club as my support network.

I'm telling Ellen, Gail, Carrie, and Doris about Deanna's departure. After getting assurances from my friends that Deanna will be fine with her other grandmother, the conversation turns to my upcoming Florida trip. They're surprisingly interested in Jerry, my Florida—dare I say—*boyfriend*. I haven't told them *all* the details. This group has a thousand words for "letting go," but orgasm isn't one of them.

They all talk at once. "But Barb, if you go to his house, how do you know he's not a rapist or an ax murderer?"

"Or has AIDS?"

"Or V.D.?"

"I thought most men after fifty didn't want it any more." Gail shrugs.

I love the attention but play down my enthusiasm. "I don't know what will happen. It's been four months. Maybe he's no longer interested."

"If you don't want sex, just wear your old underwear." Gail adds. "Works every time."

Doris looks at her disapprovingly over her reading glasses. She's paging through John Gray's book to the chapter about filling the ten love tanks, looking for where we left off.

"Barb, after all that misery Diego put you through, it's time you have some fun in your life," Gail says. Ellen nods, and I raise my coffee cup to her. Bicoastal Woman is gaining steam. I feel myself growing younger, prettier, and sexier by the minute.

"Enough about me," I say as if I really do want them to stop.

Carrie picks up the baton. She is telling the group how much I helped her get through her break-up. Which, when you think about it, is really ironic.

"And now I've rented space at this salon, and I can't believe how much money I'm already making," she says. "In just two months."

I'm super proud of her, yet I'm envious at how she and Jay have moved from separation to divorce and they're still friends, doing things with the kids together.

"Carrie, you've helped me as much as I helped you." *Yep, that's how we roll.*

"Oh dear me, look at the time, we better start reading," Ellen says.

I'm basking in vacation anticipation and recovery pride when Doris pricks me with a question.

"But Barb, what would you do if Diego decides to come back?" They all stare at me waiting for an answer. I freeze. I can't tell them how I really feel. Not after they think I've moved past bitterness. How *do* I feel about him? "The separation, it's working, for now. We share a joint checkbook."

Doris raises an eyebrow. "Barb, you need closure. And if he moved in with the other woman, how long do you think she's going to want him paying for your house?"

"Diego and I, we trust each other. I'm over him." My stomach twists at the lie.

"So you've forgiven him?" Doris's question goes for the jugular. And all four women look at me with their open books. It's been drummed into me that you can't remain bitter and still forgive. And bitterness is not part of your "authentic self."

I half smile while my rump squirms on Ellen's taupe upholstery. "All is forgiven." Almost. Their heads nod but I'm not sure they believe me. Hell, I don't believe me.

I look at Carrie and she looks so together, confident, and genuine. I wonder how come she got to bypass bitter and I didn't. Maybe it's age-related. If I were in my thirties, maybe I'd get to bypass bitter too.

"Chapter Seven: "Filling the Ten Love Tanks," Ellen announces.

Joanna is right. Thoughts of handsome, available men, like Jerry, *do* work like a drug. And getting just one full tank would feel pretty good right now.


After book group I remind myself that I told Diego he could take my name off his separate property beneficiary forms. That's something, isn't it? But does my beneficiary concession qualify as forgiveness? It just seemed like the right thing to do—proper Emily Post splitting-up protocol. But you don't get forgiveness points for manners. I get that he just doesn't want to be married to me any more. It's rational. It makes sense. I get that. He has a right to live his life the way he wants. Even a responsibility to pursue his own happiness. I can accept that. But rationalizing his right to leave isn't the same as forgiving him, is it? If I totally forgave him, I wouldn't be waking up feeling lonely and vacant with this constant feeling that I'm missing something that I can't find. And I'm still terrified of running into the two them together, holding hands on

Main in Walnut Creek. What's that about?

I've heard Joanna say it a thousand times. "Barbara, you have to forgive. Not for him. But for *you*." Forgive. Forgive. Forgive. It's like that damn Energizer Bunny that won't shut off. I heard on a talk show that you're allowed a year to grieve the death of a relationship, but after that grief turns pathological. Truthfully, after a year, I am nowhere near forgiving him. It's like telling me to fly to the moon.

"If you want a healthy new relationship, you have to forgive the old one," they say. But that doesn't sound fair. Aren't some really terrible acts that hurt multiple people, including children, unforgivable? I also heard that for every five years someone is in a relationship, it takes one year of recovery time before the person can start dating again. I do the math. That means in six years when I'm sixty-four, I'll be ready to date. *Oh, crap.*

Arriving home that afternoon I know what Doris was thinking: Poor delusional Barbara; she's attached to suffering. Truthfully, I'm not sure what I'd do if Diego wanted to come back. But he doesn't want to. That's almost a relief. I decide I need to get cracking and get this friggin' forgiveness thing done. Get it over with. I don't want to have to wait six years before I can date.

I write Diego's name in my journal. "*Diego*, I forgive you." I say it in my mind, then out loud to hear what the words sound like.

"I forgive you, *Diego*. I *really* have forgiven you." My nasal passages constrict saying his name. No sincerity. The words ring as hollow as my thudding doorbell that lost its chime.

I try another tack. A Unity pastor I heard preach at Joyce's church suggested that I write forgiveness letters. Write to both the betrayer and the other woman, she said. I write a letter to her even though Diego hasn't told me her real name yet.

*Dear Sochi, Kay Kay, LaShondra, or Kathy the names I've found out so far ...*

*You should know that Diego is a two-faced liar with a mean temper. I think you should be careful.*

A real honest woman-to-woman letter.

*And he'd rather lie to your face than tell you the truth. I do understand why you're dating a married man because I'm sure he lied to you too. And he smokes pot.*

*But I forgive you.*

Reading it over, the draft doesn't sound, well, saintly. Do I really need to warn her about Diego's multiple faults? Sounds kind of manipulative and jealous. She might think I'm trying to get her to leave him. Am I?

I scratch the warning parts off. Now the "I forgive you" at the end sounds cheesy. Like Mommy forced me to write it.

This letter sucks. I crumple up the paper and toss it in the wastebasket. The letter I try to write Diego sounds insincere too, even angry, even though I'm done with anger. Crumple and toss.

Who am I kidding? I can't forgive them. Not today.


There's a saying Joanna taught me. First you detach with anger, then with indifference, then you can detach with love. Detaching with love sounds a lot like forgiveness. A year after he left I believed that I could never forgive Diego. I didn't realize that I could take forgiveness apart into little baby bites. I didn't have to swallow it whole. Later I heard forgiveness defined differently. It's the time during our day when we don't think about what they did to us anymore.

I liked that. That definition of forgiveness was do able.

Someday, I thought, I'll be able to see Diego and LaShondra together without it friggin' killing me. Maybe. It's possible, I suppose. Someday. Just not today. After all, it didn't turn out too pretty the first time I saw them together. I decided I would give myself a gift. The gift of never having to see them together. I don't have to force myself to attend any far-off family functions in the distant future. Why kill myself? Why future-trip? Why worry about it constantly? Why shove forgiveness down my throat?

I did ask God to show me how to forgive, but I decided to give him time. Perhaps complete forgiveness isn't a human power but a grace. The big word version of Grace with a meaning stretched beyond human understanding—in the same way human ears detect only a fraction of sound waves. Perhaps that's true. But I still have to be willing. Today I can't say what part of forgiveness belongs to me and what part belongs to God. But it does seem to me that one part can't do it without the other.

Time heals, they say. But time didn't heal my hurt, it just buried it. I clung to Joanna's saying: First you detach with anger, then with indifference, then you can detach with love. After a year I felt that my anger was over, most days anyhow. But had I arrived at indifference toward Diego? Obviously I needed to work on my indifference. Going to Florida would be a good place to do it.

. . .

I HAD ONE LAST LUNCH session with Joanna before Florida. She was still nagging me about the Munchausen's thing. Give a dog a bone ....

"Barbara, why do you think you were the only kid in your family who had so many doctors and medical procedures?" Joanna asks. "Did you ask your sister about it?"

I nod. Whenever I'm about to visit family, Joanna always brings up my childhood surgeries. She looks at me across the wooden table at Cherubini's as we finish our sandwiches.

"So Barb, what did your sister say?"

"Patsy said, 'Mom took you to doctors because you were sick and we weren't.' End of story."

"So-oo you were the designated patient in the family." Joanna smiles smugly as she stirs her tea.

"I did the research like you asked." Looking up MSbP (Munchausen's syndrome by proxy) online made me feel worse.

"What did you find out?"

"Well, I found out I didn't have one-third of a clubfoot. I had a turned-in foot that doesn't require surgery." I shrug. "Back in the fifties they did surgeries for lots of things."

Joanna shrugs. "Are you going to ask your parents?"

"Joanna, my mother can barely talk. She's eighty-four with dementia."

"Guess that's like talking to the alcoholic."

I wrap up the other half of my chicken sandwich in a napkin, preparing to go.

"So why don't you ask your father?"

"My Dad?" *Absolutely not.* "I can't suggest to Dad that Mom took me for unnecessary surgeries. Joanna, my Mom isn't doing well. There's a limit to what Dad can handle. Dad doesn't need me bringing up hospitalizations that happened fifty years ago."

"Well, he was there, wasn't he?"

This is getting uncomfortable. Especially now that I know my three surgeries were unnecessary.

"Dad worked back then. And he golfed. He was too busy to visit me in the hospital." I cringe, knowing that "father never visiting the child in the hospital" is one of the identifying characteristics of MSbP.

"When Miguel was in the mental hospital, didn't you visit him?"

"Of course. We both did."

She doesn't understand. It was hard enough to ask Patsy. The thought of embarrassing my father sickens me.

"Barb, asking your father is an inquiry, not an inquisition. If I had unnecessary surgeries as a child, I'd sure want to know why, wouldn't you?"

I wish she'd drop it. Still, I can't forget about what I read. What really shook me was the high death rate of MSbP children. Ten percent. I recall three times in my childhood, due to accidents, overdoses, or my mother's rage that I came dangerously close to being one of those statistics. And those incidents didn't include the surgeries.

A fogginess descends. I see Joanna's lips moving but her voice drifts into the distance. My brain turns to slush. A brain freeze. A white-out. I've had these before with probing therapists. And whenever I remember the prongs.

"Sorry. I'm running late." I put on my sweater.

"Barb, running off to Florida again won't help. Don't you think you might be using men to feel okay about yourself? Why not have a relationship with Barbara right now?"

Yadda yadda yadda.

I need fresh air. Maybe I need a new sponsor. Someone without a medical license.

"I gotta go. It's after two." I push my chair in.

The sunlight outside the dark café blinds me but the fresh air and blue sky clear my head. I don't need her advice. I'm done with this. Stick a fork in me. I'm done.

· · ·

THE FLIGHT TO PALM BEACH is eight hours with a layover in Houston where I surrender to fast food, a Burger King cheeseburger and a diet Coke. No one has to know. In the air I usually write in my journal but on the second leg of this flight I'm relaxing. Deanna's fine, I tell myself. She told me in our last phone call about feeding apples to the horses over the fence next door to her grandparents' house outside of Seattle. Sounds nice. A suburban-rural area. Horse pastures. Two-lane roads. Like where I grew up in Wisconsin.

Out the window Houston's green coastal islands pull away into a net of white clouds. I gaze at a man's bald head two rows ahead in coach. The head doesn't move; it's a stationary head as heads go. It's not his muted plaid scarf or his boomerang flight pillow that intrigues me. It's his shaved head. So perfectly smooth, it tingles my fingertips. The way the light bounces off it, it's almost, well, winking at me. Would it feel rough like my father's shaved stubble, or soft like a baby's skin? Something about that head transfixes me. It's the antithesis of Diego's dark thick graying curls or Jerry's short-cropped mop of sandy hair. Shaved is so millennium. Sleek. Sexy. Handsome. In a smart, urban, Egyptian sort of way. I know just by the back of his shaved head that this man must be good-looking. I bet he wears one of those short beards, carries a briefcase, maybe a San Francisco trench coat, no leather bomber jackets for him. He has to be handsome, I can tell by his erect posture. That head is no slouch.

Now that I'm single and bicoastal, I'm allowed to fantasize about men I could have casual, stimulating conversations with. No need to exchange phone numbers. I might not even look at his left hand—although I admit that it's becoming a habit of mine.

I have an entrepreneur friend, Karen, whom I've known since the seventies. She began the tabloid magazine *The Berkeley Monthly*, and then another sister pub in Boston. "I'm bicoastal," she told me back when I worked for her as art director. We're the same age but she divorced, kept the mag, and traded in her bell bottoms and Birkenstocks for designer suits and high heels while I was raising three kids. I'm not ready for stilettos, but I admire the way Karen can strut in them.

Her fiftieth birthday was a posh affair with all the *Who's Who* in the Bay Area. Diego and I were invited and I saw faces that before I'd only seen on television. Karen was the knockout belle of the ball, and men, younger men, like the man in front with the shaved head, turned their heads to look at her. She never remarried. I imagine her bicoastal lifestyle kept her busy meeting famous artists and writers. Sometimes I heard rumors about her liaisons. Karen grew too smart and effete to be tied down with children or men who expect you to belong to them.

And now at fifty-seven I'm the one flying coast to coast. Bicoastal Woman feels free as a bird.

· · ·

IT'S A HOT MUGGY JULY evening when Dad pulls into the condo parking lot.

"Barb, your mother fell down trying to go to the bathroom," he says before getting out of the car. "I bandaged her up the best I could. She can't get to the toilet by herself anymore."

I knew Dad would need me. I'm happy to help.

Then he drops a bomb. "I think it's time we look for a nursing home," he says.

I'm shocked. He never mentioned a nursing home before.

"Dad, don't you think a box of Depends Overnights would be cheaper than a nursing home?" Mom may not be able to say it but I know she doesn't want to live in a home. "Did you talk to Patsy about this?"

"Not yet. I thought we could check out some facilities while you're here."

"Okay, Dad. we'll look into it." He's jumping from A to Z, like couples who have a bad fight and hate each other in the moment and start talking divorce. There's no use arguing with him.

I tug my suitcase over the wheelchair ramp into my parents' condo. Mom is wearing her pink housecoat, sitting in her wheelchair, watching *The Golden*

*Girls.* Her right arm has three big bandages on it. Looks like a shark attack. I kiss her on top of her thinning web of white hair. It's flat in the back and uncombed and sprayed. It's been a while since she's been to the salon. She smiles up at me but I notice her teeth don't quite line up with her lips. Her top denture is loose. She sucks it, snaps it into place, then turns back to the TV. A commercial comes on and Mom looks up at me like a child. "Baaaa-bara." She smiles.

Twenty years ago Grandma Miller, my mom's mother, was removed from her Florida condo and put in a nursing home where she died. Mom called me from Wisconsin very upset about her mother's death. "I'll never let that happen to you, Mom. You'll never have to go into a nursing home," I promised her. The thought of looking at homes with Dad makes me shudder.

Dad wheels Mom into the bedroom and I follow. "She goes to bed before seven now," he says. An hour earlier than four months ago. Dad has placed a line of pillows along the bedroom wall that leads to her bathroom.

"Okay Barbara, let's see you get her into bed," Dad says as if this is some kind of test. "Sometimes her legs won't hold her; they give way and it's a son-of-a-gun getting her up off the floor."

I remove my high heels to show my father my strength.

"At her last hair appointment, I dropped your mother on the asphalt getting her out of the car. The salon ladies had to call the police. You try and lift her." I bristle when he talks about Mom right in front of her, as though she's a ninety-pound bag of dog food.

I get Mom to stand up out of her chair and have her hold on to a table near her bed. Then I swivel her rear end around to land on the mattress. Plop. Home run. Now all I have to do is lift her legs up and use them as a lever to pivot her butt so she's straight with the bed. With her legs up her head falls down on the mattress but just a wee bit short of her pillow. "I almost got this," I tell Dad. I lift her under her arms. Jesus, she weighs a ton! Slowly I edge her head up to meet her pillow.

Mom's blue eyes twinkle at me. "Th-th-th-thank you,"

*Awww, so sweet.*

"Beginner's luck," Dad scoffs.


My parents have always lived a quieter, slower, less messy life than I have. Cocktails at four, dinner at six, golf on Thursdays, church on Sundays. Even today their two-bedroom condo remains spare and uncluttered. No papers, books, bills, dishes, or cat medications left on the counter. Even Mom's ashtrays have always been clean and buttless. Mom never kept live plants. When I asked her why, as a child, Mom said that she couldn't keep any living things in our house because they always died, which wasn't encouraging to an eight-year-old. As an adult I developed more appreciation for her spare decorating. She was a minimalist without ever knowing it.

Dad and I watch a tribute show to Johnny Carson. There's nothing in the world I'd rather do than sit on the pink and tan sofa with Dad watching Johnny like we used to do when I was in high school. Even the AC-ed air laced with cigarette smoke relaxes me somehow—it's a feeling of being taken care of. And with Mom happy that I'm here, I'm happy here too. For the first time I feel like I belong to both of them. Like I found a piece of lost personal property. A piece apart from Diego that belongs to me.

And it feels important somehow to cook my soups and Mexican stew recipes for Mom and Dad, to give them something besides high-sodium TV dinners. Dad appreciates my cooking, I suspect, because Mom always hated to cook—she was the opposite of my Grandma Buehler, who baked her own bread, sweet rolls, and coconut cream pies. I did, however, have to adjust Mexican recipes for Wisconsin tastes. Mom says guacamole tastes like spit. But I find that Florida markets have abundant mahi, tilapia, marinated Cajun catfish, and shrimp that are fresher and cheaper than in California. Even Dad's frozen sheep's head (he likes to show me their rows of flat fish teeth that resemble people teeth) are fabulous pan-fried in butter. I'm cooking more seafood: scampi, cioppino, halibut Florentine—the seafood recipes that felt indulgent in California when I was cooking for five.

We hold hands at the table for grace. The thin top skin on Mom's small, blue-veined hand slides around under my fingertips like loose wrapping paper. She lifts her head and looks intently into my eyes for the Catholic prayer. "Bless us, O Lord, and these thy gifts ...." I'm surprised that she can say the whole five lines without a stutter. Maybe holding her hands and eyes helps her words flow out. When she makes it through to the "Amen," the sides of her thin lips curl up. She's pleased as punch with herself.

The next day while Dad is out fishing at high tide, I sit at the table with Mom filling out my week's shopping list. Mom takes dainty, shaky bites from her bologna sandwich.

"So Mom, what would you like for dinner this week?" I'm thinking I'll buy her whatever she wants, jumbo peel and eat shrimp, barbecue ribs, filet mignon, the cost is no consideration.

Mom looks up from her sandwich and says, "TV dinners."

. . .

I CALL PATSY AND EXPLAIN that Mom's worse off than we thought and I tell her Dad's rash nursing home solution.

"I can't come out now," she says, "Summer is our busy season." She sounds a tad indignant. Minocqua in the summer is filled with tourists who break teeth or need new crowns. And summer is short in the Northwoods, only two months, July and August. Actually it's only one month of good Wisconsin weather because half the time it rains. I suspect Patsy is also saving vacation time to visit her new long-distance boyfriend Frank; they met online. Patsy expanded her Internet search radius to Texas.

"Barbara, it's not your choice; Dad's her caretaker. You have to do whatever he wants."

"I know."

She's not saying what I want to hear. She's right. I hang up feeling a bit selfish to expect her to drop everything and come to Florida. She has a dental practice to run and a relationship. And I could hear the worry and regret in her voice.

Another upsetting development occurred before I left California. I opened an email from Oakland School for the Arts. During the last school days in June they offered me another contract for the upcoming school year, but this new email began, "We regret to inform you ...." Both the fine art and literary art departments have been eliminated.

My signed contract beginning in September means zilch. No job. I'm upset about it for a whole twenty-four hours. Now I'm thinking being unemployed frees me to stay in Florida longer to help Dad figure things out. I could stay into September if I want. Maya doesn't need me, Deanna is starting school in Washington.

. . .

I PUT OFF CALLING JERRY for three days. The piece of cardboard with Jerry's phone number is still in my wallet, stored for four months in a zipper pocket, like it's a safe deposit box. Will he even remember me? I hold my breath and call him. He's coughing on the phone.

"I caught some kind of bug that knocked me out," he says in a weak voice. I offer my homemade chicken soup but he declines. "I do wanna see you Barb, *cough cough*, but I gotta shake this thing." He sounds *so* sincere, and *so* sweet over the phone, and *so* really sick in bed, that I believe his every word.

I'm disappointed; I expected to see Jerry on the weekend. Although I feel useful, staying at the condo, cooking meals, changing Mom's Depends, and planning nursing home visits isn't exactly a vacation. Lorraine's advice drums in my ears. "Start dating. Have fun."

I visit Debbie and Dave, who own a unit at the ocean end of the condo complex, old friends; we're both second generation at the Barbican. Deb suggests lunch at the Banana Boat tomorrow afternoon. "There's an outdoor tiki bar. It's a nice family place," she adds, thinking I've never been there. "Sounds delightful, Deb. You don't even have to give me directions.".

# CHAPTER EIGHTEEN
## RAINING MEN

Diego calls when I'm rushing out the door to meet Debbie for lunch. I'm already late. He wants to know when I'm coming back to California.

"I can't talk. I have a date." I don't say with whom.

"Oh," he says quietly. I catch the subtle inflection, the tiny sigh in Diego's "oh." Not exactly regret, but a close cousin. Though I am twelve months and three thousand miles away, I can still translate the minute inflections in his voice. I detected a faint little prick.

"I gotta go, Diego. I'll call you back later." I hang up first. I did it! I hung up first! After so many excruciating, sobbing, bleeding phone calls that ended with me yanking barbed arrows out of ego, I feel like I finally shot a zinger. Strutting out of the room in my short white skirt and heels, I fist-pump the air. "Yes!"

At lunch we're exchanging stories about our aging parents the way I used to swap kids' stories at playgroup. Debbie, in her sixties, is one of the "young ones" on the island. The average age here in South Palm Beach is a young eighty-something.

"We had Mom in a home in Delray but they told us she wouldn't eat."

I'm thinking I wouldn't eat nursing home canned food crap either. Actually the Caesar in front of me isn't half bad, but where are the anchovies? Caesar seems like the only salad they know how to make in Florida, besides iceberg garden.

"That's how residents die in those homes, Barb. They won't eat, that and infected bedsores."

My fork hangs sick in mid briny air.

"They stop eating and get transferred to hospice. Death certificate reads 'failure to thrive.' I couldn't do that to Mom."

"Is that legal?" I ask. "To starve someone?"

"It is in Florida."

"Mom's a good eater." I say as if she's a one-year old.

Debbie says that she and Bill keep her mother for six months and then they trade her to brother Bill in Michigan.

"Our girl, Alma, comes in during the week. Mom really likes her even if she doesn't understand much English. The agency charges by the hour, but it's worth it. We've had great women. Haitian and Hispanic mostly."

An in-home agency worker seems the ideal choice to me, but I can't picture Mom getting along with someone who doesn't speak English. And Haitian? Mom won't even shop at Winn Dixie because she says that's where "the colored" shop. Dad is more open-minded about race, and I've suggested in-home care, but he's dug in his heels to find a nursing home. Because that's what his Wisconsin friends did. But here in Florida, with many Haitian and Hispanic newcomers, it's a different ballgame.

Deb has to leave because Alma gets off at three, but I decide to hang out at our waterside table and finish my virgin margarita while the band sets up. I scan the tiki bar room as the seats fill up, but I don't see Jerry.

*Just checking.*

. . .

THEN THERE'S JOE. I can't help but notice him as he sits at the bar close to my table. Tall, Tommy Bahama shirt, sharp features, and shaved head—all put together in a macho un-put-together Florida way. He raises a finger to order with professional precision, confidence, and sober alertness. Florida yuppie, I guess, a man whose job requires an education and a three-digit IQ score, which is, as far as I can tell, a notch above a few other patrons getting sloshed.

After he's served, Joe swivels toward me. "You visiting?" he calls over. It's that kind of friendly place.

"I'm from California, San Francisco area." I smile knowing my teeth are my best feature. He's too young for me. Early forties maybe.

"Joe."

"Barbara." He's gorgeous.

His full lips open in a grin that reveals perfect teeth. "So, you like it here?"

"Love the heat. You know the quote attributed to Twain, 'The coldest winter I ever spent was a summer in San Francisco.'"

He laughs. I'm surprised he gets my reference. Joe gestures to my table. "Do you mind?"

"Not at all." I can't believe he's coming over. *Thank you, Dr. Prescott.*

Joe parks his beer bottle, wearing a slip-on foam sweater, across from me. I'm staring into the most gorgeous blue eyes. A genuine smile. Clean-shaven smooth tan cheeks. His left hand lifts his amber import, slight head. No ring. Since when did I start doing the man-scan: first the face, then the stomach, then a shot to the left hand, third finger?

"So why leave San Fran to come here?" he says.

"No one in the Bay says *San Fran*. We say *the city*. San Fran sounds almost as hokey as saying *Frisco*." Still I smile and fall into his exotic, sky-blue eyes. Clear eyes, since I smile, I can swim in.

I give Joe my usual résumé: poster designer, writer, a couple of cookbooks, high school teacher. Three kids. Grandkids. He left after thirty-one years. Younger woman. I don't say black.

"Give the lady another one," he calls to the barista.

"Soda water with lime and an olive."

Joe tells me he's a pilot and his wife is living in Calgary, Canada. He's separated. Like me.

I picture tall, straight pilot Joe in a sharp blue serge suit. Brass buttons, epaulettes on the shoulders. Those little winged pins.

"So you wear a suit to work?"

"I pilot chartered planes, actually we wear jumpsuits." He flies celebrities to Costa Rica and Cozumel and once he flew John Travolta to the Bahamas. "Ever been to Costa Rica? Beautiful country to fly over. Green mountains right up to the coast." He describes a harrowing flight over the Andes; I'm enthralled. As he leans in close, he touches my thigh once and I catch his scent, a mix of Cool Water cologne and toothpaste. Just then a tinny Beethoven symphony chimes from my purse under the table.

"Barbara, I think that's your cell phone."

"That's okay."

"Go ahead, answer it. I don't mind."

But to hear over the music, I have to step outside and I really don't want to leave, especially with three attractive younger women on the other side of the bar doing shots.

"Go ahead," Joe encourages. I pick up just to stop the annoying ringing. He raises a quick eyebrow, unmistakable on a bald head, which I interpret as an interest in my caller.

"Maya, my daughter."

Before walking off, I shoot Joe the look. I still remember the look, the one that says, "I'll be back." I feel his blue eyes follow my backside as I slide between the tables heading down the plank floor toward the exit.

"Hi Mom, you're at the Banana Boat, aren't you?"

"I came with a friend for lunch."

"So did you meet anyone?"

"Well, not really."

"Mimi, Mom met someone at the Banana Boat. Mom, who is he?"

"He's a pilot, but I just met him ... honey, I'll call you later."

"Mimi, Mom's going out with a pilot." I hate these three-way conversations with Maya and Mimi. I'm outnumbered.

"Mom, remember to use protection."

*Oh, sweet Jesus.* "Bye, Maya."

When I return to the table, Joe is gone. Figures. He left without finishing his Heineken. The three Spandex girls across that bar are still doing shots. Joe's nowhere in sight. He must have left through the indoor restaurant. Stupid me to get my hopes up. I pick up his beer, just to remember the smell. A musty heady import, a macho beer like Diego drinks, stronger than the NA I order. Then I remember, shit, I left my purse under the table. It's gone. *That asshole.* I run to the exit scanning the parking lot. He's gone. Damn why am I so gullible? I'm about to walk to the restaurant entrance and report the theft when I hear a voice.

"Hey, where are you going?" It's Joe, grinning, carrying two plates of wings and celery sticks. My purse is tucked under his arm.

"Oh, I thought you left," I say.

"Why would I leave? I just met a beautiful woman." He hands me my purse. "And it's happy hour."

I shoot Joe a giant grin that says, of course I trusted you the whole time.

At the table Joe is already digging in with man fingers. I pull a drumstick from the stack and dip it into a tub of creamy chunky blue cheese. A dainty bite. Mmmmm. God, this is good. A bigger chomp. The tender flesh falls off the bone. Too *muy sabroso* to worry about the red sauce coating the sides of my lips. Florida is all about wings, pizza, and beer. Just like college again.

"Barb, if you like water views, you'd love my back patio. I can barbecue and we can watch the lights of the boats go through the canal. I'm a good cook too."

Sounds like an invitation, but I can't go home with a man I just met. Don't you have to wait for three dates? But I long to smell smoke in a man's hair again. But Joe is bald. Still.

He orders me an NA beer to go with the wings. We eat every one. I stop counting calories. We hang on into the evening talking, laughing, dancing. By now the sky is turning from sunset orange to lavender.

"C'mon, Barb, let's go. I'll make you dinner." His second try.

"I'm not hungry after *two* lunches." The prospect is exciting and bewildering at the same time. He walks me to my car without touching.

"You can take your own car, leave whenever you want."

Joe lists a menu like a waiter: barbecued steaks, restuffed baked potatoes, grilled vegetables. No man has ever cooked for me before, just me. I lean against Dad's station wagon looking up at Joe. He's over six feet. Taller than Diego. He kisses me. Soft and long, and I find myself kissing back. Feeling almost petite, almost cute and liftable.

"C'mon," he says. "It's not far in Boca."

I sit in my front seat, pulling my white skirt down over the narrow space between my thighs.

"Barbara, come back here tomorrow afternoon? Monday I fly to Costa Rica."

"Bye, Joe." I drive off without a time to meet or giving a phone number.

The next afternoon I find Joe's backyard to be everything he'd said it was.

I'm a sucker for a man with a water view who barbecues. After his steak dinner, we lounge in twin lawn chairs and watch the boats pass by in the canal. The yard hums with summer crickets and anticipation in the warm erotic night air scented with charcoal and gasoline. Conversation comes easy with Joe. Especially when the subject is boats and planes and boy toys that go "Rrrrrr."

He slips a muscular arm over my bare shoulder and his mouth comes down for a soft landing. I let Joe pilot, and it isn't long before both of us are kissing seated in one lawn chair, me on his lap. Joe's lips, full like Diego's, yet strangely naked, make "mmm" sounds, as if I'm dessert. His fingers comb through my hair; that too feels new. I think I should play with Joe's hair too, but he doesn't have any. Back in my college dating days, all men had hair, real hair, long pale straight hair, thick wavy dark Jesus hair, curly Afro hair—and I knew all the words to *Hair*, the musical. So what do I do with bald? I slowly bring my hand up the back of his neck.

It's shiny smooth and hard as a wok pan. Do I rub it? Or stroke it like I would Diego's beard? My fingers, feeling inept with bald, move to the safer territory of a shaved cheek. I kiss a spot behind his ear that offers an airy blue scent of spring water and apples. My fingertips move down to a top button, something I can play with. One button twiddles open. Then another. My surprised index finger hits gold: thick, curly chest hair. Cushy-soft. One more button comes loose, then another. Touching another man's chest feels illicit. Dangerous. My hand pulls aside his silk floral shirt. That's when I see it. A tattoo. A pilot's wings with bleeding blue letters just above his left nipple, the spot above his heart.

"You have a tattoo."

"Uh-huh," he smiles continuing to kiss my neck. My head straightens to read the blurry blue letters melting across his chest. "V-I-C ...Vicky. Who's Vicky?" He keeps pressing kisses into my neck. I pull back slightly, waiting.

"She's my wife." I knew Joe had a wife, but I didn't expect a name—Vicky—

to be written across his chest and literally shoved in my face.

"Ex-wife, we're separated," he says correcting himself. I instantly forgive him because I too am learning how to say *ex-husband.* In the same breath he puts his full, soft lips on mine. I'm kissing a bald man with a tattoo. This is incredibly daring. I'm halfway to the Hell's Angels.

I slide my finger over the letters as if they were Braille. "This should say Barbara," I whisper. He chuckles and I realize how presumptive I sound. How can I expect a tattoo when I don't even have a phone number or a last name? I close Joe's shirt over the tattoo so I don't have to see it. He laughs and continues his smooth, gentle touching, moving lower on my cami top. Looking down, I notice my left nipple has fallen out of its bra cup. I leave it there all pink and naked in the moonlight.

Soon we find ourselves en route to more comfortable seating inside on the sofa, but somewhere on the white tile from the patio to the living room I lose my shorts. By now I'm seeing myself as the star in my own romance movie.

*She lies back sinking into soft palm tree pillows. He kneels down on the tile like a bowing prince, doing things to her that her husband never did. And she surrenders her embarrassment, because he is so gentle, so kind, so sweet, and so adorably bald. Most of all she is so incredibly grateful just to be wanted again.*

Joe leans back and says something nice about my long legs, and suggests more wine. *Now?* He kisses the inside of my thigh, gets up, still fully clothed, and heads to the kitchen. *Wait a minute, Joe. Did I ask for a commercial break?*

"Just seltzer for me." His living room, in beige neutrals, gleams with spotless chrome and glass tables. Lush potted palms are doubled in size by floor to ceiling mirrors. I get up to find the bathroom but I don't know the layout.

Joe points me to the left, off the family room, but I'm irresistibly drawn to the moonlit water shining through the patio sliding glass doors. Two sailboats slowly pass each other, sails down, as they motor in for the night, and a tall leggy silhouette of a heron stands still on a neighbor's dock like a statue. I investigate and follow the glass windows through a closed door. In the dim light I make out a king-size bed piled with pillows; beyond is an open walk-in closet.

In the dim light I check the door next to the closet expecting a bathroom. My hand gropes the wall for a switch. Click. The brilliance blinds for a second. Seated to relieve myself, I'm eye to eye with a doorknob. Draped on the silver knob is a red print bikini. The skimpy kind that ties at the hips. I touch it. Not damp. The fabric weight and the tag print say it's new. Size five. There's a collection of perfume bottles, lavender soap, makeup, a blue bottle of lavender Secret deodorant with its cap off lying on its side on the counter, and a large red roller brush, like mine, wrapped with blonde hair. A hair dryer is still plugged in. The scent of face powder and Dove soap. Recent smells. It takes a moment to register.

This is a woman's bathroom. A woman lives here. I don't want to see what I'm seeing. Maybe she does have a home in Calgary but she also lives here. This is *her* house. I'm in *her* bathroom. Using *her* toilet paper. Kissing *her* husband. Walking out I peer into the closet. A silky white kimono hangs on the door. High heels, higher than I'd wear, and the curves of a small body-hugging dress appear in the shadows. Her headless, shapely silhouette catches me in my underpants in her bedroom.

*He's married.* Maybe they had a breakup fight and she just left in a hurry. But no woman leaves her thirty-dollar hairbrush behind. In the living room Joe, now down to his boxers, has spread out on the sofa with a goblet of black-red wine.

"Joe, you're married."

"I told you I was." He shrugs. I stand there. My pilot fantasy has just been dive-bombed by a size five red bikini.

"C'mere Barbara, sit." He takes my hand and pulls me down next to him on the couch. I want him to say something that will make the hair dryer and the smell of lavender Secret go away. I want him to be *really separated*, like me, who has none of Diego's smells or his red chile shorts in my bathroom.

I want a rewind to ten minutes ago when Joe was my future boyfriend.

"Barbara, we're open."

*Open?* He kisses up my arm again. I want this. My lower body aches for this.

"Relax, its just sex," he says.

I close my eyes and feel myself melting into his butterfly kisses, but my spine holds back.

"Babe, no need to worry. It's cool." He tries to pull me on top of him but I resist. "It is what it is," he says.

And what is *it?* I'm thinking, *"it"* sounds an awful lot like cheating.

Seated on the sofa, Vicky's sofa, I lean back to think.

"So you *are* married. You're not really separated." I want him to admit he lied to me.

"So?" he shrugs. "Who is going to know?" His hand slides up my back under my cami.

Joe's full lips don't look so tempting any more. They're lying lips. Lips that tell lies to a loving wife. Lies that could drive a woman crazy—in a bad way—in a trip-to-the-mental-hospital sort of way.

"I have to go."

Joe blinks. Does he even care about me at all? I walk back towards the patio scanning the floor for my tan shorts. I find them crumbled on the tile like a large bruised magnolia. I pull on my clothes and grab my sandals from the patio. If this is "just sex," then what does that make me?

He follows me as far as the front door. "Okay. Drive safe," he calls out and closes the door. My bare feet cool in the damp grass.

Of course I want Joe. My body still aches for the love it almost had. I'm driving out of his two-car Boca subdivision. Dad's station wagon radio reads 11:32 p.m. Too late to call anyone. Then I remember it's only 8:32 in California. Maya is probably eating supper with Deanna, or watching Benji for the nineteenth time. Then I remember Deanna is gone. I miss my girls so much, my heart hurts. But Maya and Mimi are probably both out with their respective boyfriends. It's so easy for them, I think, in their twenties. I pull over at the end of the block and call anyway.

"Hey, Mom." Maya answers. "When are you coming home?"

"In three weeks. I put it on the fridge. You're picking me up, right?" Now isn't the time to tell her I might stay longer. I know she'll fight me.

"So did you have sex with him?"

"Who?"

"You know, the pilot."

"I just stayed for the reggae and went home. Never saw him again"

"Sure, Mom."


I didn't walk out on Joe that night because he was a jerk and I had claimed some moral high ground, although that's arguable. Maya's friends thought differently. One of them said, "It's not my responsibility to hold someone's marriage together." It wasn't my job to save Joe's marriage, but it wasn't my job to stick a fork in it either. They took vows. "What God joins together, let no man (or woman) put asunder." I'm not sure what *asunder* means, but I'll bet canoodling another woman's husband is doing some pretty nasty *asundering*. Wives find out eventually. Whether it's a condom wrapper, a receipt for two dinners, a discovered email, or an Internet order for Viagra, we find out. We always find out.

I really did want Joe that night. But there was Vicky, who owned the same thirty-dollar red hairbrush as me.

I couldn't do it to her.

. . .

I'M SITTING ON DAD'S BED counting the men's business cards I've collected over the last ten days. It was never so easy to meet men before. Lorraine is right. She said when you're happy, people will be attracted to you. Jerry has been sick all week, but I'm not even thinking about him with all the other offers that have mysteriously been handed to me.

As I fan out the cards on Dad's chenille bedspread, I'm thinking this is downright uncanny. I had no idea South Florida had so many older single men. When I took Mom to have her hoof-like toenails clipped, even Mom's podiatrist, his name was Raj, asked me to call him and handed me his card. I assume it wasn't for a toenail trim. I pull the newest card from my wallet. Tony, a boat captain, and I add him to my collection. I'm feeling like Sophia Loren in *Grumpier Old Men.* This feels like counting money, or admiring my fourth-grade baseball card collection that included a wrinkled Hank Aaron and a dog-eared Eddie Mathews. Although these Florida men aren't my type, still I'm keeping every card, so when I go back to California I can remind myself that these ten days really happened.

My cell rings. It reads "Restricted." Oh, no. I wish I could say please don't bother me, but I pick up and his familiar voice sucks me in. It's been a while.

"How's the vacation, Barbara? How are your mom and dad?" Diego sounds like we're still married. Yet there's something different.

"Diego, do you know that you have an accent? Really, you have a slight Spanish accent. I never noticed it before." I must have noticed it thirty-four years ago and then forgot. When I grew up in Wisconsin, we only heard accents on TV.

"Yeah, some people say that."

"So then why do you have a Spanish accent and your sister has a Texas accent?"

"Uh, because Tita lives in Texas, I guess." It's weird to suddenly hear a foreign accent in a voice you lived with for more than half your life. And suspicious, as if Diego showed up in Florida with a handlebar mustache. But he'd never do that—show up in Florida.

"So Barbara, the reason I called ...." I hold my breath. I know he wants to talk about *settling things*. He already sent me a formula from his pension fund that would award me nearly 40% of his retirement funds. I'm not ready. Not now.

"... I'm going to Cuba on Monday and, uh, if anything happens with the kids you won't be able to reach me."

Whew! I'm relieved this isn't about money, but still his voice sounds way too married. Way too familiar. I stare at my business card collection to get grounded. But he's talking about his sprinkler system and how I shouldn't try to use the front yard hose. *Okay.* And he cleaned out the pool filter. *Thanks.* And the Creepy-Crawly vacuum in the pool is working fine. *Okay.* And he'll be gone three weeks, he says, and he'll be back when his classes start the end of August. *Fine.* And yes, it will be really hot in Havana this time of year. The same conversation we always have whenever I visit my parents. Nothing is different and everything is different.

"Okay." All I manage to say is okay. Something about his leaving the country tugs at my heart. It saddens me, not crying sad. More like a slight sick feeling.

"Okay. Thanks for telling me," I say flatly.

"Barbara, you don't have to worry. She's not going with me."

What did he just say? Now I'm rattled. I want to reply, "Hell if I care," but I do care and I'm relieved she's not going. What did he mean? Could he have a layover in nearby Miami? Then I realize he's just thrown me a crumb. A crumb of hope. Hope is the worst. Hope will kill me. *Why do you do this to me?*

"I gotta go, Diego." I can't let him know I still care. Not now. Not over a year.

"Okay then, Barbara."

"Bye. Thanks."

I hang up. When my haze clears, I stare down at the ten cards on the bed: John, the insurance guy, Dr. Gupta, Mom's podiatrist, Rick, the school administrator who said Florida needs teachers, Allen, the bearded New York photo booth salesman and Jerry's number on cardboard (my souvenir), the receipt from Larry, the drunk guy on a bike. Looking over each one, I feel numb. I don't want any of them. No one melts my heart like the voice on the phone. I have to stamp out hope.

# CHAPTER NINETEEN
## THE GIRL WHO PLAYED WITH FROGS

Sunday afternoon, the day Dad and I are to visit the nursing homes I sit with Mom in her bed with her photo albums across her lap. This is our thing; we've been doing this for nearly sixty years. The album pages are falling out, the bindings have separated, and the softened black mounting paper tears like wet cardboard. I keep pushing pages in and stacking them to keep them together. Mom points to her sorority sisters and old boyfriends by name. Her memory is very acute with a photo album across her lap. The old scalloped-edge black-and-white photos keep popping out, and I tuck them back into their little black stick-on corners. Mom's favorites are baby pictures of my little brother, Bobbie. We find song sheets of Mom's favorite songs and she begins singing "What a Friend We Have in Jesus." She gets through two whole verses without a single stutter. I'm dumbfounded. She smiles contentedly.

My kid pictures show snapshots of a bonneted baby. There's a large eight-by-ten studio shot of a little girl with cropped straight blond hair, a baby-toothed smile—all show eyes straight ahead. No trace of a wandering eye in any photo, except the three-month-old looks a tad spacey and cross-eyed as if she'd been hit over the head. Mom stares intently at each picture with a sweet little smile. A black and white snapshot slips out from the album. It shows a skinny girl around twelve with cat-eye glasses, a frizzy perm, and a gap-toothed grin. It's me holding a large frog by the leg at a campsite. I tuck the photo back into its corner holders. Someone, likely Mom, wrote under the photo, "Which one is the frog?" I admit it's not my most glamorous shot.

I guess Joanna is right; in regard to Mom's MSbP. Mom got a get-out-of-jail-free card. After several weeks I find myself missing Joanna. Despite her medical obsession, she always pulls me back on track.

I turn the black pages back to the four-year-old girl with fine straight blonde hair, little baby teeth, and straight aligned eyes. There is something so trusting, so innocent, and precious about her.

I tuck Mom in for her nap, remove her denture, loosen the blue blanket around her feet to make her more comfortable, and kiss her pale waxy forehead that has lost its eyebrows.

"Mom, do you ever dream about us kids when we were little?"

"Yep, all the time." A serene smile spreads across her face with no teeth behind it. Since she seems to be so happy in her dreams, why is it so important that she be awake and conscious? That's my world, not hers.

"Anything else I can do for you, Mom?"

Her eyes dart madly. Two bluebirds trapped in a cage. "I-I-I don't want to go to a h-h-home."


The ladies at the three nursing homes handed Dad and me their ad-agency-designed brochures. They were pleasant enough and the lobbies were well appointed with good lighting and spotless Florida coral and turquoise upholstery, but the chairs were empty. The few residents we saw stationed in the halls had hanging heads, shaking hands, and drool dripping from their mouths. They looked half dead. In contrast to my parents' condo, these homes were mausoleums.

Mom's physical shape may not be much different but we could still connect with her. There was life in her blue eyes. In the three homes we visited I witnessed attendants showing kindness and attention, but it wasn't family love, the kind that comes from a daughter, a son, a husband. It wasn't home. I hated being party to putting Mom in a nursing home, especially when I promised her it would never happen. I felt like Judas, betraying my own mother.

At the third home, Dad explained my mother's condition to a lady in a blue suit.

"She'll need special care in 'C' building." And she showed Dad the price list based on tiers of care. His golf-tanned face blanched at the figures. Similar to the prices at the other two facilities. As we walked out the brightly lit lobby to his Ford station wagon, he was sullen and silent. I think he was shocked that the loving care he gave daily to Mom cost a high price in the marketplace.

"Dad, please let me talk to some agencies about getting a woman to come in? I can interview women while I'm here," I asked. "I can do this. I speak Spanish."

"Okay, kiddo." He looked relieved and he called me kiddo not "Dr. Barbara."

· · ·

EVER SINCE I CALLED Joanna this afternoon, I can't shake her voice in my head. I want to ask Dad what he remembers about my childhood surgeries, but I can't work up the courage. I hate being a whiner, like some gripers in program meetings who go on and on about their miserable childhoods. I'm over my childhood. I'm no complainer. Dad never had patience for complainers. And there was another symptom on the MSbP list that I didn't discuss with Joanna. *The mother is comfortable in hospital settings.* Yep, that's mom. She was always visiting people in the hospital, and going to nursing homes getting all the residents to join in singing old songs she printed on song sheets.

About the time I was thirteen, when I balked about doctor visits and refused to take the prescribed tranquilizers, mom began working at our local hospital as a volunteer nurses aid. She told me she especially loved visiting the children patients. I knew some of them. There was the sweet brown-haired little girl in the Sunday school class I taught at St. Paul's and the little brother of my boyfriend in high school. Mom would sit at their bedsides and talk and play just like she did for me when I was in the hospital. When I left for college in Madison, Mom always filled me in on the local news when I would call or return home on school breaks.

Both those children died of cancer. Mom cried. We cried together.

Yes, Jeannette Buehler was comfortable in hospital settings.

But was that a symptom or a blessing?


That evening Dad and I sit on the couch, at our usual spots. The day's date, mid-August, on the *Palm Beach Post* reminds me that my alone time with Dad is running out. Only a few vacation days left. "Now or never," my travel-size Joanna voice prods.

"Dad, do you remember the cast on my foot the summer before third grade? You straightened a coat hanger so I could scratch inside the cast after I played in the sandbox."

"Vaguely."

"A year later I had an eye surgery for lazy eye when I was nine. But Dad, I never had a lazy eye. Look at the photo albums." He's not annoyed or dismissive. He looks sincere, as he tries to think back.

"Gee Barb, I don't remember."

This is harder than I imagined. I feel like I'm unraveling some invisible thread that held our family together for over fifty years. I wish I didn't remember those operations either.

*"Ether will put you to sleep," the man in a white coat said placing a greenish gas mask over my eight-year-old face.*

*"Count backwards, little girl, from a hundred." I breathed in the awful smelly gas.*

*"Ninety-nine, ninety-eight, ninety ... seven ..."*

Dad looks at me blankly. He doesn't remember.

"Dad, I had three surgeries and you never once visited me in the hospital."

For a man who remembers every detail about his ship, the USS Harris in the Philippines in 1945, it's surprising he can't recall his first daughter being in the hospital. Ten days for the foot surgery. But then Mom handled all my medical affairs.

In my research, I read the mother taking charge of all the child's medical conditions is a symptom of Munchausen's syndrome by proxy and the father rarely, if ever, visits the child in the hospital.

Mom matched every symptom on the list: *The mother seeks out different doctors. These mothers often grow up with a sibling who has medical issues, someone who gets all the attention:* Mom's younger sister Joyce had polio.

This is agonizingly painful to talk to Dad about. Why am I doing this? I'm throwing my sick mother, napping peacefully in the next room, under the bus.

I'm about to say, "Never mind, Dad. It's not important."

But that photo. That little girl with the straight blond hair stares at me from the photo album. She really *was* cute. Once years ago while we watched our old home movies Mom said, "Barbara, I don't know why I didn't think you were cute. You were cute." That little girl in the photo never knew she was cute. And her eyes were straight. Not crossed or wandering.

There was nothing wrong with her. *Why did they do it to her?*

I wasn't going to talk to Dad about the dental chair. I never even told Joanna about the prongs.

It just came out. "Dad do you remember the prongs?" It was likely Mom who wanted me to have straight baby teeth, but Dad was my dentist. I can't find words that don't sound like accusations.

"The prongs you put on my front teeth?" The memory chokes like hands squeezing my throat. I can't swallow. I take a breath becoming the little girl crying on her father's red leather dental chair. Her tongue speared by two metal prongs whenever she tried to swallow.

*"Don't cry. Be a big girl, Barbara."*

My thoughts slog through green quicksand mind, heading into a white-out.

"That was for tongue thrusting." Dad nods.

I push through. "Dad, I found an article in a medical journal, they called the prongs hay rakes: two metal prongs were applied to the back of a child's front teeth in the 1950s." I take a breath. "The article called that procedure child abuse." Saying the words "child abuse" kills me.

My father's face looks pained. My eyes well with guilty tears. I steady myself and straighten my wobbly backbone on their well worn, too-soft sofa.

He doesn't know what to say. I'm feeling damn crappy for hurting him like this. I want to let him off the hook. He never meant to hurt me. None of the doctors did. Mom didn't either; she was sick. So why am I doing this? Dad's the only man left on the planet who still loves me, and now I'm accusing him of doing terrible things to me.

I exhale. "I just wondered if you remembered, that's all, Dad."

"Not very well, kiddo, I'm afraid." He knocks his head with his palm and gives me a weak smile, then picks up the remote. And I lose him to golf.

What just happened? I'm staring blankly at the coffee table. Lost.

. . .

I'M CHECKING THE PHONE book the next day for senior care businesses and Dad looks over my shoulder. "Barb, how do you know that these in-home nurses won't be more expensive?"

"Dad, in-home care depends on the hours you need. Debbie says the agencies charge from twelve to fifteen dollars an hour. We don't need anyone twenty-four seven."

I know how to do this. This used to be my job. Back in the eighties when Mimi was a baby I quit my art director job to stay home with the kids more and do volunteer work with Central American refugees. I helped found Manos, a Bay Area Hispanic work cooperative loosely associated with the sanctuary movement. For five years I conducted interviews in Spanish, wrote "seeking employment" ads, and translated on the job. Those five years working with Manos not only improved my budding Spanish, but I grew to admire and respect the immigrant women I met, many who were forced to leave their children behind with relatives. It took courage—beyond courage.

Within the next few days I hire Nora from the agency. Piece of cake. It turns out the language problem I worried about with Mom isn't an issue. Nora treats my mom like her own mother, styling her hair and putting on her makeup. Mom is just as thrilled with compliments in Spanish as she is in English. Dad decides Nora will come five days a week and he'll be fine handling evenings and weekends.

"My hiring Nora is working out just great," he tells me after a few days of in-home care, as if it were his idea. I have to admit that finding Nora makes me feel a bit like a hero. A hero who saved Mom from a dreaded nursing home purgatory ridden with horny, perverted interns, the AIDS virus, and canned green beans. A hero who saved us all from guilt.

. . .

DURING ONE OF MY LAST dinners with Dad, Mom went to bed early and we're sitting at the kitchen table together. He tells me a story about Mom cooking his supper some years back. At first he's smiling, recounting how she put their TV dinners in the oven.

"But by dinnertime she burned them until they were nothing but charcoal flakes," he says. "It was during one of her depressions." His face turns serious.

I notice how Dad never laughs out loud the way Mom does or did when she told her crazy stories about eating the salt and pepper packets on the sanitarium tray or finding the milk in the cupboard. I suspect her sanitarium stories may have embarrassed him in public.

"Those TV dinners, there was nothing left of them," he says, shaking his head. He's silent a moment, then he looks up at me. "I don't know how I could have left you kids alone with her." His usual twinkly blue-gray eyes are wet with regret.

This surprises me. Regret for the past isn't my father.

*I don't know how I could have left you kids alone with her.*

It was as close to an apology as he could get.

I didn't think I needed my father to admit that I had experienced a dangerous childhood, but I was wrong. I did need to hear him say it. I needed his acknowledgment that I wasn't the sick one. I wasn't the difficult defective child who caused her mother to go crazy.

. . .

READING THE SUNDAY NEWSPAPER was a family tradition that began before I could read. After church, mom would sit between Patsy and me and read us the funnies, every page—Li'l Abner, Blondie, Beetle Bailey, Dennis the Menace, Little Lulu, Pogo, and gray-haired Mary Worth, who wasn't funny, but we listened anyway.

This, my last weekend day in Florida, is going to be relaxing, no cooking dinner, no meeting men in tiki bars, and no pushing Mom's chair around in the ninety degree heat. Nora comes tomorrow and she takes Mom out for a walk every morning. In Florida I read the whole paper, even the throw-away sections: advertising, classifieds, and the sports page. In the classifieds I notice a rental ad.

"Where's 4201 South Ocean?" I ask Dad.

He peers over the stock report. "Must be right before you get to the bridge. Two condos south of here."

I think for a moment. It's a crazy idea but I'm thinking that I'll walk over and look at this condo for rent. Just out of curiosity. In private I call the number listed. "You're practically next door," says the owner. "Come over right now." I'm surprised that the owner and the listing agent are the same person. She's probably used to nosy people in this retirement community who have nothing better to do on a Sunday afternoon than poke around in other people's homes.

I mention to my parents that I'm going to the beach and I might look at the unit for rent down the street. Dad will be interested in the going rental rates in his area of Palm Beach. Dad, being a man of few words, smiles. If Mom were normal, she'd be quizzing me, "Why do that? You're not moving here, are you? You can't afford two homes."

I step into the humid August heat grateful for my mother's new calm senility. I'm glad she's not asking questions about my motives, because to tell the truth, I'm not even sure what they are. The Palm Beach Villas is closer than I thought, a half block away, although this narrow part of the island doesn't have blocks, only condo driveways. The address leads me upstairs to a quaint second-story villa with a wide balcony facing Lantana Beach. The second story doesn't have an ocean view but just across A1A, also known as South Ocean Boulevard, a warm aqua sea stretches into forever.

Vera, an attractive blonde realtor in her sixties, opens the door. "Barbara, come in. Come in."

Her spacious bright one-bedroom has white tile floors, black granite counter tops, and shiny stainless appliances.

"Wow. This is amazing."

"I just remodeled," she says graciously. Her accent and last name tells me she's Finnish. "It's partly furnished," she says, "with two baths." I peek into a guest bath painted china red, with slate floors and a pedestal sink.

She guides me into a sunny bedroom. "Here's a walk-in closet with floor to ceiling shelves for shoes."

"Honestly, I'm not planning to move," I explain.

"In the season you don't need the AC," she continues, "just open the sliding glass doors and the sea breeze floats right through." I tell Vera that my parents live in the Barbican, two condos down. Turns out Vera knows the same people my parents know, including Debbie and Bill and my Aunt Dorothy and Uncle Bing, who took over Grandma's unit in the next-door Tropicana.

I'm feeling guilty for wasting her time. I'm used to real estate agents who say, "Just have a look for yourself," which means they know I don't have money and they can't be bothered. That's what I hoped for. A quick peek, thank you, and good-bye. But Vera is giving me the V.I.P. tour. "Washer and dryer here in the hall and I keep this tray under the AC in the summer. I just add a few drops of bleach once a month, that's it. Do you have a dog?" Vera guides me back into the open living area.

"Yes, Lola's a little Westie."

"Perfect. You know most condos on the strip don't accept pets. There are only two pet-friendly condos on the intracoastal side—here and the Barbican where your parents live. None at all oceanside."

The sunshine tumbles through the white blinds in lazy diagonals across the white tile floor. The sea only steps away. I can smell the salt air. Being in a real beach apartment with the smell of the sea floating through intoxicates me.

"Sit, Barbara, sit." It seems impolite to leave. Not only is she a neighbor, but she's Scandinavian. My grandmother was Swedish, so we're practically family.

"Well, only for a minute. I leave for California day after tomorrow."

She pulls out a velvet-cushioned chair and I sit at her gleaming circular glass table afraid to leave a fingerprint. We make small talk about the area. I tell her Grandma Miller bought one of the town's first condos in 1960 when I was eleven. I loved it here even then. I was here when the Beatles stayed at the Fontainebleau in Miami.

"Barbara, I'm so glad you came by. I want to rent to you."

I'm taken aback. She just met me.

"Uh, I can't move here; I have family in California." Could I really do this? Stay in Florida, not for a few weeks, but maybe for a few more months. I expect her to tell me to think about it, thank me for coming, and say hello to Mia and Sven over at the Barbican.

Could I? Of course not. It's ridiculous. What if something goes wrong in Washington and Deanna comes back home? I suppose I could extend my vacation into fall while Deanna stays with Nicki. But I can't sign a lease. And "month to month" doesn't exist in South Palm Beach. Not during the season.

"Well, I could extend my vacation into the fall...."

"Perfect," she says. "The unit is available in two weeks, September first, and the lease is only for four months, after that it's month-to-month."

I'm walking across the street to the beach. *What on earth did I just do?*

Grass and patches of sand are firm under my flip-flops as I ascend the dune. I'm feeling discombobulated. From the top of the dune, the aqua ocean spreads beneath me. The warm salt air, inhaled, feels part of me. I can't believe I'm coming back.

. . .

I END UP HAVING DINNER with Jerry on Tuesday, the last night before I leave. I chose the restaurant; I'm sick of wings and pizza and maybe a bit sick of feeling blown off. We drive North to one of my favorite Cuban restaurants, Havana. I've visited Cuba three times with Diego and we always ate in nice places. Still, I say if you want great Cuban food go to Miami. But Havana has the best Cuban food in West Palm Beach.

Jerry looks at the menu, puzzled. Maybe he never saw one without hamburgers on it. Our waiter, Enrique, is surprised at my Spanish, but in the Latino way, he politely defers to Jerry, making sure he translates what he says to me.

I have my usual, *carnitas* and sweet plantains. Jerry has *bistec*, which is Spanish for beefsteak. He seems surprised when it arrives with yellow rice, not a baked potato. Jerry mentions that the construction workers he employs should learn to speak English, because this is America.

"Not in Miami," I chide. In the Miami airport the announcements come first in Spanish, then in English. Midway through our meal I'm about to tell Jerry about my condo lease when he calls our waiter for another Budweiser, "Hey, José."

"Jerry, his name is Enrique." I whisper.

He shrugs. "Enrique, José, same difference."

I wince in embarrassment when Enrique, who is within earshot, comes to our table. I honestly don't remember another word said at the table after that. Our budding romance was over before the second Bud.

Jerry had no idea how insulting he was. That's the problem with living in the Bay Area bubble; we don't realize how much of America thinks outside of our elitist politically correct sensibilities. But at the moment he said it, I wasn't thinking about appreciating cultural differences. I bristled. Terry hit below my Hispanic surname belt. He could just as easily have said, "Miguel, José, same difference."

I would have slugged him.

I declined his after-dinner drink invitation saying I have to pack for my trip. I vowed when I returned to Florida to be more discriminating about whom I dated. A free *carnitas* dinner and gaga blue eyes wasn't worth it. Never again. And I don't give *caca* if he spoke out of racism or out of ignorance.

Racism. Ignorance. Same difference.

. . .

MAYA PICKS ME UP AT the Oakland airport two days later, on August fourteenth. It's our thirty-first wedding anniversary. Diego is still in Cuba, celebrating without me no doubt. As we tunnel through the Oakland hills, I'm thinking there's plenty of time, two whole weeks, to tell Maya about my extended vacation. I sit in the passenger seat with a Cheshire cat grin on my Florida-bronzed face.

"You're glad to be home, aren't you, Mom."

"Yep. Sure am." Maya hasn't mentioned Deanna yet or how she is adjusting to life with Jesse and her grandparents. "I thought you told me Deanna's school starts early in Washington."

"She's fine." Maya doesn't want to talk about Deanna. A sore subject, I'm sure.

"Is Houston still staying with us?"

She nods. "Guess what, Mom. He got a job as a plumber."

"A plumber? Really? Don't you need training to be a plumber? I thought he was in jail since he was seventeen."

"Not jail, prison," she corrects. "He got trained there. Now he has to do a certain amount of hours with the company. Then he gets his license."

"Wow. That's terrific." I don't ask her if her brother is working yet. He's had a hard time since Quinton's death and he always gets depressed when his kids visit and they leave for Utah when school starts. Generally Maya is more talkative in the car. Maybe Deanna being gone is upsetting her. Me too, the house will seem empty without her.

My condo lease, hidden in my luggage, feels a little less dangerous knowing that they are both working and getting on with their lives. My plan will work out fine. I'll ask Diego for my 40% of the retirement money, the portion his pension fund calculated is legally mine. It'll be enough to live on in Florida if I count pennies. Maya and Houston can pay Diego rent money for the Glenside house to help out. Diego should agree because he's always saying he wants Maya to take on more responsibility for herself. This will be a great opportunity for all of us. And I'll have myself a four-month extended vacation in the tropics, maybe more.

Just thinking about those green highway signs that read MIAMI SOUTH excites me. Four long luxurious months to lie on the beach, drink virgin margaritas, and before long I'll be calling Diego "my ex." Patsy approved of my move. When I called her from Florida at first she was surprised, then she asked, "Barbara, are you going to Florida for a man?"

"Yes," I said truthfully. "Our dad."

When our screen door clangs behind my suitcase, Lola jumps all over me, turning circles nonstop, her tail going into overdrive. I sit in a kitchen chair trying to calm her nonstop wiggling, but she can't control herself from plastering doggie kisses all over my face.

"Somebody's glad to see me, aren't you, big girl." You'd think she'd been locked in a cage for the last three weeks.

"I hope you've been walking her, Maya." I said it like a question.

"Uh, we can't find the leash."

"Maya, dogs need to—" I'm about to deliver the "what dogs need" lecture but she interrupts.

"Mom, there's something you need to know."

"Oh no. You're not pregnant?"

Maya suppresses a smile and turns toward the dining room door. "Okay, now."

"What's going on?"

"Surprise, Gramma!" Deanna bounces in and wraps her arms around me.

Maya is bent over laughing. "Gotcha, Mom."

"Uh, you sure did." I pull her up on my lap, but Lola won't budge and my thighs in skinny jeans have to accommodate them both. Deanna's arms feel thicker somehow, less like sticks, and she feels heavier, more solid for her nine years. I snuggle my nose into her hair scented with strawberry shampoo, little girl sweat, and peanut butter. I can't say that Lola smells that delightful. Even Tigger wakes up from his nap and rubs his fur against my calves. I bask in their welcoming attention. But it also feels like a conspiracy to make me feel guilty.

"Is Deanna staying?" I ask.

"Yeah Gramma, I'm back for permanent! You happy?"

"Ecstatic." This is getting complicated. I'm shocked, relieved to see Deanna home safe and sound. But I'm thrown off my horse. Maya tells me that in Washington Deanna refused to ride the bus to school.

"That's all?" I imagined police, jail, Tasers.

"I'm not taking some dirty ol' bus to school, Gramma."

Good God, the preteen years have started already.

This is not a good moment to tell them. Not with everyone so thrilled that I'm home. Why didn't they treat me like this when I wanted to stay here? Even Lola won't budge off my lap. My arms stay wrapped around my granddaughter, while my head searches for exit strategies.

.  .  .

THE REALITY OF BEING HOME slowly seeps back in. A week passes and I still can't bring myself to tell Maya I'm leaving in a week. She's on her best behavior and Deanna starts fifth grade in a few days. Mimi, the daughter who doesn't need a man, moved into an apartment in Walnut Creek with Javier and she's talking about enrolling in the California Culinary Academy. Great idea, but that will be more money out of the pot. Diego is back from Cuba, but I'm suddenly reluctant to call and ask for my share of his retirement account. *Don't rock the boat.* I'm still afraid he'll want to sell the house.

With California real estate still skyrocketing, I have neither the funds nor the income to buy him out. Our retirement account checkbook still sits in my bedroom drawer with both our names printed on it. I still grovel and ask permission before using it, and only for family expenditures like pool chlorine, Roto-Rooter, or Deanna's swim lessons. But using our joint checkbook for an eleven-hundred-a-month rent check for a condo in Palm Beach isn't exactly pool chemicals. He'll think it's frivolous. If I bring up that 40% is legally mine, he'll want to discuss "settling things" again—the nail-in-the-divorce-coffin-conversation that I'm not ready for. I don't know why. To go to Florida I have to make it sound like my poor mother is taking her last dying breath on her scavenged cigarette butt. I'll have to bend the truth, maybe even have to beg to use *his* retirement money. This is not only scary, it's humiliating and degrading.

After cleaning the dishes, glasses, and Taco Bell bags left on the counter, I find two realtors' cards behind the toaster. Maya says some dude her father brought over left the cards, and she didn't tell me at first because she didn't want me to get mad at Dad. And Miguel told her that Dad brought LaShondra over to the house too.

"*What?* He brought *her* into my house!" My face feels like it's on fire.

"Miguel was really pissed about it too," she says, "he pushed Dad in the pool, right in front of the realtor. Dad was so-oo embarrassed." She chuckles.

"I don't see anything funny about your father trying to sell our house while I'm in Florida. That's just dirty pool. And bringing her here...." I shiver as if he had brought in bed bugs.

"Is he serious, Mom? He can't sell our house, can he?"

"Not without me, he can't." My head is spinning. "Don't worry, sweetheart. It's not going to happen." I toss the realtor cards in the trash compactor with the moldy cat food cans left in the fridge. Still, Diego bringing a realtor and *her* into my house while I'm gone, that's a stab in the back. I can't stop thinking about it.

No way. Diego is not selling our home, over my dead body. Not with a pack of lascivious realtors circling my home. I decide to tell Vera that I've changed my mind and I won't be sending her the deposit. Renting a Florida condo now is bad timing. I can't leave with Deanna starting school and Miguel going crazy. Worse, my suspicions that Maya is working in a San Francisco strip club have turned out to be true. Who will watch Deanna if Maya is working until two a.m.? I can't leave. What was I thinking? Running off to Florida, dating tanned construction workers, pretending that strange middle-aged bald men really care about me. That's absurd. A ridiculous, selfish, post-menopausal fantasy of a woman cruising too fast toward sixty. I can't move to Florida. I can't.

Diego is out on the front lawn, hose in hand, watering his Meyer lemons when I return early from Saturday morning Jazzercise. Usually I go with Joyce to Peet's afterward but she flew to Tucson this weekend to visit her grandson. I park in the drive and sit a moment behind the wheel. He waves at me with a cockeyed grin. I can't avoid him. And it's such a nuisance having to pretend to be friends.

I walk down the driveway in leggings and a T-shirt, knowing I still have a good butt.

"Diego, I can't believe you brought a realtor to the house while I was gone?" Put him on the defensive. Go for guilt.

"Barbara. This guy approached me." Diego stands there in his cargo shorts, his hose dripping.

"So you let him and your girlfriend in the house? In *my* house, without asking me?"

"Look Barbara, I can't go on paying for an apartment and a mortgage while you're sitting on your ass. Something has to give here."

"Seriously? You want to sell our home out from under us? Put Maya and Deanna out on the street? Put Deanna in some bad school with gun violence and no swim team?"

"I thought Deanna was staying in Washington."

"I should have known you'd pull something like this, Diego." I walk into the house in a huff and clang the screen door shut. *Better change the locks.*

Both Deanna and Maya are gone so I don't bother closing the bedroom door behind me. My T-shirt and leggings are still damp and sweaty from Jazzercise. I peel off the T-shirt over my aching shoulders. I can't find the energy to unhook the back of the water bra I bought in Key West. When I modeled it for Diego a couple of years ago he commented in the tone of a physics professor, "Well, it certainly does add volume." My butt plops on the edge of the bed and I see the folded papers on my drawing board desk. My Florida lease agreement. Tears dampen my cheeks. Now I can't go to Florida.

Diego could legally force the home sale if he wanted. I know that. I cry for my house, for my family, and for the mom and dad and their three beautiful children who used to live here. A gut-rolling cry bends me over like a rotten apple that finally collapses in on itself. And it hurts. I cry because I have to let go of the fairy tale that I am the rock foundation on moral high ground of this family. Just yesterday I would have abandoned my children for some new sexy, single life just like he did. Now I'm no better than he is. And I'm crying because there is still a little girl inside me with her little pug nose pressed up against the window glass waiting for him to come home. A depleting cry, a shedding cry, a what-the-fuck-I-give-up cry.

There's a knock at the kitchen screen door, more of a metal shudder.

"Can I come in?" he asks.

"Yes." The girl's small voice. I wipe my soppy grief onto my sweaty T-shirt in my lap. I'm staring out the window when I hear him enter. I don't get up. It's the first time we've been together in our bedroom in two years. Sitting in my water bra, I'm embarrassed but I don't bother to put on my T-shirt. Embarrassment is beside the point.

I want to wail at him for making me feel so sad, humiliated, and defeated. And beat his chest with my fists, the way I overheard him in the van, then push him down on our bed and have sex, great sex ... but I can't find any will to move. I peer up at him through the wet strands hanging in my face. A hot mess.

He stands at a distance between the doorway and the bed, our bed. If he wants me right now he can have me. But he doesn't come closer. He's afraid I might hit him. Or throw the coffee cup on the nightstand.

I'd do it, though, surrender to him, betray myself, just to feel his muscled arms around me once more. But then I'd feel shitty afterwards. I turn and glance up at him.

His brown eyes are wet. A tear escapes. "I never wanted to hurt you, Barbara."

"I know." I allow his truth to take root in me. I know now that it's over. Not just with him, but with us. And with everything I wanted for us. With everything that is being sucked out of my grasp. I can't live like this. I can't pretend to live in a memory of what was. I gaze out at my potted impatiens blooming red and coral on the patio and our turquoise pool beyond. This is my dream house and I have to let it go. He's a good man. He'll be fair in a divorce settlement. I'll get through this.

I sit up, sniff, and say with full water-bra volume, "Diego, I'm moving to Florida and I want my share of the retirement money."

I don't know who is more surprised to hear me say it, him or me.

# CHAPTER TWENTY
## PALM BEACH

"Two hundred twenty-two, two hundred twenty-three, two hundred ...." I'm counting steps to the ocean as I stroll across South Ocean Boulevard with Lola in tow. It's 6:30 a.m., just before sunrise. I'm averaging about a hundred steps a minute, and it's less than a four-minute walk to the crest of the dune. The blue-green sea and milk-blue sky spreads before me divided by an indigo horizon line that stretches beyond my vision and sets the world straight.

Below on the beach, I remove Lola's leash and plant myself just far enough behind the surf to keep the towel dry. Lazy, luminous clouds rest on the horizon, like sleeping cherubs draped in gold. A blinding white disk emerges behind the gilded clouds and shoots a spray of gold cannonballs across the sea. A sudden warmth washes over me. This magnificent morning coronation only lasts a minute. But my blinking, burning eyes savor every second.

Lola is happy too, running back and forth in the sand kicking up her own illuminated dust storm. She darts close to the towel, daring me to swipe her black nose, then dances around doing doggie figure eights. Life on the beach feels very full. I like being alone in the seaside villa; that's something I thought

I'd never say. An empty nest feels calm and peaceful when you've learned how to fly. I love no dishes in the sink except one coffee mug. And the warm, briny scent of the ocean and how the morning sun spills through the cracks in the blinds to caress my bed linens and paint the walls with light. Light in the tropics shines brighter than in the Bay Area. Even the palm tree shadows on the front walk glow a pastel lavender.

When my girls were newborn, Pabla would let herself in early when the house was asleep and I'd awake to the sounds of her washing dishes and putting them away in their places. Those gentle kitchen rattles told me all was right with the world; I was being cared for.

It feels like that here.

I boarded the plane for Palm Beach with only two suitcases and a doggie carry-on. I left a whole house behind me in California, a whole life really. Perhaps the feeling of being so full is related to having so little to carry.

Before I left California I twisted the truth and lied to Diego. I told him that my father needed me in Florida to help him take care of Mom. And I felt guilty for lying. When Dad picked me up at the Palm Beach airport, I confessed my lie to Diego.

"Barbara, that wasn't a lie," he said.

I don't know what is ahead, whether I'll stay in Florida when my four-month lease is up. Perhaps I'll meet someone new, maybe not, anything is possible. I'm in an in-between space between lives, taking a breather, getting a tan, resting on that narrow indigo horizon line.

It's okay.

I breathe in the warm salty ocean air. Ahhh. I say my usual prayer: "God take care of Diego and help me let go." Today I add, "Let LaShondra take care of Diego, because I can't."

The hush-sh-sh-sh of waves lulls me into deep, slow, hypnotic breaths. My eyes close and I sit in the peace of not knowing, the silvery space of waiting for life to happen.

Under orange sun-warmed eyelids, a vision appears. A sailboat is drifting away from me out to sea. Diego is on the back of that boat, waving wildly to me. Not the husband I know, but a cherub-faced, curly, dark-haired boy excited to leave on an adventure. As the boat grows smaller gliding on the waves, he appears happy. Oh so happy. Then I see myself, my child self, on the edge of the shore, where I am now, but I'm excited too, jumping, waving back to him.

A sudden flash of love for him courses through me. And, it's hard to put into words, but in this instant, I am aware, not only of my love, but all the love the world holds for him. Helen's deep love for him. His sisters. Our kids. LaShondra. This overwhelming cloud of love envelops me.

Not regretful love, but a deep, tender love of ... no words .... I try to hold on to this feeling. I won't open my eyes. I don't want to leave. Or return to that person I really am. I want to stay here. *Please let me stay.*

"Arf." Lola's barking jars me awake. And the sailboat that carried Diego, and the cloud that carried the love, and the love that carried me, it all fades away into blue sky of here. Of now. A coolness washes over my toes. The rising tide has reached me.

"Arf! Arf! Arf! Rrrrrrr-oof." Lola snarls at the advancing foam. A line of bubbles undulates over the coral sand and Lola is chasing it. For her, the sea is alive, a white bubbly snake that slithers toward her, retreats, and disappears. She's down on her sandy front paws, snarling and snapping at the foam as though she could bite and hold on. Spellbound, I watch her, like watching a puppy shake a stuffed toy tiger. Even with a nose full of salt, sand, and foam, Lola will not give up trying to bite the sea. Silly girl, it's only water, harmless water, a wave coming in, going out. A wave pretending to be fierce.

. . .

I'VE REMAINED IN FLORIDA for two years now. After the birth of Diego's fifth child Diego turned to a lawyer who skillfully managed to delay our divorce for yet another year. He calls me about minor divorce wrinkles and complaints that his lawyer costs too much. I hear a baby crying in the background. "I'm doing child care," he says as if he's a seventy-year-old working in a daycare center. Or he'll tell me he's "babysitting" in a not-so-thrilled voice. For thirty years I tried to tell him that it's not babysitting when it's your own kid. Now I zip it.

The divorce is finally settled. I agree to send him the remaining checks from our joint account. As I watch the waves wash over my coral pedicure and hear his kid crying in the background, I can't help but reflect on this odd twist of fate. All I wanted when this mess began was to keep my home and family in California intact. And Diego wanted his freedom from family to enjoy his retirement. Did Santa Claus mix up our Christmas lists? As I adjust the beach umbrella and search for Deanna's brown legs sticking up out of the ocean, the Stones' lyrics roll through my head.

"You can't always get what you want ... but you get what you need."

· · ·

FOR DINNER TONIGHT I'M sautéing teriyaki salmon and assembling Greek salad. Maya always asks for Greek: spinach, tomatoes, parsley, red potatoes, imported feta, and calamata olives. Whatever coast I'm on, I'm dicing red onion, Italian parsley, and cherry tomatoes; it relaxes me. Home is where the cutting board is. The one I use most every night is in Dad's condo.

The year after I moved into the Florida condo I switched to a two-bedroom and Deanna moved in with me. Later, in 2008, Maya and Houston moved into an apartment five minutes away. The three of them followed me across the country like puppies.

Two pats of butter melt into a transparent pool in the black cast-iron skillet I brought from California. A wee drop of spit sizzles, then disappears in the butter, signaling me to slide in the cool pink salmon slices that mold to the palm of my hand. Dried oregano is rubbed between my palms to release their aromatic oils before adding the dry leaf to the olive oil and lemon juice salad dressing. I toss the salad in Mom's wooden bowl.

I miss her. She passed last January. I had just returned to Florida after spending Christmas in California. I made us dinner and watched Dad spoon-feed Mom her mashed potatoes and gravy. Before bed she sat in her wheelchair and watched turtle hatchlings head for the sea on *Animal Planet*. Then, for no apparent reason, she stopped breathing. I had been back only two days. I believe Mom waited for me to come back from California before she died. On nights like this, with a home full of family, it feels like she's still here.

The salmon steaks take a bit longer than our usual Friday night fish fry, but I catch them at just the right moment, when their flesh yields to the fork's silver prongs and flakes apart like pink flower petals. A very blonde Maya, who looks like Anna Nicole Smith, sets out the plates while Houston and Dad discuss the 49ers and the Packers. I don't try to keep up. Dad, at ninety, still possesses an encyclopedic knowledge of every sports event known in America.

Dinner's ready and I'm kind of a mess, my face oily from the stove, my hair piled on top of my head after a swim. I'm wearing men's shorts, a yellow T-shirt, and no makeup. But it's fine, it's just family. I ask Deanna to close the computer. "Okay, G-Mama," she says, using her new nickname for me. At eleven she's into Myspace, rap songs, and dancing to "Soulja Boy."

Our table is set with five plates. The centerpiece is a salad mandala of spinach greens, red cherry tomatoes, black olives, thin strings of purple onion, and creamy feta. The aroma of salmon steaks, blackened from a caramelized marinade, fills the busy living room. Next to a platter of gold baked potatoes sits a bowl of charred jalapeño salsa. It's no longer tainted by my loss of Diego and with him the loss of my adopted Mexican heritage. The salsa on the table belongs to all of us now.

I call the troops. "Everybody, come and eat!"

I just love saying that.

# EPILOGUE
## AN ELEGY OF LOST THINGS
### *June 2018, Palm Beach*

*"Your pain is the breaking of the shell that encloses your understanding."*
— Kahlil Gibran

I was packing a carry-on to join Mimi and my husband George in our new home in Livermore, California, when Deanna, now twenty-two, blew in my condo front door with her five-year-old, Giselle Solis, my partner in crime. Giselle tackled me on my bed—a game we call "morning hugs" that she initiates anytime, day or night. Deanna and Giselle had moved into to Dad's condo when he went to live with Patsy. He'll be ninety-nine, and still kickin' this year.

Usually when Deanna drops off Giselle, I only hear her voice from the door. "Her backpack's on the counter, Gramma, bye." That morning Deanna stayed to chat and surprised me with a question.

"Gramma, is it okay if I get tattoos of you and Papa?"

"Together?" I asked indignantly.

"No, separate." The way she moved her bare shoulders and tossed her long straight auburn hair lead me to believe that Diego and I would be occupying separate real estate on opposite sides of her tall, lean body. Tattooed images on her pale, perfect skin have grown into a marker map of us. Our family. So far her ink is hidden under her Key Lime House restaurant uniform, but covered skin space is running out.

Deanna's upper back belongs to her uncle Miguel, sadly a 2012 victim of the opioid crisis. He's now immortalized in a full spread of blue wings on my granddaughter's back. Though my mother taught me tattoos were for degenerates and sailors, I have a special affection for these blue wings. Miguel always called Deanna Little D. "I got your back, Li'l D," he'd say.

And now he does.

Deanna's lower back had been a two-rifle tribute to her former Texas boyfriend, Luis Andrés Solis, Giselle's father, but she had the rifles reworked into trailing flowers. Smart choice. Her left upper arm is Maya's place, the most exquisite tattoo yet, a magnificent tree in full foliage, its trunk wound with vines. It reads "My Mother's Keeper." At this moment neither Deanna nor I know where her mother is living—she has had a tough time since her brother passed away.

Written on her upper arm, left side, is "Giselle," her daughter's name in a sweet, feminine cursive, not exactly true to Giselle's truck and dinosaur personality. A new tat appeared recently; this one is small—a map of California tucked behind her right ear.

Although Deanna's tattoos of late have become more tasteful—I never liked the one of Hello Kitty holding an assault rifle—I tell my granddaughter that I don't want to be a tattoo.

"Deanna, your body is already beautiful; besides I heard it's painful."

She thinks a moment, then asks, "Well ... is it is okay then if I get one of Papa?"

Old resentments flood back. I suppress a hurt look but my green eyes betray me. She wraps her arms around me and says, "Oh, Gramma."

Diego tells me a few days later, during a discussion of Maya's whereabouts that he doesn't want to be a tattoo on Deanna either. But Deanna's going to do what Deanna's going to do.

. . .

THERE ARE A FEW LOSSES in life, losses so deep, so painful, and rich to the core, they bring you to your knees. Losing Diego was like that. I felt wrung out like a dishrag, then slammed against the wall, Whap! Whap! Whap! a few times for good measure. At first I believed it was my moral wifely duty, part of the Latin code, to reclaim my *Mexicano* husband. But that didn't work so I tried to join the "I will survive" jilted-female chorus, belting out "Walk out the door … cause you're not welcome anymore." But the rebounded, successful, single woman archetype was always out of reach. My heart didn't match the "F him—you go, girl" model presented to me by many well-meaning friends. I couldn't permanently skew my vision to see my best friend for thirty years as the vicious, monstrous tiger who had finally shown his stripes.

I tried a thousand ways to leave Diego behind, prayed ten thousand prayers seeking peace. I wanted a safe haven from grief, a new life for myself without him or thoughts of him in it. I expected that with time my thoughts of Diego would disappear down the tub drain, I'd flush out the dirty water, scrub out the brown oil ring, and I'd have a fresh, faintly Chlorine-scented white tub I could fill up with new love.

But love doesn't work like that, at least not for me. If I have one regret, it's that I wish I had given myself more time. And that I'd been kinder and gentler with grief. My Swedish Grandma used to say, "Baa-bara, you've got all the time there is, and there isn't any more."

Another adage on loss is that "God never gives you any more than you can handle." That didn't sit right with me. God gave me an "unbearable endless" that proved more than I, my ego *I*, could handle. I had to surrender the old me and hope a new *I* would arise from the ashes of my life left on Glenside Drive.

It didn't happen in one year, or even ten, but painfully, slowly, by trial, prayer, and error. I don't understand the spiritual alchemy, but eventually, through forgiving him and giving myself space, time, and tenderness, a new person popped out on the other side of grief. Amazingly, this new, God-reconditioned *I* feels less defensive, open, and more compassionate. Like a gift of new oversize flannel pajamas I'm growing into.

. . .

IN PROGRAM WHEN WE lose precious people in our lives to illness, drug addiction, or death, we're taught to let go. "Let go and let God" is a constant drumbeat theme at every twelve step meeting.

But who or what is really lost?

I regularly lose things. My checkbook, my phone, Giselle's library books, sunglasses, the darn remote, my lemon squeezer. Not long after Miguel's death I was searching for a missing signed check. I turned my condo upside down looking everywhere: inside drawers and folders, digging through pockets, sifting through office trash: papers, dust, and used yogurt cups. I dumped out my purse and all six zipper pockets on the bed, and searched my car. The whole while I'm badgering myself with interrogation. Where did you put it? Where did you last see it? What were you doing when you saw it last? Then I start the search all over again, looking, looking, looking in the same places for that check I endorsed but forgot to deposit. It's exhausting.

At some point during this frantic dance of lost things my mind switches from where did I put it to *who* took it? Who came in and out of my house? Who is to blame? Usually my kids, ghosts, and, of course, me. Most of all me.

Out of frustration bordering on a meltdown, I finally give up and sit. I call sitting on the sofa stage two: reassurances. I remind myself that 99 out of 100 times, it was me who misplaced something. And I'm not poor, I can always replace it. Perhaps someone who found it needs it more than me. Then the question comes. What is lost?

The check isn't lost. It's somewhere else.

Where I can't see it or hold it right now.

Sometimes what I lose can be replaced, like keys, my glasses, a Bay Area home, a job, or a husband. Sometimes what is lost joyously reappears on its own. Like when Maya, Deanna, and Houston moved to Florida to be near me. And the last time I met Deanna at the airport she was carrying a baby. A double return.

But not everyone I've lost comes back.

In program we learn that holding onto our loved ones with tight fists turns to pain, so we practice letting go. I've come to prefer the word *release*. *Releasing* someone feels more comforting somehow than *letting go*. More serene, less forced and generous.

*Palms open*

*Fingers uncurl like the petals of a lotus blossom*

*A white bird takes flight*

Yet releasing a lost one takes practice. But I've discovered that it leads to a gift beyond easy replacements or unexpected homecomings. The gift of new perspective and an understanding that what I thought was lost, was never lost.

The severed chain left behind freed us both.

For whom I release, also releases me.

# ABOUT BARBARA FLORES

Barbara Flores is known internationally as the designer of over thirty iconic food art posters for Ten Speed Press. She has authored three non-fiction books: *Confusion Is a State of Grace*, *The Great Sunflower Book*, and *The Great Book of Pears*, which was nominated for an IACP (International Association of Culinary Professionals) award. Her literary work has appeared in many publications including the *San Francisco Chronicle*, *Diablo Magazine*, and *More*. She has taught writing for twenty years at institutions in California and Florida, including UC Berkeley Extension, Moraga College, Diablo Valley College, Oakland School for the Arts, and currently she is a professor at Palm Beach Atlantic University. Flores is a frequent speaker at literary and food events and has been a guest speaker on *Dining Around with Gene Burns* (KGO, San Francisco) and *Splendid Table* (NPR). She lives with her husband in Palm Beach, Florida, and Livermore, California.

Books by Barbara Flores and Barbara Flores poster art are available at www.barbaraflores.net